HUMOR IN THE MIDST OF MARK

EARLY CHRISTIANITY AND ITS LITERATURE

Emerson B. Powery, General Editor

Editorial Board:
Ronald Charles
Kylie Crabbe
Mary F. Foskett
Jennifer A. Glancy
Lynn R. Huber

Number 36

HUMOR IN THE MIDST OF MARK

Jon Carman

SBL PRESS

Atlanta

Copyright © 2025 by Jon Carman

All rights reserved. No part of this work may be reproduced or transmitted in any form or by any means, electronic or mechanical, including photocopying and recording, or by means of any information storage or retrieval system, except as may be expressly permitted by the 1976 Copyright Act or in writing from the publisher. Requests for permission should be addressed in writing to the Rights and Permissions Office, SBL Press, 825 Houston Mill Road, Atlanta, GA 30329 USA.

Library of Congress Control Number: 2025945454

Contents

Abbreviations	vii
1. Humor and the Gospel of Mark	1
2. Method	25
3. Script-Oppositions in Mark 4:35–6:6	59
4. Humor Effects in Mark 4:35–6:6	123
5. Summary	171
Bibliography	179
Ancient Sources Index	197
Modern Authors Index	202

Abbreviations

AB	Anchor Bible
ABD	Freedman, David Noel, ed. *Anchor Bible Dictionary*. 6 vols. Doubleday, 1992.
Aen.	Vergil, *Aeneid*
A.J.	Josephus, *Antiquitates judaicae*
AJA	*American Journal of Archaeology*
Andr.	Terence, *Andria*
Apol.	Plato, *Apologia*; Seneca, *Apocolocyntosis*
b.	Babylonian Talmud
Bacch.	Plautus, *Bacchides*
Bib	*Biblica*
BibInt	*Biblical Interpretation*
BibInt	*Biblical Interpretation*
BQR	*Baptist Quarterly Review*
BTB	*Biblical Theology Bulletin*
CBQ	*Catholic Biblical Quarterly*
CH	*Church History*
Char.	Theophrastus, *Characteres*
CJ	*Classical Journal*
ClQ	*Classical Quarterly*
CurBR	*Currents in Biblical Research*
CW	*Classical World*
De an.	Aristotle, *De anima*
EBib	Etudes bibliques
Epigr.	Martial, *Epigrammata*
Eq.	Aristophanes, *Equites*
Flor.	Apuleius, *Florida*
FRLANT	Forschungen zur Religion und Literatur des Alten und Neuen Testaments
GTVH	General Theory of Verbal Humor

Hist.	Herodotus, *Historiae*
HSCP	*Harvard Studies in Classical Philology*
Il.	Homer, *Iliad*
Inst.	Quintilian, *Institutio*
JBL	*Journal of Biblical Literature*
JECS	*Journal of Early Christian Studies*
JGRChJ	*Journal of Greco-Roman Christianity and Judaism*
JQR	*Jewish Quarterly Review*
JSJSup	Journal for the Study of Judaism Supplement Series
JSNT	*Journal for the Study of the New Testament*
JSNTSup	Journal for the Study of the New Testament Supplement Series
JSP	*Journal for the Study of the Pseudepigrapha*
JSPSup	Journal for the Study of the Pseudepigrapha Supplement Series
JTI	*Journal of Theological Interpretation*
LCL	Loeb Classical Library
Leg.	Plato, *Leges*
LNTS	Library of New Testament Studies
LXX	Septuagint
Lys.	Aristophanes, *Lysistrata*
Marc.	Plutarch, *Marcellus*
Men.	Plautus, *Menaechmi*
Metam.	Apuleius, *Metamorphoses*
Nat.	Pliny, *Naturalis historia*
Neot	*Neotestamentica*
NICNT	New International Commentary on the New Testament
NIGTC	New International Greek Testament Commentary
NovT	*Novum Testamentum*
NovTSup	Novum Testamentum Supplement Series
NRSV	New Revised Standard Version
NTL	New Testament Library
NTS	*New Testament Studies*
Nub.	Aristophanes, *Nubes*
Od.	Homer, *Odyssey*
Op.	Hesiod, *Opera et dies*
Or.	Cicero, *De Oratore*
Perik.	Meander, *Perikeiromene*

Pesah.	Pesahim
PGM	Preisendanz, Karl, ed. *Papyri Graecae Magicae: Die griechischen Zauberpapyri*. 2nd ed. Teubner, 1973–1974.
Phar.	Lucian, *Pharsalia*
Philop.	Lucian, *Philopseudes*
Poet.	Aristotle, *Poetica*
Prog.	Apthonius, *Progymnasmata*; Nicolaus, *Progymnasmata*; Pseudo-Hermogenes, *Progymnasmata*; Theon, Progymnasmata
PRSt	*Perspectives in Religious Studies*
Ran.	Aristophanes, *Ranae*
Res gest. divi Aug.	Res gestae divi Augusti
Resp.	Plato, *Respublica*
Rhet.	Aristotle, *Rhetorica*
Rhet. Her.	Rhetorica ad Herennium
RHPR	*Revue d'histoire et de philosophie religieuses*
SBT	Studies in Biblical Theology
SemeiaSt	Semeia Studies
SNTSMS	Society for New Testament Studies Monograph Series
SP	Sacra Pagina
SSTH	script semantic theory of humor
Symp. caus.	Galen, *De symptomatum causis*
SymS	Symposium Series
Theog.	Hesiod, *Theogonia*
Tim.	Plato, *Timaeus*
TynBul	*Tyndale Bulletin*
Vesp.	Aristophanes, *Vespae*; Suetonius, *Vespasian*
Vit. Appoll.	Philostratus, *Vita Apollonii*
WBC	Word Biblical Commentary
WGRW	Writings from the Greco Roman World
WGRWSup	Writings from the Greco Roman World Supplement Series
WUNT	Wissenschaftliche Untersuchungen zum Neuen Testament
ZNW	*Zeitschrift für die neutestamentliche Wissenschaft und die Kunde der älteren Kirche*

1
Humor and the Gospel of Mark

Introduction

"If the scriptures are God's revelation of himself and his will for human beings, humor has no place in God or in his plan for human beings."[1] With this sweeping statement, John Morreall dismisses any hope of finding humor in the books present in the Hebrew Bible or New Testament. Nor is Morreall alone in this evaluation. Other scholars have remarked on the "total absence of humour from the Bible" and its seeming ability to claim the title of "the world's least amusing book."[2] The tendency to interpret Hebrew and Christian scripture as ahumorous finds further accent in the New Testament, as this collection of texts orbits around the central fact of Jesus's death. In light of this heavy subject matter, Stephen Halliwell concludes:

> We should therefore not be surprised that the evidence of the New Testament as a whole suggests the activation of a general suspicion of laughter in the development of early Christianity.... Laughter, as a metonym for the soul's elation, is here displaced from the current life of the body onto the spiritualized joy of an eternal afterlife.[3]

---

1. John Morreall, "Sarcasm, Irony, Wordplay, and Humor in the Hebrew Bible: A Response to Hershey Friedman," *Humor* 13 (2001): 293–301.
2. Lucian Price, ed., *Dialogues with Alfred North Whitehead* (Little, Brown, 1954), 199; Ralph Wood, *The Comedy of Redemption: Christian Faith and Comic Vision in Four American Novelists* (Notre Dame University Press, 1988), 1.
3. Stephen Halliwell, *Greek Laughter: A Study of Cultural Psychology from Homer to Early Christianity* (Cambridge University Press, 2008), 475–76. I am indebted to Kelly Iverson, "Incongruity, Humor, and Mark: Performance and the Use of Laughter

While many scholars maintain this view, one wonders whether this verdict is too pessimistic. After all, what are the odds that a collection of documents as varied as those found in the Hebrew Bible and New Testament contains little to no humor? It is far more likely that this is an overdetermined perspective, possibly shaped by later Christian theologians' suspicions concerning humor. Indeed, biblical scholars have been making the case for nearly two centuries that this is, in fact, not the case. Terri Bednarz illuminates this stream of scholarship in her collection of humor research regarding the canonical gospels. Upon surveying the literature, Bednarz notices a curious pattern:

> As I studied a vast collection of Grecian, Roman, and Jewish works ... it became apparent to me that a lack of humor in the Gospels would be, in fact, a striking anomaly from the perspective of ancient circum-Mediterranean literature and culture.... As I read through various publications on humor in the Bible, I noticed that scholars frequently qualified their work by saying that little research about humor in the Bible had been done. While I knew that was not accurate.... It then occurred to me that no one had ever compiled a comprehensive *history* of scholarly study of humor in Scripture, especially the Gospels.[4]

Bednarz's statement here underscores two critical points: First, it would certainly be odd for the cultures embedded within and represented by the Hebrew Bible and New Testament to abstain from a phenomenon otherwise demonstrated throughout the ancient Mediterranean. Second, while scholarship on biblical humor is not at the center of the discipline, it is still present. Bednarz's history of humor scholarship and the Bible demonstrates that there has been a sustained conversation on this topic for some time now.[5]

Most importantly for the present study, Bednarz's work demonstrates that not only is one likely to find some form of humor in the Hebrew Bible or New Testament, but also that the gospels are particularly fertile ground for such analysis. In addition to demonstrating this possibility, Bednarz's

---

in the Second Gospel," *NTS* 59 (2013): 2–19, for this helpful collation of scholars' views of humor and the Bible.

4. Terri Bednarz, *Humor in the Gospels: A Sourcebook for the Study of Humor in the New Testament: 1863–2014* (Lexington, 2015), 2–3.

5. By my count, Bednarz provides an analysis of 120 sources on humor and the gospels. This is to say nothing of her broader works consulted pages, which demonstrate even more sources touching on the topic of humor and the Bible.

work yields another key insight: while work has been done on humor and the life of Jesus, what remains uncovered are the dimensions of humor wielded by the evangelists themselves. That is, there have been attempts at documenting the humor of the historical Jesus.[6] However, studies of the ways in which the evangelists utilized humor alongside historical Jesus traditions are wanting. Indeed, this turn occurred late in gospel studies, beginning in earnest in the 1980s as New Testament scholarship focused increasingly on synchronic methods, thereby raising the profile of the evangelists and highlighting their role in shaping Jesus traditions.[7] Thus, while scholars have advanced their understanding concerning the use of humor by the evangelists, much work remains to be done. Mark, in particular, lags behind its canonical counterparts in this regard.[8]

This, then, is the task of the present study: to move the conversation forward regarding Markan humor by offering a study focused specifically on the use of humor by the Markan evangelist. The challenges in accomplishing this are considerable. Not only is the topic of humor generally

---

6. See, e.g., George Wright Buckley, *The Wit and Wisdom of Jesus* (West, 1901); Henri Cormier, *Le Humour de Jésus* (Editiones Paulines, 1974); John Dominic Crossan, *Raid on the Articulate: Comic Eschatology in Jesus and Borges* (Harper & Row, 1976); Sheppard Knapp, "Traces of Humor in the Sayings of Jesus," *The Biblical World* 29 (1907): 201–7; Humphrey Palmer, "Just Married, Cannot Come," *NovT* 18 (1976): 241–57; William Romaine Paterson, "The Irony of Jesus," *The Monist* 9 (1899): 345–58; Elton Trueblood, *The Humor of Christ* (Harper & Row, 1964), among others.

7. Bednarz, *Humor in the Gospels*, 294. To provide just a few examples of the scholarship happening in this period: Blayne Alexander Banting, "Proclaiming the Messiah's Mirth: A Rhetorico-contextual Model for the Interpretation and Proclamation of Humour in Selected Gospel Sayings" (DMin thesis, Acadia Divinity College, 1998); Terri Bednarz, "Humor-neutics: Analyzing Humor and Humor Functions in the Synoptic Gospels" (PhD diss., Texas Christian University, 2009); Bednarz, "Status Disputes and Disparate Dicta: Humor Rhetoric in Luke 16:14–18," *BibInt* 21 (2013): 377–415; Harry Boonstra, "Satire in Matthew," *Christianity and Literature* 29 (1980): 32–45; Joseph Grassi, *God Makes Me Laugh: A New Approach to Luke* (Wipf & Stock, 1986); Bruce Longenecker, "A Humorous Jesus? Orality, Structure and Characteristics in Luke 14:15–24, and Beyond," *BibInt* 16 (2008): 179–204; Doris Myers, "Irony and Humor in the Gospel of John," *Occasional Papers in Translation and Text Linguistics* 2 (1988): 1–13; Earl Palmer, *The Humor of Jesus: Sources of Laughter in the Bible* (Regent College Publishing, 1987); William Phipps, *The Wisdom and Wit of Rabbi Jesus* (Westminster John Knox, 1993).

8. Of the fifty-eight sources that Bednarz discusses with regard to humor in biblical scholarship from the 1980s onwards, only six focus on humor in the Gospel of Mark, and even some of these are more indirect treatments of the topic.

regarded as too subjective to study across time and culture, but there is no systematic theory or approach that scholars have adopted when looking at the gospel texts themselves. Scholars are still in a constructive phase regarding theory and method.

In the present chapter, I will explore what work scholars have undertaken in dealing directly with the subject of Markan humor, looking both at systematic approaches as well as their nonsystematic counterparts. I will supplement this with a brief glance at the history of humor studies vis-a-vis humor-adjacent approaches to Mark (e.g., satire, irony). This review will demonstrate that a study of the topic at hand is long overdue and a more systematic approach is required if the topic of Markan humor is to succeed as a line of scholarly inquiry. In chapter 2, I will describe the methodology I use to approach detecting humor in a textual artifact from Greco-Roman antiquity, including a brief overview of humor theories with an emphasis on incongruity as a primary way to locate humor in a text. I conclude with an articulation of my own model: a combination of the General Theory of Verbal Humor working in conjunction with ancient humorous comparanda. In chapter 3, I focalize my analysis of Markan humor through the miracle stories located in Mark 4:35–6:6. I give special attention to the presence of script-oppositions as well as potential humorous touchstones evident in Greek, Jewish, and Roman sources that appear to comically engage subjects raised in these script-oppositions. In chapter 4, I sort the script-oppositions highlighted in the previous chapter into a three-tiered system ranging from the most to least humorous. With this assortment complete, I analyze the ways in which the Markan evangelist might deploy humor throughout the miracle stories, paying particular attention to physiological, psychological, sociological, and pedagogical effects of humor. In chapter 5, I conclude the study, highlighting the most salient elements of Markan humor that emerge and outline potential lines of future research for the gospel and humor studies.

Humor Studies and the Gospels

The study of Markan humor rests in a broader stream of gospel studies focused on humor.[9] Bednarz documents how this topic was initially

---

9. A very light, diachronic sketch of this period illustrates the tendencies of historical Jesus studies as it focused on the figure of Jesus himself and the type of humor he employed. Much more could be said, but this suffices to capture some of the general

concerned primarily with questions regarding the life of Jesus.[10] Students of Jesus's humor as it presents in the gospels were found among specialists and nonspecialists, as the topic fascinated scholars, pastors, and poets alike. They analyzed Jesus's teachings for their potentially humorous elements, paying particular attention to apparent incongruities, absurdities, hyperboles, and reversals, among other features. For the most part, interpreters characterized Jesus's humor as positive, or at least oriented toward a positive telos (e.g., correction of misunderstanding, attacking problematic theological positions). The renewal of historical Jesus studies that arose in conjunction with synchronic approaches to the gospels in the 1980s inaugurated a new movement in humor studies with gospel scholars paying more attention to the humor of particular evangelists. Additionally, scholars broadened the scope of how they perceived Jesus's humor could function, with attention given to its more tendentious qualities. Ultimately, this synchronic turn, combined with a more robust understanding of humor's positive and negative qualities,

---

observations of scholarship in this time. In the 1880s, Marion Shutter explored the use of humor in the Bible, including the teachings of Jesus. Marion Shutter, "The Element of Humor in the Bible," *BQR* (1885): 443–53. Contemporaneously, Thomas Hyde offered an analysis of the wit of Jesus, focusing on his capacity as a skilled, humorous orator. Thomas Alexander Hyde, "Christ as Orator," *The North American Review* 156 (1893): 750–53; Hyde, *Christ the Orator, or Never Man Spake Like This Man* (Arena, 1893). This trend continued into the twentieth century alongside historical Jesus inquiries. George P. Eckman argued in a series of lectures that the Bible, because it is literature, likely included the presence of humor. Part of his analysis centered on Jesus's speech, which he viewed as utilizing irony, wit, and mockery, among other humorous forms of speech. George P. Eckman, *The Literary Primacy of the Bible*, The Mendenhall Lectures, second series (Methodist Book Concern, 1915), 117–21. Dudley Zuver, offering his own analysis of philosophy and humor, maintained that Jesus's humor was found primarily in his wit and satire. Zuver also underscored the importance of the hermeneutical dimensions of humor when interpreting New Testament texts, suggesting that one consider whether a text might be serious or comical. Dudley Zuver, *Salvation by Laughter* (Harper & Row, 1933). Decades later, in a focused study on Jesus's wit, Elton Truebold highlighted the universality of Jesus's humor as it came through in irony, parables, and humorous dialogue. Elton Trueblood, *The Humor of Christ* (Harper & Row, 1965). Further historical Jesus studies such as those undertaken by Crossan underscored Jesus's use of comic speech as a key part of his strategy in delivering the message of the kingdom of God (Crossan, *Raid on the Articulate*).

10. The synopsis of humor studies in this paragraph is a summary of Bednarz's overview of scholarly contributions. For more, see Bednarz, *Humor and the Gospels*.

accelerated the tendency for scholars to consider the following: If Jesus could be humorous, could not the editors or narrators of his traditions also employ comical elements in their renditions of Jesus's life?

Humor and the Gospel of Mark

While the amount of scholarship documenting humor in the speech and actions of Jesus is impressive, it is only in the last generation or two that scholars have turned their attention to the ways in which the gospel texts deploy humor. This is particularly true with respect to the Gospel of Mark where there remains a considerable dearth of analyses regarding the humor of the evangelist. As it stands, only a handful of scholars have undertaken a systematic study of the gospel's humorous elements. Beyond such studies, one finds scholars who make passing observations about humor in various Markan passages. I will consider each of these types in turn, taking up the latter first.

Nonsystematic Humor Analyses

Scholars have historically made passing remarks about humor in the Markan text. Often, when something in the text either does not cohere with the surrounding narrative or some other apparent incongruity arises, the possibility for humor presents itself. Scholars who have noted such incongruities include Rudolf Bultmann, R. Alan Culpepper, Paul LaMarche, Joel Marcus, Mary Ann Tolbert, and Tom Shepherd.

Bultmann, LaMarche, Marcus, and Tolbert have all commented on the possible use of humor in the pericope involving Jesus's encounter with the man afflicted by spirits in Mark 5:1–20. While discussing the oddities of this pericope, including elements such as an inverted exorcism formula, Jesus's possible powerlessness, and the ambiguity regarding who conquered whom (i.e., whether Jesus tricked the demons or they tricked him), Bultmann suggests that the original tale may have been comical at Jesus's expense.[11] Marcus, in his commentary on the narrative of the Gerasene demoniac, makes a number of observations regarding potential humor in the passage. He notes, for instance, the parodic nature of the demoniac's attempt

---

11. Rudolf Bultmann, *The History of the Synoptic Tradition*, trans. John Marsh (Harper & Row, 1963), 210.

to adjure Jesus in 5:7.[12] Marcus also suggests that, as the demons further negotiate with Jesus, the reader finds "an element of burlesque comedy."[13] LaMarche and Tolbert similarly characterize the story in broadly humorous terms, or at least note that the story carries a kind of comical weight. LaMarche, for instance, remarks that the pericope maintains "un humour blasphématorie."[14] Tolbert states that "the humor ... is thoroughly evident."[15]

Culpepper and Shepherd locate humor in a neighboring pericope: the account of Jairus's daughter and the woman with an affliction (Mark 5:21–43). Culpepper, in a dictionary article on humor and wit, makes a passing remark about the activity of the doctors in 5:26, suggesting that the evangelist plausibly makes a joke at their expense.[16] The humor derives, presumably, from the stark incongruity drawn between what the doctors should be able to accomplish for the suffering woman (heal her) and what they actually do (rob her). Shepherd also comments briefly on the possibility of humor, seeing its potential at a number of places in the narrative. In a footnote, he suggests that the scene involving Jesus's ignorance regarding who touched him (5:30, "Who touched my clothing?") "is ... truly comical. It is really very funny that Jesus says, 'Who touched me.'"[17] This comedic moment is not alone. Rather, it adumbrates humor in the outer-story of the intercalation concerning Jairus's daughter where, in verses 39–40, the crowd laughs at Jesus for stating that the dead girl is actually asleep. The humor here occurs at the expense of the mourners, for "Jesus is not the one to laugh at, death is."[18] Ultimately, for Shepherd, "comedy is interjected along the way in both stories"[19] for the purpose of keeping the narrative fresh and engaging.

---

12. Joel Marcus, *Mark 1–8*, AB 27 (Doubleday, 1999), 344. The demoniac's adjuration is a subject of considerable confusion. Most scholars agree that it is strange to find the formula of an exorcist on the lips of the one being exorcised. I will explore this incongruity further in chapter 3 and chapter 4.

13. Marcus, *Mark*, 350.

14. Paul LaMarche, *Evangile de Marci*, EBib 33 (Gabalda, 1966), 145.

15. Mary Ann Tolbert, *Sowing The Gospel: Mark's World in Literary Perspective* (Fortress, 1989), 167.

16. R. Alan Culpepper, "Humor and Wit: The New Testament," *ABD* 3:333.

17. Tom Shepherd, *Markan Sandwich Stories: Narration, Definition, and Function*, Andrews University Seminary Doctoral Dissertation Series 18 (Andrews University Press, 1993), 148–49 n. 1.

18. Shepherd, *Markan Sandwich Stories*, 162.

19. Shepherd, *Markan Sandwich Stories*, 169.

These examples illustrate the idiosyncratic nature of some approaches to humor when analyzing the Markan text. While they are interesting and potentially important observations, especially insofar as they point up incongruities, they do not utilize a specific theory or methodology for examining humor in the narrative.

Systematic Humor Analysis

A handful of scholars have undertaken a systematic analysis of humor in the Gospel of Mark. They include Dan Via, Stephen Hatton, Jason Robert Combs, Kelly Iverson, and Sarah Emanuel, with each offering a study of the Markan text that is either conversant with contemporary methods or theories of humor, ancient comedic comparanda, or both, thereby offering a more robust analysis for determining humor in the gospel texts.

In his 1975 monograph, *Kerygma and Comedy in the New Testament: A Structural Approach to Hermeneutic*, Via argues for the presence of comedy in the worldview of both Paul and Mark. Via adopts a structuralist-literary approach to his analysis whereby he argues that both apostle and evangelist view the kerygma in light of a basic death-resurrection motif extant in ancient Greek comedy.[20] Via is particularly concerned with the *gattung* of Mark, ultimately suggesting that Mark is a "dramatic history" that tilts toward comedy.[21] However, given the balance of both serious and humorous elements, Via fine-tunes his discussion of genre by positing that the gospel's classification should fall under "tragicomedy," as both tragic and comic elements are present throughout the entire narrative.[22] Notably, while there are comical elements present, "Mark does not really exploit the comic side of these patterns. He lets it remain implicit. Mark is primarily tragicomedy."[23]

Via's analysis of Mark as tragicomedy is inviting, and he hits upon several critical ideas when approaching the topic of humor and the gospel. To begin with, Via's work is seminal for its attempt to locate the Markan genre along a comedic axis. While his work predates the *bios* consensus, it offers tantalizing possibilities in reading the gospel with comedic cotexts

---

20. Dan Via, *Kerygma and Comedy in the New Testament: A Structuralist Approach to Hermeneutic* (Fortress, 1975), xi.
21. Via, *Kerygma and Comedy*, 97–98.
22. Via, *Kerygma and Comedy*, 99.
23. Via, *Kerygma and Comedy*, 101.

in mind. There is a limitation in this, however, in that Via is primarily in conversation with Old Comedy. He relies on an Aristophanic model of comedy, even making direct points of comparison between Old Comedy conventions and the Gospel of Mark.[24] Via's work would benefit from an expansion of comedic comparanda given the vast shift in conventions that comedy underwent as a genre. Via's argument is laudable, too, for its reading of the gospel as a tragicomedy. Such a reading helpfully illuminates the texture of the gospel which, for all of its poignancy, also maintains several odd episodes. Finally, Via's work represents an attempt to track humor through a contemporary theory, namely, structuralism. This has the advantage of grounding comedy in a theoretical framework.

Hatton has offered one of the most sustained analyses of humor in Mark's Gospel. In three articles spanning nearly two decades, Hatton has addressed humor across the breadth of the Markan text. Significantly, Hatton has utilized both contemporary methods and ancient comedic texts when examining humor in Mark.

In his 2001 article, "Mark's Naked Disciple: The Semiotics and Comedy of Following," Hatton takes up the puzzling episode of the disciple who fled naked when authorities seized Jesus in Gethsemane (14:51–52).[25] For Hatton, the key to interpreting these verses rests in a close semiotic analysis of the concept of following, a critical idea alluded to repeatedly throughout the gospel. Through consistent reference to this theme, the evangelist generates a broader understanding of this term that directly links not only to the physical act of trailing behind someone, but the very act of discipleship itself. The actions of the young man, in combination with the jarring details of the episode, act as a mimicry of the disciples and even the entire subtext of discipleship. The evangelist's aim in adopting this rhetorical technique is possibly that "it downplays the importance of discipleship and 'following.'"[26]

Following his analysis of one of the stranger episodes in the Markan text, Hatton offers a comparative study of the gospel and ancient comedic

---

24. See, e.g., Via, *Kerygma and Comedy*, 124, where Via makes a connection between the convention of parabasis (chorus) in Aristophanes and the gospel. Yet the parabasis was eventually phased out of comedic works as it transitioned into New Comedy.

25. Stephen Hatton, "Mark's Naked Disciple: The Semiotics and Comedy of Following," *Neot* 35 (2001): 35–48.

26. Hatton, "Mark's Naked Disciple," 47.

devices in his 2002 article "The Gospel of Mark as Comedy."[27] In this article, Hatton argues that the dramatic genre of Mark leans in the direction of comedy (opposed to tragedy) because of the presence of critical comedic elements such as self-referentiality, internal commentary, costuming, and the addressing of the readers.[28] These elements reflect similar tendencies in Aristophanic comedies. Upon locating these features, Hatton turns to those characteristics that typify tragedy and argues that they are either not present in Mark or do not function in the way scholars typically assume they do when found in Mark's Gospel.[29] Hatton determines that, in light of comedic elements in the Markan Gospel (especially the presence of self-referentiality), "one must conclude that insofar as the Gospel of Mark is modeled after Greek drama, its model or influence is comedy, not tragedy."[30]

Finally, Hatton has written an important article regarding the presence and function of humor in the intercalation involving the woman and sleeping daughter of Mark 5:21–43.[31] In his 2015 article "Comic Ambiguity in the Markan Healing Intercalation (Mark 5:21–43)," Hatton argues that a comedic reading of both stories offers a more satisfactory way of understanding the intercalation than other interpretive avenues. Hatton keys in on elemental ambiguities in both narratives, observing that the story of Jairus's daughter intentionally asserts that the girl is sleeping *and* dead, while also raising questions about the nature of the older woman's touch. By centering ambiguity in this manner, both stories interrogate surface level interpretations of Jesus as an effective miracle-worker:

> But there is much incongruity and self-referentiality in this text that call into question the cogency of the usual interpretations. Jesus may not heal the woman—perhaps she heals herself by touching his garment. The twelve year old girl may not be raised from the dead—perhaps Jesus merely wakes her.[32]

---

27. Stephen Hatton, "The Gospel of Mark as Comedy," *Downside Review* 120 (2002): 33–56.
28. Hatton, "Gospel of Mark as Comedy," 37–46.
29. Hatton, "Gospel of Mark as Comedy," 46–51.
30. Hatton, "Gospel of Mark as Comedy," 51.
31. Stephen Hatton, "Comic Ambiguity in the Markan Healing Intercalation (Mark 5:21–43)," *Neot* 49 (2015): 91–123.
32. Hatton, "Comic Ambiguity," 116.

Taken together, Hatton's articles represent the most consistent analysis of humor apropos of the evangelist. Several notable elements surface in his work. First, Hatton's analyses raise critical questions about the potential presence of humor across the entire gospel. He argues for its existence in two discrete chapters, as well as throughout the entire gospel when tracking patterns of self-referentiality. Hatton has thus advocated for the idea that the evangelist is not only coincidentally funny but is adopting comedic elements throughout the narrative for particular rhetorical ends. Second, Hatton utilizes both contemporary methods and ancient comparanda to make his case. Hatton interprets humor within the framework of semiotics, while drawing upon Aristophanic humor to better elucidate the highly self-referential Markan text.

Hatton's work is invaluable for the study of Markan humor. However, there are some limitations. To begin with, while Hatton does use a modern method, he does not use any identifiable form of humor theory. Interpretations of gospel humor working from contemporary methods would do well to incorporate the findings of such studies. Additionally, Hatton's work, like Via, is limited to Old Comedy. Utilizing Aristophanes is helpful, but it does not account for the dramatic shifts that Greco-Roman comedy experienced in the intervening years between Aristophanes and the gospels. In particular, this model does not account for the domestic comedies produced by Menander or their emulation by Latin playwrights such as Plautus and Terence.

Ultimately, Hatton offers a sustained reading of Markan humor (opposed to historical Jesus humor). Few scholars have undertaken this topic of study, let alone done so across the breadth of the text. Hatton's scholarship does much to suggest the possibility that humor is, indeed, present and that it likely resides in the ambiguous, incongruous elements of the text.

Combs, in his 2008 article "A Ghost on Water? Understanding an Absurdity in Mark 6:49–50," takes up the question of how best to interpret the reaction of the disciples in Mark 6:49–50 where they are terrified of seeing what they think is a ghost (*phantasma*)—when in reality it is Jesus walking upon the water.[33] In particular, Combs pursues the query of why, when there is a wealth of texts bearing witness to divine men walking on

---

33. Jason Robert Combs, "A Ghost on the Water? Understanding an Absurdity in Mark 6:49–50," *JBL* 127 (2008): 345–58.

water without clear cases of ghosts doing likewise, the disciples interpret Jesus as the latter rather than the former.³⁴ He focuses especially on the salient detail of a *phantasma* walking on water. Not only do ghosts not walk on this substance (according to relevant sources), but based on his reading of several ancient ghastly narratives, Combs argues that water was thought to hinder the movement of ghosts noting that "no one familiar with any of these accounts [of ghosts and water] would believe that a ghost *could* walk on water."³⁵ Combs concludes that the Markan evangelist has intentionally set up all the proper features for a ghost story only to switch one key element, thereby introducing an intentionally absurd incongruity. To explain why the evangelist has done this, Combs analyzes the comic play *Mostellaria* by Plautus where a ghost story is a key element of humor in the comedy. Combs argues for a formal similarity between Mark and Plautus, insofar as both construct plausible elements of ghost stories, only to introduce aspects totally incongruous to such stories with the purpose of playing up the credulity of key characters.³⁶ In the case of Mark's Gospel, this effectively underscores "to the extreme, their [the disciples], failure to believe in Jesus."³⁷ Indeed, so acute is the disciples' misapprehension that

> the disciples clearly want Jesus to be something that he is not, to the point that they are willing to believe the absurd when Jesus approaches them as something much grander than they had imagined. God and divine men walk on water; ghosts do not. But when the disciples see Jesus walking on water, they believe the impossible rather than the obvious.³⁸

Combs's analysis raises key issues for the present study. To begin with, Combs notes that the evangelist achieves humorous effect by introducing

---

34. Combs, "Ghost on Water," 347.
35. Combs, "Ghost on Water," 356. Upon surveying stories of ghosts, Combs summarizes their condition thus: "Water is a hazard for ghosts. The sea serves as the final resting place for the phantom driven into it and presumably destroyed. Water is a boundary for spirits. Rivers function to impede the unburied dead from entering their rest and the buried dead from escaping their realm. Water is foreign to ghosts, and one who dies there must remain forever lost unless called to a cenotaph on the shore. Finally, since water is dangerous for the ghost, it can even be used as a defense to ward off unwanted spooks" (356).
36. Combs, "Ghost on Water," 356–58.
37. Combs, "Ghost on Water," 358.
38. Combs, "Ghost on Water," 358.

an incongruity into narrative elements that would otherwise be familiar to an audience: the image of a *phantasma* walking on water. Furthermore, Combs refers to similar features in an ancient comedy. He strengthens his case by drawing comparisons from an intentionally humorous ancient text, noting that both form and content are similar to Mark's own account. In so doing, Combs implicitly adopts an incongruity-based approach to humor and locates Mark in the ambit of other ancient comedic sources.

Iverson has offered a reading of Markan material that is vital in discussions of Markan humor. In his 2014 article, "Incongruity, Humor, and Mark: Performance and the Use of Laughter in the Second Gospel," Iverson unpacks the rhetorical strategy and effect of humor as deployed by the evangelist when recounting the story of Jesus and the disciples' third sea-crossing.[39] Iverson adopts the General Theory of Verbal Humor (hereafter GTVH), a method crafted by humor theorists Viktor Raskin and Salvatore Attardo, to act as the principle tool in detecting Markan humor. In particular, Iverson focuses on one key element of this method: script-opposition. Script-oppositions are rooted in the fundamental ambiguity of linguistic scripts wherein a given lexeme or text often maintains multiple meanings at the same time. The possibility of humor occurs when overlapping and opposed scripts are activated at the same time.[40] Such activation generates incongruity which, in turn, can lead to humor.[41] Iverson focuses on Jesus's statements concerning food in Mark 8:14—21, ultimately arguing that the statement about bread, though it "might appear to be an innocent piece of background information ... is a humorous jab line that exposes the disciples' paradoxical misunderstanding."[42] Ultimately, Iverson argues that the humorous stupidity of the disciples initially elicits laughter from a Markan audience, only to challenge the audience to consider their own potential misunderstandings as disciples.[43] Indeed, through clever use of humor, the evangelist invites the audience "to accept that the laughter derived at the disciples' expense is, ultimately, a joke on them."[44]

Iverson's article marks a step forward in Markan studies by making the gospel conversant with contemporary humor theory. Such a dialec-

---

39. Iverson, "Incongruity, Humor, and Mark," 2–19.
40. Iverson, "Incongruity, Humor, and Mark," 7.
41. Iverson, "Incongruity, Humor, and Mark," 7.
42. Iverson, "Incongruity, Humor, and Mark," 7.
43. Iverson, "Incongruity, Humor, and Mark," 17.
44. Iverson, "Incongruity, Humor, and Mark," 19.

tic is critical for considering potential humor in the text as it adopts a theory that is currently in use by contemporary humor scholars. Historically, one of the most consistent shortcomings in analyzing humor in the biblical text concerns a lack of methodological rigor. Iverson's work offers a tantalizing solution to this problem by approaching the biblical text with a coherent and systematic theory in hand. Indeed, as I will show, not only can Iverson's use of the GTVH track humor in one instance; in fact, it can be applied across significantly larger portions of the gospel narrative. When brought into conversation with ancient, comedic cotexts, the GTVH is a promising method that can yield fresh interpretive insights.

Emanuel, in "On the Eighth Day, God Laughed: 'Jewing' Humour and Self-Deprecation in *Crazy Ex-Girlfriend* and The Gospel of Mark," offers an intertextual reading of the Markan text that interacts with the expression of humor in a contemporary television show and the ways in which it illuminates humorous aspects of the gospel.[45] In an intricate analysis, Emanuel shifts between both texts with a focus on humor and identity. Emanuel's analysis engages critical aspects of the Markan narrative. In particular, she focuses on the incongruities latent within the text. Most notably, given that the Markan Gospel is plausibly a Jewish text, it appears strange that Jesus fails to live up to his title of Christ, and his followers are generally clueless about what is going on. When combined with other narrative oddities, such characterizations push against the boundaries of what one would expect from a panegyric focused on the life and legacy of Jesus. However, rather than accepting Mark as either farce or a satire of the Jesus movement, Emanuel suggests that such incongruities are likely an intentional form of humor. Drawing upon similar observations in *Crazy Ex-Girlfriend*, she notes:

> If we consider the absurdities within Mark's Gospel to mirror Jewish self-disparaging humour, which I think it does, then it is also worth considering the types of openings that humour creates ... self-disparagement creates space for implied readers to navigate on their own terms in what ways Jesus does or does not fit their needs ... such humour might even

---

45. Sarah Emanuel, "On the Eighth Day, God Laughed: 'Jewing' Humour and Self-Deprecation in *Crazy Ex-Girlfriend* and the Gospel of Mark," *Journal of Modern Jewish Studies* 19 (2020): 29–50.

leave room...for implied readers not only to remember that they suffered, but to also, in doing so, consider how much suffering impacted them.[46]

Emanuel's analysis of the Markan text is helpful for exploring humor in the narrative. To begin with, Emanuel helpfully touches on profound incongruities that lay at the root of the gospel, namely, that a story about the Christ involves a protagonist who suffers tremendously in his passion and that, though a teacher with followers, they rarely seem to know what is going on. Furthermore, Emanuel identifies a specific form of humor (self-deprecation) and explores how it might be functioning within a community grappling with the tragedy of 70 CE.

The work of the scholars above reveals that reading Mark from a comedic angle has potential to yield new insights, even possibly offering better ways of explaining such narratival oddities as the disciples' mistaking Jesus for a ghost or the cryptic statement regarding the disciples' forgetting of bread. Simultaneously, they signal that there is much work to do. While scholars occasionally make off-hand reference to elements they find humorous in the Markan text, a point to which I will return below, these authors represent sustained and methodical readings of humor with respect to the evangelist. Though their approaches differ, common elements can be found in the work thus far—humor scholarship on Mark has involved using some type of method, comparison with ancient comedic texts, or a combination of the two. Of these options, the attempt to combine contemporary methods with ancient comparanda offers the best way forward. More specifically, Iverson's use of the GTVH stands as a promising theoretical framework, drawing as it does upon a humor model that has been tested in various ways over three decades. When utilized alongside ancient comedic texts, the ability to discern humor in an otherwise ancient medium rises considerably.[47]

Humor-Adjacent Approaches to Mark

In addition to scholars working either systematically or nonsystematically with the topic of Markan humor, several scholars have worked in fields that I term *humor-adjacent*. Such studies explore aspects of Mark that function as necessary, if not sufficient, conditions found in humor and include ele-

---

46. Emanuel, "On the Eighth Day, God Laughed," 44.
47. For a more detailed explanation of methodology, see chapter 2.

ments such as satire, irony, ambiguity, and misdirection. Put another way, wherever ambiguity and multiple meanings present in a text, there often resides comedic possibility. This is due to the fact that incongruity remains one of the most important engines for humor, and such elements often generate incongruity.

For decades now, scholars have argued that the Markan text reflects a satirical outlook on Roman imperial power. Hans Leander's recent work on Mark illustrates this stream of scholarship.[48] In his postcolonial reading of Mark, Leander explores the ways in which the Markan Gospel both criticizes and reifies imperial power, even as the evangelist has written the gospel for lower-class urban populations in the empire. Leander argues that Mark's Gospel challenges imperial authority, especially Flavian imperial ideology.[49] This is most evident in the story of Jesus and the man afflicted by spirits in Mark 5 where Roman military might and ideology clash spectacularly in a confrontation between Legion and Jesus. Leander's emphasis on this pericope finds accent in other anti-imperial readings of Mark.[50] J. D. Derret argues for the presence of satire in this episode by focusing on the military terms in the passage.[51] Others such as Warren Carter explore the ways in which Jesus's actions emasculate and humiliate the imperial force.[52] Carter's contribution is noteworthy as it not only posits a satirical reading but draws upon the Greek comedic corpus to do so.[53]

---

48. Hans Leander, *Discourses of Empire: The Gospel of Mark from a Postcolonial Perspective*, SemeiaSt 71 (Society of Biblical Literature, 2013). Leander outlines four major interpretive trajectories regarding the relationship between the Markan Gospel and Rome: "(1) Mark as a Roman apology; (2) Mark as anti-imperial Gospel; (3) Mark as an imperial Gospel; and (4) Mark as a combined reproduction of and resistance against imperial ideology" (17). On the topic of Markan critiques of imperial power see Fernando Belo, *A Materialist Reading of the Gospel of Mark*, trans. Matthew O'Connell (Orbis, 1981); Richard Horsley, *Hearing the Whole Story: The Politics of Plot in Mark's Gospel* (Westminster John Knox, 2001); Ched Myers, *Binding the Strong Man: A Political Reading of Mark's Gospel* (Orbis, 1988); Hermen Waetjen, *A Reordering of Power: A Sociopolitical Reading of Mark's Gospel* (Fortress, 1989).

49. Leander, *Discourses of Empire*, 297.

50. Leander, *Discourses of Empire*, 298.

51. J. D. Derrett, "Contributions to the Study of the Gerasene Demoniac," *JSNT* 3 (1979): 2–17; Derrett, "Spirit-Possession and the Gerasene Demoniac," *Man* 14 (1979): 286–93.

52. Warren Carter, "Cross-Gendered Romans and Mark's Jesus: Legion Enters the Pigs (Mark 5:1–20)," *JBL* 134 (2015): 139–55.

53. Carter, "Cross-Gendered Romans," 139–55.

Other scholars have raised the possibility that the Markan evangelist intentionally utilizes sustained irony throughout the gospel. In his comprehensive work on the topic, Jerry Camery-Hogatt tracks irony as it surfaces in the Markan story.[54] He focuses especially on the social and literary functions of irony, ultimately concluding that the gospel intentionally plays with ambiguity to veil information for its characters that is otherwise available to an audience of the gospel.[55] This puts the audience in a privileged position, but also makes a demand upon hearers to embrace the evaluative point of view of the narrator.[56] This potentially impacts the life of the audience:

> If for Mark the events of Jesus' life are ciphers of a deeper reality, they are also sign-posts which can direct the reader to look more deeply into his own reality … in this way he can find the courage to affirm God in the face of a broken and suffering world.[57]

The presence of irony in Mark requires some comment; namely, what is the precise relationship between humor and irony? After all, one might object at the outset that a comical reading of Mark is nothing more than taking an ironic angle on the gospel and putting it in conversation with comedic cotexts. Unfortunately, this issue is difficult to resolve. The relationship between irony and humor is beset by a range of issues, not least of which concerns fundamental definitions of both terms.[58] Yet the two concepts are clearly related. As Isabel Ermida notes, at an essential level, "the analogy

---

54. Jerry Camery-Hoggatt, *Irony in Mark's Gospel: Text and Subtext*, SNTSMS 72 (Cambridge University Press, 1992). On irony in Mark, see also Gilbert Bilezekian, *The Liberated Gospel: A Comparison of the Gospel of Mark and Greek Tragedy* (Baker, 1977); Andrew Burrow, "Bargaining with Jesus: Irony in Mark 5:1–20," *BibInt* 25 (2017): 234–51; Robert Fowler, "Irony and the Messianic Secret in the Gospel of Mark," *Proceedings: Eastern Great Lakes and Midwest Biblical Societies* 1 (1981): 26–36; Donald Juel, *An Introduction to New Testament Literature* (Abingdon, 1978), 182–96; Geoffrey Miller, "An Intercalation Revisited: Christology, Discipleship, and Dramatic Irony in Mark 6:6b–30," *JSNT* 35 (2012): 176–95.
55. Camery-Hogatt, *Irony in Mark's Gospel*, 170–80.
56. Camery-Hogatt, *Irony in Mark's Gospel*, 170–80.
57. Camery-Hogatt, *Irony in Mark's Gospel*, 181.
58. Herbert Colston, "Irony and Sarcasm," in *The Routledge Handbook of Language and Humor*, ed. Salvatore Attardo, Routledge Handbooks in Linguistics (Routledge, 2017), 234–49, in his discussion of irony notes that "little agreement holds for a specific definition of irony sufficient for scholarly purposes. Indeed, some scholars have dismissed entirely the attempt at defining irony" (234). For a helpful discussion

between verbal humor and irony derives from a common characteristic: having one *signifier* which conceals more than one *signified*."[59] In spite of this commonality, there is significant debate regarding the intent and impact of irony and humor. One approach has been to suggest that irony has a serious telos, while humor simply makes light of a situation without offering a definitive value judgment in any particular direction.[60] Such a distinction, however, is overly simple and does not account for the constructive ways in which humor can, and often is, wielded in order to make intentional points. It very well may be the case that humor trades in the "realm of uncertainty and doubt";[61] however, comedic communication is often a powerful way to express a desired telos. Finally, in spite of the fact that there is certainly unhumorous irony and ironic humor, Attardo's observation regarding irony and humor is instructive: "With the proviso that irony need not be humorous, when it is so, it is clear that irony may contribute to the perception of humor in a text."[62] Consequently, I proceed with the understanding that both irony and humor are closely correlated and that, for the Markan evangelist, irony and humor are not mutually exclusive categories.

In addition to satirical and ironic readings of the Markan text, scholars have explored perceived ambiguities in the gospel, paying particular attention to the theme of misunderstanding that predominates the text.[63] Working with the category of the "anomalous frightful," Douglas W. Geyer examines Mark 4:35–6:56.[64] He explores the uncanny elements of the text

---

regarding definitions of irony and irony's relationship to humor, see Candace Lang, *Irony/Humor: Critical Paradigms* (The Johns Hopkins University Press, 1988), 37–69.

59. Isabel Ermida, *The Language of Comic Narratives: Humor Construction in Short Stories*, Humor Research 9 (De Gruyter, 2008), 11.

60. So Franck Evrard, *L'Humor* (Hachette, 1996) as quoted in Ermida, *Language of Comic Narratives*, 13.

61. Ermida, *Language of Comic Narratives*, 13.

62. Salvatore Attardo, *Humorous Texts: A Semantic and Pragmatic Analysis*, Humor Research 6 (de Gruyter, 2001), 122.

63. On the theme of misunderstanding, see also Jin Young Choi, "The Misunderstanding of Jesus' Disciples in Mark: An Interpretation from a Community-Centered Perspective," in *Mark*, ed. Nicole Wilkinson Duran, Teresa Okure, and Daniel Patte (Fortress, 2011); Michal Beth Dinkler, "Suffering, Misunderstanding, and Suffering Misunderstanding: The Markan Misunderstanding Motif as a Form of Jesus' Suffering," *JSNT* 38 (2016): 316–38.

64. Douglas Geyer, *Fear, Anomaly, and Uncertainty in the Gospel of Mark* (Scarecrow Press, 2002).

and argues that the evangelist intentionally characterizes Jesus as unresponsive to certainty in the text in order to draw readers' attention to this phenomenon while simultaneously resisting ideological interpretations of Jesus.[65] Mary Thompson, working with the narrative as a whole, maintains that there are two competing narrative levels of Mark that intentionally generate ambiguity.[66] This, in turn, creates a conflicted narrative by highlighting both Jesus's superlative position and his rejection and misunderstanding by persons in the story.[67] Deven Macdonald also notes the importance of misunderstanding in the Markan narrative.[68] He proffers that the evangelist crafts themes of "misunderstanding, opposition, and allegiance [that] present the reader, both ancient and modern, with a choice"[69] to acknowledge Jesus as the Son of God. Readings such as these highlight the centrality of ambiguity and misunderstanding in the Gospel of Mark.

The presence of humor-adjacent studies buttresses the studies scholars have undertaken so far to track humor in the Gospel of Mark. While they do not approach the question of humor directly, these studies raise the possibility of finding humor in the text by pointing to elements in the gospel that are often found in humorous texts. Features such as satire, irony, ambiguity, and misunderstanding function to subvert the obvious meaning of a narrative or idea. This generates multiple levels of meaning that occasionally find themselves in opposition to one another. The presence of potentially conflicting levels of meaning, in turn, gives rise to incongruity which humorists can exploit. With an overview of humor-specific and humor-adjacent approaches outlined, it is necessary to examine other preliminary considerations that impact the present study.

Mark 4:35–6:6 as Test Case

An examination of Markan humor would ideally take into account the full scope of the gospel text. This would yield the most comprehensive case for any arguments concerning what one may label Markan humor. Such a

---

65. Geyer, *Fear, Anomaly, and Uncertainty*, 19–64, 269–74.
66. Mary Thompson, *The Role of Disbelief in Mark: A New Approach to the Second Gospel* (Paulist, 1989).
67. Thompson, *Role of Disbelief*, 170–75.
68. Deven Macdonald, *Allegiance, Opposition, and Misunderstanding: A Narrative Critical Approach to Mark's Christology* (Pickwick, 2018).
69. Macdonald, *Allegiance, Opposition, and Misunderstanding*, 181.

task, unfortunately, is beyond the scope of the present study. Consequently, it is necessary to decide where in the Markan text to locate an extended study of potential humor. Though there are many promising locales in the gospel, for the present study I have chosen to examine 4:35–6:6. There are several reasons for this.

To begin with, this selection represents a discrete narrative block that is set off from preceding and subsequent material. Prior to this narrative, one encounters an extensive section on Jesus's teaching abilities focused on his use of parables and their proper interpretation (4:1–34). Immediately following the narrative block, upon Jesus's rejection in his home territory, the story shifts in order to focus not on Jesus's miraculous deeds alone but on the disciples' mission (6:6–13, 30) and the tragic death of John the Baptizer (6:14–29).

Additionally, the material is thematically linked. Mark 4:35–6:6 relates a series of stories testifying to Jesus's power over nature, demons, disease, and death. Each episode raises questions about Jesus's identity, exploring themes of his preternatural abilities, misunderstanding among followers and onlookers alike, and culminates in the rejection of Jesus by the people of his home territory (6:1–6). While narrative distinctiveness and thematic cohesion are not necessary for humor, tracking humor through such a block of material provides one with the opportunity to track patterns and motifs in how the evangelist might deploy humor.

Finally, I have selected this block of material because a handful of studies have signaled potential humor in the text. This is particularly the case in Mark 5. As noted above, scholars have called attention to incongruities in the narrative of the Gerasene demoniac (5:1–20). What is more, they have suggested that the story of the woman with an enduring illness and Jairus's daughter (5:21–43) possibly contains an ancient doctor joke alongside multilayered incongruities regarding sleep and death (5:35, 39, 41–42) that culminates in the only explicit reference to laughter in the gospel (5:40). Beyond these references, significant incongruities are present in the first and final episodes. The pericope about Jesus's calming of the raging storm (4:35–41) depicts Jesus asleep as the vessel he is on nearly shipwrecks, while his rejection in his home territory (6:1–6) finds Jesus unable to do works of power. These portraits of Jesus are arresting and warrant consideration for potential humor given their high degrees of potential incongruity. Notably, while scholars have made observations about humor in these episodes, only Hatton has studied the miracle cycle of Mark 4:35–6:6 and its humor in depth, and that study focused on the narrative of the woman and Jairus's daughter. Thus, this collection of stories is promising as a starting point for investigating potential humor. Its incongruities and oddities have tantalized scholars, flashing glimmers of humor that may yet reveal a rich vein of comedy if unearthed.

Terminology and Response

In the present study, I use the terms *humor* and *humorous* synonymously with a wide range of similar terms, including, but not limited to, *amusing, entertaining, comical, delightful, farcical, playful, funny, laughable,* and *witty*. Unlike some approaches to humor studies, there is no attempt to restrict humor to one term and view texts through this lens nor to engage in combat between one term and another (e.g., *wit* as droll vs. *comical* as farce). Rather, I have opted for a range of terms that index to a general affective domain often present when people are responding to humorous stimuli. It is also critical to note that, though such terms often are associated with laughter, I do not link humor with laughter per se. Laughter is one potential response to humorous stimuli, but far from the only acceptable or even common response.[70] For instance, one might smile rather than laugh. On the other hand, one might feel delight or mirth in response to a humorous stimulus but choose not to express this visibly for any number of reasons (e.g., social acceptability, one's own health/vigor, not wanting to reward a joke made in poor taste, etc.). Conversely, one might laugh where one finds no humor whatsoever. This decision is important when considering the ways in which humorous gospel texts might be performed, an issue which I explore in greater detail in chapter 4.

Final Considerations

For the present study, I presume that the Gospel of Mark is written for an audience of Jesus followers embedded well within the information flow and networks of the Greco-Roman world. This audience is informed by Jewish and Greco-Roman comedy, literature, and legends and shaped by the political arrangement of Rome as an empire in the second half of the first century CE. Demographically, the gospel audience may be imagined to be a mix of gentile and Jewish Jesus followers, all of whom must con-

---

70. For issues surrounding the bounding of humor, see chapter 4.

tend with the social pressures of converting to a potentially threatening religious organization, even while adjusting to new religious patterns and attempting to coordinate fellowship across cultural boundaries. There is, thus, enough commonality to bind this audience in humor, even if there is daylight that the Markan evangelist might occasionally exploit.[71]

The present study proceeds from a synchronic perspective. While I do not doubt that the Markan text has a preliterary history, the focus of the present study is on the final form of the text and the ways in which humor informs the rhetoric of this text. As a result, whatever may be said of the humor of Jesus, I include this within the purview of the Markan evangelist. I do not seek to further build on the work regarding the humor of the historical Jesus. This has already been established. Rather, I train my focus on the ways in which the evangelist deploys humor in the gospel text, with Jesus being one of many characters in this story.

Finally, I do not presume that all humor is beneficial. In an era shaped by the modern flourishing of comedy (stand-up, film, or sitcom), this is not always obvious, and many critics and scholars focus on the positive ends of humor. However, there are many ways in which humor can be used to a negative or detrimental effect. Humor is particularly adept at galvanizing deleterious attitudes towards out-group targets and obscuring deep prejudices and hatreds beneath the guise of laughter. While the accent of the present study falls on the constructive end of the spectrum, it is critical for biblical scholars to remember the two-edged nature of humor.

Conclusion

Markan humor is an idea whose time has come. The studies of the humor of the historical Jesus, the instincts of scholars who have raised the possibility of humor at one point or another in the text, and the exploration of topics such as irony, misunderstanding, and satire that suggest the possible presence of humor have presaged its arrival. In what follows, I will demonstrate that there is, in fact, a detectable Markan humor that impacts the ways in which one ought to read the miracle cycle of Mark

---

71. The question of audience remains a challenging issue in gospel studies. For a robust analysis of the evangelists' audience as fellow literary agent in the Greco-Roman world, see Robyn Faith Walsh, *The Origins of Early Christian Literature: Contextualizing the New Testament within Greco-Roman Literary Culture* (Cambridge University Press, 2021).

4:35–6:6. Indeed, being attuned to the presence of humor reveals new ways of reading these familiar stories, broadening the affective range and impact of the narrative while calling for a reevaluation of certain christological assumptions read into these stories. Humor is not coincidental to the interpretation of 4:35–6:6; rather, it is part of the very fiber of each pericope. Given its prominence, it is critical to adopt a method sufficient to locate and explain the function of humor in the text. It is to this essential issue that I now turn.

2
Method

Introduction

To laugh or not to laugh—that is the question. One of the most formidable challenges in humor studies concerns the determination of whether something is funny or not. Humor is frustratingly ephemeral in this regard. While every person has laughed at some point in her or his life, humor is implacably contextual. In spite of this challenge, it is hard to escape the sense that, at least in some moments, the Markan Gospel is comical. At the very least, as I noted in chapter 1, there are several scholars who make this case for elements of the Markan text. Unfortunately, while arguments for Markan humor are now underway, the tools one might need to detect humor remain underdeveloped. The goal of the present chapter is to address this specific issue by establishing a method that is suitable for detecting humor in Mark, or at least bringing contemporary readers into a range of probabilities regarding whether a particular saying or story might be considered humorous by Jesus followers in the first century CE. To do this, I will first discuss humor theory, paying particular attention to incongruity-based theories of humor. Next, I will demonstrate the importance of incongruity for humor as indicated by Greco-Roman philosophers, rhetoricians, and comedians. Finally, I will turn to modern humor theory and incongruity. This portion of the chapter will highlight the development of the General Theory of Verbal Humor (GTVH), tracing key moments in its history and its culmination in the work of Attardo, who has applied it to texts of varying length. I will argue that the GTVH is suited to the challenges of detecting humor in an ancient text such as Mark's Gospel, given its articulation as a theory seeking the necessary conditions for humor across cultures and social locations.

Humor Theory

There are several ways to discuss the topic of humor. Of course, before doing so, it is helpful to first define what one might mean by *humor*. The task is by no means easy, as humor theorist Attardo's survey of definitions involving the term demonstrates.[1] Following Raskin, whose work on humor I analyze below, I will utilize the term humor in an intentionally nonrestrictive sense, which may be "used synonymously with [terms such as] 'the funny,' 'the ludicrous,' 'the comic,' [and] 'the laughable.'"[2] Additionally, the broader semantic field of "humor" may include such terms as "wit," "pun," "bon mot," "satire," "nonsense," "ridicule," "mockery," and "teasing."[3] Put another way, humor may be said to refer to those words and actions that put one on the trajectory toward smiling and, ultimately, laughing, be it in a positive or negative manner (though laughter is not a necessary criterion for the presence of humor).[4] With this general definition of humor in hand, I turn to the question of how a contemporary reader might establish whether an ancient text contains humor.

Scholarship frequently approaches the study of humor from sociological, psychological, linguistic, or philosophical avenues. When tracking the development of humor theory, scholars usually break down this history into three major theories: (1) superiority theories; (2) relief theories; and (3) incongruity theories.[5] Superiority theorists argue that humor is fundamentally aggressive and functions as a way to disparage a specific target of a particular joke. What is more, individuals will often aim this humor at outsiders, powerful or otherwise, and can accomplish various sociological ends as a result.[6] Relief theorists assert that humor functions as a kind

---

1. Salvatore Attardo, *Linguistic Theories of Humor*, Humor Research 1 (de Gruyter, 1994), 2–13. See, too, the discussion in Viktor Raskin, *Semantic Mechanisms of Humor*, Synthese Language Library 24 (Reidel, 1985), 1–8.

2. Raskin, *Semantic Mechanisms of Humor*, 28. Attardo, *Linguistic Theories of Humor*, 10, also accepts Raskin's definition of humor.

3. Terms are taken from figure 0.1 in Attardo, *Linguistic Theories of Humor*, 7.

4. On the issue of laughter as an overly restrictive and even misleading criterion for detecting humor, see Attardo, *Linguistic Theories of Humor*, 10–13.

5. For a helpful overview of the historical study of humor, see Amy Carrell, "Historical Views of Humor," in *The Primer of Humor Research*, ed. Victor Raskin and Willibald Ruch, Humor Research 8 (de Gruyter, 2008), 303–32.

6. On the potential for humor to function as both a social "lubricant" (in-group formation) and "abrasive" (out-group formation), see especially William Martineau,

of release for the person experiencing humor. Such release can be social (e.g., brief relief from structures that society might impose on someone) or physiological (e.g., the burning off of nervous energy). Finally, incongruity theorists proffer that one generates humor through the apprehension of two apparently contradictory realities permeating one another. Incongruity humor theorists differ on how they understand this phenomenon. For instance, D. H. Monro defines incongruity-based humor as being rooted in the "linking of opposites."[7] For Mahadev L. Apte, incongruity may involve humor that arises from "the result of cultural perceptions, both individual and collective, of incongruity, exaggeration, distortion, and any unusual combination of the cultural elements in external events."[8] Essentially, the juxtaposition between two seemingly disconnected ideas, images, impressions, et cetera, gives rise to the perception of something not being as it should. This discordance can, in turn, engender a humorous response. Generic examples of such incongruity might include the imagery of a horse riding a man, an elephant in overly tight clothing, or a short giraffe, while more famous examples of humorous incongruity would include Monty Python's King Arthur confounded in his august quest for the holy grail by a discussion about swallows carrying coconuts or Cervantes's Don Quixote desire to joust windmills.

While each of these humor theories maintains considerable scholarly support, I anchor the present study in an incongruity approach. I do not assume that other models of humor cannot be used as well. Indeed, superiority, relief, and incongruity theories of humor often work alongside and complement one another. However, it is beyond the scope of the present study to take up all of these methods and apply them to the Markan text. Tracking the comedic elements in the gospel along this band is helpful for keeping the present study narrowly focused on the text. An incongruity-based approach also benefits from important advances in linguistic-based humor theory that have developed in the last three decades, offering strong prospects for identifying and evaluating humor in ancient texts through

---

"A Model of the Social Functions of Humor," in *The Psychology of Humor: Theoretical Perspectives and Empirical Issues*, ed. Jeffrey Goldstein and Paul McGhee (Academic Press, 1972), 101–25.

7. D. H. Monro, *Argument of Laughter* (Melbourne University Press, 1951), 248, as quoted in Carrell, "Historical Views of Humor," 303–32.

8. Mahadev L. Apte, *Humor and Laughter: An Anthropological Approach* (Cornell University Press, 1985), 16, as quoted in Carrell, "Historical Views of Humor," 311.

the use of the GTVH. Finally, an incongruity-based approach to humor benefits from approaching humor along an axis familiar to the ancients themselves.

The Ancient Roots of Incongruity and Humor

Incongruity among Greco-Roman Philosophers and Rhetoricians

When considering the subject of humor in the ancient world, scholars do not necessarily think of incongruity first.[9] Rather, many turn to a superiority model. The move is not surprising given the nature of ancient humor, which frequently traded in insulting people for mental, physical, and spiritual "deficiencies."[10] Aristotle is often quoted as providing a summative view with respect to this type of humor in the Greco-Roman world:

> Comedy, as we said, is mimesis of baser but not wholly vicious characters: rather, the laughable comprises any fault or mark of shame which involves no pain or destruction: most obviously, the laughable mask is something ugly and twisted. (Aristotle, *Poet*. 1449a [Halliwell])

Aristotle's definition here underscores comedy's negative, targeting tendencies. Yet though there is no shortage of such comedy present in the ancient world, Greek and Roman writers considered other approaches to humor. Indeed, many ancient philosophers and rhetoricians underscore elements of incongruity in their respective analyses of humor. One sees this in the works of Plato, Aristotle, Cicero, and Quintillian.

---

9. The present chapter focuses primarily on Greco-Roman texts. I have chosen these because they either explicitly deal with the subject of humor or are considered humorous by their genre. Such texts provide the firmest footing when attempting to articulate how the wider Greco-Roman world understood humor.

10. Peter Berger, *Redeeming Laughter: The Comic Dimension of Human Experience*, 2nd ed. (de Gruyter, 1997), 37–39, in a brief overview of Plato, Aristotle, and Cicero underscores the bitterness of ancient humor. So, too, do Anthony Chapman and Hugh Foot, eds., *Humor and Laughter: Theory, Research, and Applications* (Transaction, 1995), 1. This view is understandable. One does not need to look far in the ancient world to find humor rooted in seemingly cruel topics.

Plato

When interpreting Plato's examination of humor, scholars often regard the philosopher as holding a negative view of humor, principally because he construed humor in light of its pejorative capacity. After all, Plato linked Aristophanes's comedic work in *Clouds* to the death of Socrates (*Apol.* 18d, 19c). One can hardly be surprised that Plato was wary of comedy if he did, indeed, believe it played a part in the demise of his mentor.[11] While this assessment of Plato's perspective on humor is accurate, it is incomplete. Plato analyzed other aspects of humor and occasionally commented on the role of incongruity. For instance, in a discussion regarding laughable arts, Plato's Athenian Stranger states that human poets "by their senselessness in mixing such things and jumbling them up together would furnish a theme for laughter to all men" (*Leg.* 2.669e [Bury]). The tendency for poets to cleave "rhythm and gesture from tune, putting tuneless words into metre, or leaving tune and rhythm without words" (*Leg.* 2.669e [Bury]) reflects self-evidently clownish activities through inappropriate juxtaposition of artistic elements.[12] Plato develops a similar theme in his conversation between Socrates and Glaucon in *Republic*. Throughout their dialogue, Socrates offers a ridiculous picture to Glaucon in the thought experiment of imagining women, young and old, exercising alongside men in the gymnasium—a mental image Glaucon considers laughable given its sheer incongruity (*Resp.* 452b).[13]

Aristotle

As I noted above, Aristotle offers a definition of comedy that is consonant with a superiority theory of humor. Yet it is possible that Aristotle, and/or the Aristotelian tradition after him, recognized incongruity as a

---

11. Cameron Shelly, "Plato on the Psychology of Humor," *Humor* 16 (2003): 352, summarizes Plato's suspicion well: "Plato was well aware that comedy is not simply a political or social phenomenon.... Plato says a fair amount about laughter and malice and how they are combined when we feel amused about a character being derided on stage or a person being ridiculed in public. The result can be insalubrious not only for the person being laughed at ... but also for the person doing the laughing."
12. Shelley, "Plato on the Psychology of Humor," 356–57.
13. Lisa Glebatis Perks, "The Ancient Roots of Humor Theory," *Humor* 25 (2012): 119–32.

critical element of the comedic. In *Rhetoric*, amid an extended analysis of metaphors, Aristotle talks about their misleading nature, which, in turn contributes to their overall efficacy. Significantly, Aristotle brings up the tendency of humor to rely on unexpected surprise:

> And what Theodorus calls "novel expressions" arise when what follows is paradoxical, and, as he puts it, not in accordance with previous expectation; just as humorists make use of slight changes of words. The same effect is produced by jokes that turn on the change of a letter; for they are deceptive. (*Rhet.* 3.1412b [Freeze])

Aristotle's observations suggest that juxtaposition or incongruity were important for generating a particular comedic effect.[14] Helpfully, Aristotle provides an example and explanation of such humor: "And he stroed on, under his feet—chilblains, whereas the hearer thought he was going to say 'sandals.' This kind of joke must be clear from the moment of utterance. Jokes that turn on the words are produced, not by giving it the proper meaning, but by perverting it" (*Rhet.* 3.1412b [Freeze]). As Aristotle notes, the humor here derives from incongruous surprise.

In addition to Aristotle's remarks regarding humor, one finds more explicit discussion of incongruity in the *Tractatus Coislinianus*. The question of the text's relationship to Aristotle is complicated; though it appears to have some connection to Aristotle, the manuscript tradition associated with it dates to the tenth century CE. Thus, there is something of an open question regarding whether or not *Tractatus Coislinianus* faithfully represents Aristotle's supposed lost second book of *Poetics* wherein comedy is discussed at length. Though the issue is far from settled, enough scholars view it as a valuable witness either to Aristotle or an Aristotelian tradition that I consider it here.[15]

Tractatus Coislinianus is fairly concise. While it is brief, the text points consistently to the importance of incongruity for humor. It defines

---

14. Attardo, *Linguistic Theories of Humor*, 20–21; John Morreall, *Taking Laughter Seriously* (State University of New York, 1987), 14.

15. For instance, Attardo, *Linguistic Theories of Humor*; Lane Cooper, *An Aristotelian Theory of Comedy: with an Adaptation of the Poetics and a Translation of "Tractatus Coislinianus"* (Harcourt, 1922); Richard Janko, *Aristotle on Comedy: Towards a Reconstruction of Poetics*, vol. 2 (University of California Press, 1984); and Armando Plebe *La teoria del comico da Aristotele a Plutarco* (Giappichelli, 1952), maintain that *Tractatus Coislinianus* can be used to discover most or parts of the second book in Poetics.

comedy as "an imitation of action that is ludicrous and imperfect."[16] What is more, in describing the technical mechanisms of humor, *Tractatus* remarks that laughter arises "from deception, from the impossible, from the possible and consequent, from the unexpected … from the use of clownish dancing, when one of those having power, neglecting the greatest things, takes the most worthless."[17] Additionally, characters of comedy are said to consist of buffoons and the ironical.[18] Elements such as these point to the consistent use of incongruity as a mechanism for generating comedy as they speak to characters acting incongruously or ludicrously.[19]

Cicero

Moving from Greek philosophers to Latin orators, one finds an even more pronounced discussion regarding the mechanisms of humor. Cicero, through the persona of Julius Caesar, offers an extended discussion of humor in *De Oratore*. He remarks that one of the primary categories of "the laughable" (*Or.* 2.62.254 [Sutton and Rackham]) is that which is unexpected. What is more, it is one of the most ubiquitous categories: "These categories I will certainly run over. You know already, however, that the most familiar of these is exemplified when we are expecting to hear a particular phrase, and something different is uttered" (*Or.* 2.63.255 [Sutton and Rackham]). Cicero's humorous category of the unexpected relies on the incongruity between expectation and actuality, a tension that gives rise to a laugh. "In this case our own mistake even makes us laugh ourselves" (*Or.* 2.63.255 [Sutton and Rackham]). Cicero proceeds to offer several more categories of the laughable but returns once more to incongruity: "But of all these devices nothing causes more amusement than an unexpected turn, of which there are countless instances" (*Or.* 2.70.254 [Sutton and Rackham]). In addition to viewing incongruity as a key category of humor, Cicero enumerates several examples of the comedic, many of

---

16. Cooper, *Aristotelian Theory of Comedy*, 225.
17. Cooper, *Aristotelian Theory of Comedy*, 225.
18. Cooper, *Aristotelian Theory of Comedy*, 226.
19. On this point see especially Perks, "Ancient Roots of Humor Theory," 122, who points to several scholars who view *Tractatus Coislinianus* as highlighting the importance of incongruity for humor. See further Janko, *Aristotle on Comedy*, 95, as well as Cooper's extensive commentary on these elements.

which rely directly on incongruity.[20] Ultimately, Cicero offers one of the earliest extant treatments of humor that directly addresses the importance of incongruity as a key mechanism in humorous discourse. He is followed shortly thereafter by Quintilian.

Quintilian

Quintilian, a notable admirer of Cicero whom he dubs "the prince of orators" (*Inst.* 6.2.3 [Butler]), offers his own extended analysis of humor akin to that of his predecessor. In *Institutio*, Quintilian develops a taxonomy of the humorous where incongruity figures prominently. Quintilian admits at the beginning of his analysis that humor is difficult to categorize; however, in spite of this, when it comes to the topic of the "excitement of laughter" (*Inst.* 6.3.22 [Butler], he identifies three primary categories of humor, the last of which "consists in cheating expectations, in taking words in a different sense from what was intended" (*Inst.* 6.3.24 [Butler]). Thus, incongruity, much as it does for Cicero, forms one of Quintilian's primary categories of that which causes laughter. Following this statement of broad categories, Quintilian proceeds in seemingly desultory fashion to explore many examples of different humorous forms of speech, several of which contain elements of incongruity.[21] After citing various instances of humor, Quintilian returns again to the importance of incongruity: "There remains the prettiest of all forms of humour, namely the jest which depends for success on deceiving anticipations or taking another's words in a sense other than he intended" (*Inst.* 6.3.84 [Butler]). Such humor relies

---

20. It is beyond the scope of the present study to enumerate all such examples, as Cicero's study is strikingly exhaustive. For a helpful breakdown of larger categories of incongruity, see especially Perks, "Ancient Roots of Humor Theory," 123, who sets Cicero's incongruity into the categories of "deceived expectation," "misrepresenting one's own views or the views of another person," "the disjunctive relationship between the tenor of a speaker's statements and character," and "those formed from a clash between a speaker's statements and the relative gravity of a situation."

21. For instance, in remarking upon humor's capacity to be a weapon in oration, Quintilian cites Nero's joke of a thieving slave that "no one was more trusted in my house: there was nothing closed or sealed to him" (*Inst.* 6.3.50 [Butler]). This is a rather wry take on an otherwise serious problem. Not only is there incongruity in a trusted slave acting as a thief, but there is additional humor in the latter part of this statement, which was quite literally true (i.e., he was capable of stealing everything in the house, even if it had been carefully secured and shuttered away).

on incongruity by offering a different element to a saying than that which a person is expecting, and, significantly, is given a superlative position in Quintilian's explanation of humorous discourse. All told, Quintilian maintains that incongruity, while not the only element present in humor, acts as a primary category for the excitement of laughter.

Incongruity among the Greco-Roman Comedic Playwrights

The Greco-Roman world was home not only to philosophical and rhetorical reflections on humor, but it was also the cradle of a prolific and enduring comedic tradition. What is more, comedians from Athens to Rome employed incongruity as a key element for evoking laughter. One finds this tendency in the works of Aristophanes, Menander, Plautus, and Terence.

Aristophanes

Many scholars and critics regard Aristophanes as one of the most important playwrights of ancient comedy. Indeed, any discussion of Old Comedy must inevitably invoke Aristophanes as he is widely considered its most important representative, though he is certainly not its only ambassador.[22] A dramatist of late fifth-century and early fourth-century BCE Athens, Aristophanes wrote approximately forty-five plays, eleven of which survive to the present.[23] Old Comedy's most famous playwright crafted plays that touched on a wide variety of themes, including, though not limited to, war, religion, political leaders, foreigners, and sex.[24] In the process of treating these topics, Aristophanes deployed incongruity extensively.

---

22. Aristophanes's stature is remarkable, and he was already regarded by the time of Aristotle as one of the most important writers for defining Athenian comedy in the fifth century BCE. However, scholars rightly point out that there were many other comic writers at this time, several of whom beat out Aristophanes in dramatic contests. For more on this, see Jeffrey Rusten, ed., *The Birth of Comedy: Texts, Documents, and Art from Athenian Comic Competitions, 486–280*, trans. Jeffrey Henderson et. al. (The Johns Hopkins University Press, 2011), 1–456.

23. Bernhard Zimmerman, "Aristophanes," in *The Oxford Handbook of Greek and Roman Comedy*, ed. Michael Fontaine and Adele C. Scafuro (Oxford University Press, 2014), 132–59, notes the difficulty of ascertaining the precise number of plays written by Aristophanes, suggesting anywhere from forty-five to fifty-four.

24. There is debate as to how politically one should read Aristophanes. That is, was Aristophanes actively seeking to shape discussions on the topics he ridiculed, or

To begin with, Aristophanes frequently drew upon incongruity in his use of obscenities. His plays, as so many others in Old Comedy, traded frequently in bawdy themes.[25] Comedic costuming in this period might see some players wear a phallus at all times.[26] This open display of the phallus stood in sharp contrast to the general attitude of contemporaneous Athenians who regarded it as something that should remain covered.[27] The contrast between typical costumes and theatrical sanction likely generated incongruity for theatergoers. Characters within the plays exploited this mismatch. Aristophanes's prologue in *Acharnians* is emblematic of how he often dealt with such incongruity elsewhere in his canon. In the opening speech, the protagonist Dicaeopolis lists the various things he does while waiting for people to join him at the assembly, including his tendency to fart and even pluck pubic hairs—actions which Athenian society regarded

---

was he simply creating funny plays for their own sake? For a helpful take on reading Aristophanes in conjunction with ideological concerns of fifth century BCE Athens, see David Konstan, *Greek Comedy and Ideology* (Oxford University Press, 1995), 3–92.

25. In discussions of the origins of comedy, scholars often point to traditions of obscenity as comedy developed in association with satyr plays and Dionysian processions. For examples of phallic humor see Rusten, *Birth of Comedy*, 45–50. On Aristophanes's use of obscenity, see James Robson, *Humour, Obscenity, and Aristophanes* (Narr Verlag, 2006). On this topic see also Jeffrey Henderson, *The Maculate Muse: Obscene Language in Attic Comedy* (Yale University Press, 1975).

26. Halliwell, *Greek Laughter*, 252.

27. Henderson, *Maculate Muse*, 1–30, emphasizes the differentiation a fifth-century BCE Athenian audience would hold. For such persons, obscenity was defined primarily with respect to shameful or shameless acts, rooted particularly in making sure private aspects of life remained hidden from public view. The comic theater provided a space where theatergoers could see such private affairs aired openly. However, because it was not the audience member openly displaying or talking about genitalia, the matter could then become laughable. The theater created a space where an author could breach a taboo topic because of the distance between the characters and the audience. Heraclitus of Ephesus offers a helpful commentary on this distinction where otherwise shameful acts found sanction through ritual: "If it were not for Dionysus that they hold their process and sing songs to genitals [*aidoia*], then these acts would be absolutely shameless [*anaidestata*], but Dionysus, for whom they act mad and drunken, is the same as Hades [*Aidies*]" (Rusten, *Birth of Comedy*, 46). Indeed, a short time later, Aristotle would highlight both the centrality of obscenities to comedy, while encouraging students of civil life to abstain from watching comedies. Jeffrey Rusten, "In Search of the Essence of Old Comedy: From Aristotle's Poetics to Zieliński, Cornford, and Beyond," in *The Oxford Handbook of Greek and Roman Comedy*, ed. Michael Fontaine and Adele C. Scafuro (Oxford University Press, 2014), 33–49.

as embarrassing and borderline obscene.[28] Aristophanes exploited these obscenities, and many others besides, generating an incongruity between custom and comedic theater.

In addition to the utilization of obscene references, Aristophanes also depicted incongruous portraits of both gods and people. Unlike the tragedians of classical Athens, Aristophanes did not draw upon the gods as frequently to supply major characters.[29] When he did include them, he often depicted the gods in comical fashion. This is particularly evident in *Birds*. In this comedy, the cunning protagonist Peisetaerus crafts and executes a plan whereby he overpowers the gods through convincing the birds to lay siege to heaven. The birds, in turn, starve the gods into submission by cutting off their access to sacrifices. Finally, Peisetaerus, through further trickery, ultimately usurps the authority of Zeus himself. The portrait of the gods in *Birds* as finding their defeat at the hands of humans and their bird companions stands in sharp contrast to the more common view of the gods as powerful, if capricious, beings and likely acted as a source of humor for theatergoers. Such humorous incongruity was also evident in the depiction of popular political Athenian figures. Throughout his career, Aristophanes targeted several individuals in his comedies, perhaps none so famously as Socrates in *Clouds*.[30] In this comedy, Aristophanes mocks the character and legacy of Socrates relentlessly. Aside from the essential incongruity of his character, Aristophanes depicts the philosopher as a useless, pedantic, youth-deceiver whose ideas run counter to the good of society.[31] For instance, the "thinkery" he runs is said to put forward ideas such as "the sky is a barbeque lid … and that we're coals" (*Nub.* 95–96 [Henderson]), has determined "how many of its own feet a flea can jump" (*Nub.* 145 [Henderson]), and learned that "the gnat's arsehole turns out to be a bugle" (*Nub.* 165 [Henderson]). Indeed, much to the protagonist

---

28. Henderson, *Maculate Muse*, 58.

29. John Given, "When Gods Don't Appear: Divine Absence and Human Agency in Aristophanes," *CW* 102 (2009): 107–27.

30. Old Comedy, rooted as it was in the Iambic traditions, was home to sharp invective. For more on this topic, see Ralph Rosen, *Old Comedy and the Iambographic Tradition*, American Classical Studies 19 (Scholars Press, 1988).

31. Andres Willi, *The Languages of Aristophanes: Aspects of Linguistic Variation in Classical Attic Greek* (Oxford University Press, 2003), 116, notes that there is already inherent incongruity in Socrates's characterization: "*Clouds* stages a Socrates who holds Diogenean ideas, lives in a Pythagorean setting, and uses Empedoclean language. To be sure, such a composite picture is a result of much comic freedom."

Strepsiades's dismay, Socrates's teaching enables Pheidippides, his son, to rebel against his parents, even threatening to beat both father and mother (*Nub.* 1443). The presentation of Socrates in *Clouds* stands in sharp contrast to more august depictions of him as a stately philosopher.

Finally, Aristophanes often utilizes absurdly incongruous scenarios as the pretext for scenes as well as entire plays, a fact on full display in *Lysistrata*. To begin with, the plot of *Lysistrata* is based on a striking situation: the women of Athens, tired of war, are led by the titular character to initiate a sex-strike until the men of Athens cease fighting. Consequently, the entire premise of *Lysistrata* takes patriarchal Athenian concerns about the libidinous nature of women to a hyperbolic extreme, creating a contrastive portrait between actual, socially acceptable limits on female sexuality and that which occurs in the play. It also plays on the incongruity between idealistic assumptions about male self-control, depicting a juxtaposition in the male characters who will pursue peace if only to attain sexual pleasure.

Aristophanes, along with several playwrights of Athenian Old Comedy, utilized incongruity to generate much of his humor. Notably, though Greek comedy would undergo significant shifts from Old to Middle Comedy, the use of incongruity would remain an important feature for comedic authors.

Menander

One of the most important comedic writers of Greek theater was Menander (ca. 343 BCE–291 BCE). The Athenian dramatist lived during a particularly tumultuous period of Athens' political life and was likely the student of Theophrastus who himself took over Aristotle's peripatetic school. Menander's writings represent a key shift in the tone of Greek comedy. Indeed, many scholars hold that his style is illustrative of the shift from Old and Middle Comedy to New Comedy.[32] Several key changes occur in this transition impacting both formal and thematic elements of com-

---

32. Scholars of Greek comedy divide the genre into three major time periods: Old, Middle, and New. These periods demonstrate the changes comedy underwent from the fifth to the third centuries BCE in Athens. Scholars study Old and New Comedy primarily through the writings of Aristophanes and Menander, while Middle Comedy remains significantly lacking in sources (though Aristophanes's later work is sometimes viewed as a transition to Middle Comedy).

edy.³³ For example, the chorus, a critical element of plays in Old Comedy, shrinks to a space between each act, rather than persisting throughout the entire play. Thematically, contemporary politics and events vanish from the comedic stage, with a focus on domestic affairs and troubles appearing in their stead. The writing itself becomes more chastened, with farce and obscenity cast to the wayside. Such changes result in a form of comedy much less overtly absurd in its topics, language, and plots.³⁴ Indeed, scholars frequently praise Menander's work as "realist" or "mimetic," celebrating in particular his sharply drawn characters. As a result, the use of incongruity in Menander is subtle when one views it against Aristophanes. Yet in spite of more nuanced craft and contrived plots, Menander still relies on incongruity to generate humor. Menander employs incongruity in jokes and dialogue, plots, and characterization. These techniques are all present in the play *Perikeiromene*.

In the comedy *Perikeiromene*, the female protagonist Glykere is in a love-triangle with a hot-tempered husband, Polemon, and her brother, Moschion (though they do not know they are related). The comedy builds from this conflict until the play finally reveals that Glykera and Moschion are siblings, Polemon learns his lesson to be a gentler man, and Glykera and Polemon marry while receiving a blessing from Glykere's long-lost father, Paitaikos. Throughout the play there are several one-off jokes and back-and-forth exchanges derived from incongruity. For example, in a confrontation between Polemon's and Moschion's respective retinues, Menander adopts militaristic language to characterize the conflict. This rhetoric pushes into the realm of double-entendres, which provide the basis for several jokes, while the scene itself incongruously compares the scrappy retinues to fully decamped armies.³⁵ Menander also utilizes incongruity for longer, comical back-and-forth exchanges. For instance, in an extended dialogue between Moschion and his slave Daos, the two

---

33. For a helpful treatment of Menander and particular compositional issues such as the relationship of his work to tragedy, the topic of Menandrian choruses, pacing of plot, etc., see Alain Blanchard, *Essai sur la composition des comédies de Ménandre* (Les Belles Lettres, 1983).

34. One might dispute whether the plots are not farcical or at least absurd as they so often hinge on woefully convenient deception and recognition. Indeed, the degree to which *anagnorsis* predominates New Comedy plots can be frustratingly predictable, at least for the contemporary reader.

35. William Furly, *Menander: Perikeiromene or The Shorn Head*, Bulletin of the Institute of Classical Studies Supplement 127 (Institute of Classical Studies, 2015), 75.

men have been discussing Daos's attempts to secure an audience for Moschion with Glykera, who herself has moved in with Moschion's mother Myrrhine. Comically, Daos insinuates that he helped make this happen, but also admits that the mother does not want Moschion to interact with Glykera. This leads to a humorous exchange between the two:

> Moschion: What's that you say? [Didn't take] her in by choice? Or why then? Not on my behalf? [You said] you persuaded her to come to my house!
> Daos: Have I said [I persuaded] her to come here? By Apollo I did not—[You're accusing me] of telling lies about you, master, [now].
> Moschion: Did[n't] you just now allege that you [yourself] had helped to persuade [my mother] to allow the girl to stay with us, all for *my* sake?
> Daos: Look, I said that. Yes, I do remember. (*Perik.* 484–485 [Arnott])

Menander crafts a comically incongruous scene here, particularly in the character of Daos who initially takes credit for Moschion's fortune, then tries to distance himself when Myrrhine dismisses him, only to remember what he said after Moschion confronts him.

Menander often uses incongruity as the foundation for scenes and even entire plays. In act 3 of *Perikeiromene*, Menander sketches a comical portrait in the rag-tag band of ruffians who consist of Polemon's army (*Perik.* 467–550). This army consists of a slave, a courtesan, and a slightly inebriated Polemon. Menander is comically juxtaposing these characters with an actual army—a fact noted within the play itself when Moschion declares: "*They* couldn't wipe a nest of swallows out—what pansies these Devils are! They'd got mercenaries, he said—These celebrated mercenaries amount to Sosia here and no one else!" (*Perik.* 526–531 [Arnott]). In addition to incongruous scenarios generally, Menander often creates humor by cutting an otherwise comical scene from tragic cloth. This is evident in the recognition-scene between Glykera and her father Pataikos in the fourth act of the play (*Perik.* 708–827). The emotional scene wherein father and daughter finally reunite is written in a tragic register, but it is juxtaposed by comical asides in the person of Moschion who learns his own identity while eavesdropping throughout the speech.[36] Indeed, this is a technique

---

36. Netta Zagagi, *The Comedy of Menander: Convention, Variation and Originality* (Indiana University Press, 1995), 51, notes: "The recognition scene between Glykere and Pataikos in *Perikeiromene*, with its stichomythical structure, its lofty expressions and its unchanging metrical pattern, well illustrates the advantages

Menander adopts elsewhere, blending and contrasting tragic form with comical scenes and likely engendering laughter as a result.[37] Notably, Menander does not apply such incongruity only to scenes but extends this through entire plays. *Perikeiromene*, while it touches on important themes and is realistic in its presentation of characters, stands on an incongruity that drives the plot forward and accounts for comical misunderstandings, namely, that the love triangle is in fact really only one-sided, for Moschion can never be with Glykera. It is fitting that the prologue is given by the goddess Misunderstanding (*Agnoia*), for the play's entire conflict turns on misunderstanding.

Menander also uses incongruity in his characterization. This technique is especially evident in *Perikeiromene*'s Polemon. Polemon, Glykera's common-law husband, cuts off her hair in a fit of jealousy, his rashness touching off the precipitating action of the play. Notably, rather than being a competent, capable military man as a soldier should, Menander portrays him as a petty, distraught man who cannot manage his own affairs and needs constant help and encouragement from friends. Sosias, his slave, wryly observes: "Our swaggering soldier of an hour ago ... now lies upon his couch in tears" (*Perik.* 172–174 [Arnott]) whose "friends have mustered there together, just to help him soldier through this business with less pain" (*Perik.* 175–177 [Arnott]). Later, in act 3, Polemon enlists the aid of Pataikos in hopes that he can help turn Glykera's affections back to himself. Polemon, in contrast to a manly soldier, is beside himself: "I don't know, by Demeter, what to say, except, I'll choke! Pataikos, Glykera has left Me, left me—Glykera!" (*Perik.* 505–507 [Arnott]). Polemon's grief gives way to an awkward exchange between the two men as he harps on about the clothes he bought for Glykera:

> Polemon: ... if you could see her things ...
> Pataikos: No need for that!
> Polemon: Just look, Pataikos, *please*—You'll pity me more!
> Pataikos: In heaven's name!
> Polemon: Do come here—such dresses! How she looks when she slips one of these on! Perhaps you won't have seen ...

---

inherent in presenting a comic situation (note the farcical element of Moschion's eavesdropping!) in tragic guise."

37. See, for instance, the dramatic exchange between Daos and Smikrines in *Samia* where Demeas quotes tragedies only for Smikrines to mock them for their overly dramatic nature (Zagagi, *Comedy of Menander*, 53).

Pataikos: I have.
Polemon: Of course her height's remarkable—but why Should I now introduce her height? I'm crazy, Going on about irrelevances! (*Perik.* 515–524 [Arnott])

In this portrayal, Menander depicts Polemon as a humorous character through the use of strong contrast between his character-type (soldier) and his actual character (weeping lover). Rather than commanding his emotions, Polemon is powerless and hardly able to help himself.

Menander's comedies represent a significant turn in the development of Greek comic traditions. However, despite significant departures from Old and Middle Comedy, incongruity remains an important engine for humor in New Comedy. From brief quips to entire plays, incongruity is a mainstay for Menander, even as his writings turn to more nuanced techniques. The use of incongruity in New Comedy would persist as a feature of Latin comedy.

Plautus

Titus Maccius Plautus is the first of the two comedic, Roman playwrights whose corpus of *comoediae* has survived to the present era.[38] Born in the middle of the third century BCE, Plautus worked in the Roman theater before going on to become a commercially successful dramatist.[39] Twenty-one of Plautus's comedies are known and represent Plautine comedy. While there are many elements to Plautus's comedies, his plays often draw upon incongruity in order to achieve a comic effect.[40] Indeed, Erich Segal has

---

38. While there were other Roman comedic writers in this era, all that remains of these dramatists are fragments. Thus, while scholars have access to literature from playwrights such as Naevius, Caecilius, and Titinius, the fragmentary nature of their work causes scholars to approach the topic of Roman comedy through the larger, more complete works of Plautus and Terence. For a general overview of the difficulties in coordinating Plautus within a broader stream of fragmentary works see Wolfgang David Cirilo de Melo, "Plautus' Dramatic Predecessors and Contemporaries in Rome," in Fontaine and Scafuro, *Oxford Handbook of Greek and Roman Comedy*, 447–61.

39. Although Plautus's relationship to the theater is somewhat unclear, scholars generally believe that Plautus held some position in the theater early on in his career. Whether an actor or set-builder, Plautus's familiarity with the technicality of the theater shows up often through his various works.

40. Studies on Plautine comic technique abound, whether looking closely at the language of Plautus or more broadly at his form and use of "meta-theater." For more

argued that Plautus offers a primarily Saturnalian take on Roman values, drawing laughter from his audience by the sheer incongruity of lauding values such as disrespect for elders, marital discord, parricide, and even direct blasphemy.[41] While not all scholars agree with this interpretation of Plautus, Segal's characterization stands as one of two major paradigms in Plautine scholarship.[42]

Plautus deploys incongruity in manifold ways. Like other comic writers, incongruity is the primary humorous fulcrum ranging from one-liners, to scenes, to entire plots. At the elemental level of jokes, one finds a helpful example in *Bacchides*. In a passionate monologue, the young Mnesilochus is distraught that the woman he loves, Bacchis, has fallen for his friend. However, upset as he is, Mnesilochus cannot bring himself to stay angry:

> It's completely unclear whether I should believe that my friend is more of an enemy now or Bacchis. She preferred him? She can have him. That's fine. Seriously, there will be a price to pay for doing that … *and I'll pay it*…. I'll take care that she won't say she's found someone to make fun

---

on this, see Michael Fontaine, *Funny Words in Plautine Comedy* (Oxford University Press, 2010), who takes up the question of Plautine neologisms and their comedic effects; Allison Sharrock, *Reading Roman Comedy: Poetics and Playfulness* (Cambridge University Press, 2009), who offers a literary take on Plautus, paying careful attention to comedic form, plot, and repetition; and Niall W. Slater, *Plautus in Performance: The Theatre of the Mind* (Princeton University Press, 1985), who explores performative dimensions of Plautus.

41. Erich Segal, *Roman Laughter: The Comedy of Plautus*, 2nd ed. (Oxford University Press, 1987). It should be noted, too, that whether or not one views incongruity as a prime paradigm for understanding Plautus, his use of incongruity is extensive. As George Duckworth, *The Nature of Roman Comedy: A Study in Popular Entertainment* (Princeton University Press, 1952), observes of Plautus: "Incongruity of character is everywhere evident" (318) and "The fun of Plautus is characterized by haste and vigor; he delights in incongruities and irrationalities" (328).

42. Michael Fontaine, "Between Two Paradigms," in Fontaine and Scafuro, *Oxford Handbook of Greek and Roman Comedy*, 529–30, states: "Named for Rome's winter festival as the spirit in which Plautine comedy was performed, the Saturnalian paradigm emphasizes freedom in a number of respects. It emphasizes Plautus's independence from or subversion of his model, it emphasizes the temporary freedom from Roman social mores that his audience enjoys while watching the plays, and within the dramatic illusion of the plays it emphasizes a 'topsy turvy' world free from mimetic reality itself." This paradigm stands in contrast to a "Hellenistic paradigm," which sees greater continuity between Plautus and his Greek source material.

of: I'll go straight home and ... *steal something from my father.* (*Bacch.* 500–507 [de Melo], emphasis added)

In this construction, Plautus leads the audience down a garden path in one direction only to pull back in the opposite direction through the jarring endings I have emphasized above. Indeed, scholars frequently cite this passage as evidence of Plautus's clever use of incongruity. William S. Anderson, for instance, notes that "the most striking device used to produce this unevenness by the poet is what is known as the unexpected or surprise ending.... Mnesilochus ... is made to break away and blurt out the comic reverse of what we expect."[43] This creates a comically incongruous scenario with Mnesilochus even raising the possibility of financially ruining his father.

Incongruity also plays a key role in longer forms, extending to scenes and even entire plays. *Menaechmi* offers examples of both comedic techniques. With regard to the former, Plautus crafts a humorous scene in act 5 of *Menaechmi* that depends entirely on the incongruity of mistaken identity. Frustrated that her husband Menaechmus is unfaithful and acting oddly cagey, Epidamnus presses her father to confront Menaechmus about his behavior. But what neither Epidamnus nor her father knows is that this is not Menaechmus, but Sosicles, the long-lost twin of Menaechmus who has just happened to show up in the same town as his estranged brother. This leads to a comical scene where Sosicles, confused at accusations of being someone's thieving husband, embraces the assertion that he is insane in order to get out of trouble (*Men.* 819). This precedes a drawn-out encounter between the *senex* and Sosicles in which Sosicles pretends that Bachus and Apollo have possessed him, even attempting to run down the *senex* with his invisible chariot (*Men.* 860–870). Notably, Plautus compounds the incongruity of the scene through comical asides. For instance, after Sosicles threatens him, the *senex* states to the audience: "I really have to be on my guard against that and be careful. I'm horribly afraid, given the nature of his threats, that he could do me some harm" (*Men.* 860–861 [de Melo]). The incongruity here derives from the fact that the *senex* is deathly afraid of a man who himself is so afraid that he is pretending to be insane—a fact that he too discloses to the audience: "I'm stuck. Unless I get hold of some trick, they'll carry me off to their house" (*Men.* 847–848 [de Melo]). This

---

43. William S. Anderson, *Barbarian Play: Plautus' Roman Comedy* (University of Toronto Press, 1993), 11–12.

incongruity resides not just in this scene, however. Rather, it extends to the whole of *Menaechmi*, functioning as the primary plot device whence the play derives its humor. Characters consistently confuse Menaechmus with his twin and vice versa, causing trouble and confusion for them and those around them until the mix-up finds resolution at the end of the play.

Finally, Plautus derives humor not only from incongruous turns of phrase or plot points but possibly through playing off incongruities in Roman values. All throughout, Plautus's comedies display an irreverence for Roman social mores. As Segal observes:

> In sum, the very foundation of Roman morality is attacked in word and deed on the Plautine stage. What is more, in subverting filial devotion, marital concord, and respect for the gods, Plautus' characters express their awareness of the outrages they are perpetrating.[44]

Such incongruities, masked as they are by their location in fictive Greek settings, are a corner stone of Plautine comedy.

Ultimately, Plautus makes extensive use of incongruity, a fact easily recognizable in his exaggerated and farcical comedies. Plautus's successor, Terence, while significantly more subdued than Plautus, also deployed incongruity throughout his comedies.

Terence

The second major figure in Roman comedy was Publius Terentius Afer, also known as Terence. Living in the early second century BCE, Terence enjoyed a brief career as a comedic dramatist that quite possibly ended as quickly as it precociously began.[45] Unlike Plautus, only a handful of Terence's plays have survived. Indeed, just six comedies form the basis of the Terentian canon. Limited in number as they are, Terence's plays are striking and provide an interesting contrast to Plautus, while underscoring Terence's unique use of incongruity.

---

44. Segal, *Roman Laughter*, 31.
45. Traditionally, Terence is believed to have begun his career possibly in his late teens and died young as well, cutting short a very promising career as a dramatic writer. However, there are good reasons to be cautious about such a reconstruction as the sources regarding Terence's life are unclear. For a helpful introduction to and overview of such issues, see Walter E. Forehand, *Terence*, Twayne's World Authors Series 745 (Twayne, 1985), 1–12.

Scholars often describe Terence as a writer of significantly greater restraint than Plautus. They characterize him as a dramatist who avoids techniques such as farce, buffoonery, exaggeration, impropriety, and the like, preferring instead to write with a more subtle humor focused on realistic, nuanced characters.[46] Additionally, though both writers worked within the *palliatae* tradition, Terence follows his Greek models more closely than Plautus, thereby resembling Menander more than Plautus.[47] Consequently, there are less exaggerated examples of incongruity-driven humor in Terence, whether at the levels of language, characters, or social mores.[48] Yet while Terence may be more restrained in his comic tone, the playwright still develops humorous incongruity, particularly at the levels of "character and situation."[49] The comedy *Andria* illustrates this technique well.

---

46. There appears to be, at times, an argument among scholars as to who is the greater playwright. Gilbert Norwood, *Plautus and Terence* (Cooper Square, 1963), 19, offers a striking example of this in his less than flattering portrayal of Plautus: "The construction of some among his plays is so incredibly bad that even stupidity alone, even ignorance alone ... seem insufficient to explain it. We can but suppose that he neither knew nor cared what a drama is."

47. Terence's motivation for deviating from the Plautine tradition remains a point of interest for scholars. Sander M. Goldberg, *Understanding Terence* (Princeton University Press, 1986), 29, in exploring Terence against his Roman background remarks that "Terence altered his models not simply to appeal to a semi-literate rabble, but because he cared for the subtleties of his originals and sought effective Roman equivalents of them." One of the most striking elements of Terence's plays is his use of prologues. Rather than directly set up the play or initiate the plot, Terence uses his prologues to take up arguments against his work. Thus, it is not unusual to find translations of Terence's plays omit the prologues altogether.

48. One sees this contrast between Plautus and Terence, for example, in Duckworth, *The Nature of Roman Comedy*, who offers a close reading of both dramatists. When considering the use of incongruity in characterization, he notes "Incongruity of character is everywhere evident—but carried by Plautus to greater lengths than by Terence" (318). Or, when examining the use of humor and wordplay, Duckworth must draw much more from Plautus than Terence as the latter exhibits far more restraint in his dialogue (331–61). Though Terence lacks the verbal humor of Plautus, scholars widely note and celebrate his linguistic skill. For a careful study of the features of Terence's use of language see especially Evangelos Karakasis, *Terence and the Language of Roman Comedy* (Cambridge University Press, 2005).

49. Duckworth, *Nature of Roman Comedy*, 359, offers this evaluation in conjunction with a discussion of verbal humor in Plautus and Terence. However, it applies equally well to Terence's use of incongruity.

Andria centers on the plight of the young man Pamphilus who, against the wishes of his father, has fallen in love with Glycerium, the sister of the courtesan Chrisis from Andros. As a result, his father, Simo, has arranged a marriage for Pamphilus in hopes of reigning him in. Amid this predicament, Davus, the slave of Pamphilus, crafts a plan that will allow the young man to marry Glycerium. The rest of the comedy unfolds from this initial set of events, with Pamphilus eventually marrying Glycerium, who turns out to actually be the sister of the woman Pamphilus was to have married, thereby allow Pamphilus to honor his father's wishes and marry the woman he loves.[50]

Andria contains incongruous humor both with respect to its characters and the situations in which such characters find themselves. To begin with, Terence does not completely deviate from earlier comedians in depicting an incongruously funny social scenario. For instance, in act 2 of *Andria*, one encounters a humorous exchange between Charinus and Byrria, respectively master and slave. In this scene, the former asks the advice of the latter, hoping that the slave will help him figure out a way to convince Pamphilus to let him marry Philumena, the woman to whom Pamphilus is betrothed:

> Charinus: Byrria, what do you think? Shall I approach him?
> Byrria: Why not? If you can't persuade him, you'll give him the idea that you're all set for a spot of adultery after marriage.
> Charinus: Go to hell, you and your insinuations, you villain! (*Andr.* 315–317 [Barsby])

The scene continues, with Charinus and Byrria clashing until Charinus, exasperated at the lack of advice from Byrria, finally remarks:

> Charinus: But I don't get any from you, god knows, except what I don't want to hear. Make yourself scarce.
> Byrria: I will, gladly. (*Andr.* 338 [Barsby])

This exchange is comically incongruous in its depiction of Greco-Roman master-slave relationships, for the latter is supposed to be helpful and invested in the affairs of the former. Byrria, however, cannot seem to

---

50. Sander M. Goldberg, "The Dramatic Balance of Terence's *Andria*," in *Oxford Readings in Menander, Plautus, and Terence*, ed. Erich Segal (Oxford University Press, 2001), 216–23, observes that this contest of wills is the central, driving action of the play.

muster the slightest concern for his master's situation and is more than happy when Charinus dismisses him. Terence sharpens the incongruity through a contrast to Davus, a slave who works tirelessly to aid his master Pamphilus. Notably, in the case of Davus, one also finds a clear example of comedic incongruity.

In act 4 of *Andria*, Davus's scheming begins unraveling as Pamphilus is now on track once more to marry Philumena rather than Glycerium. In an attempt to fix this problem, Davus enacts a highly convoluted plot to get Chremes, father of Philumena, to stop the wedding. To do so, Davus retrieves Glycerium and Pamphilus's bastard son and has Mysis, Glycerium's servant, lay the baby out on a doorstep. Davus then leaves, waits for Chremes to stumble upon the child, and conveniently returns pretending not to notice the presence of Chremes. Upon his return, Davus launches into a conversation with Mysis where he pretends not to know who the child is in order to have Chremes figure it out by accident, while occasionally leaning in to remind Mysis that this is all a plot. Mysis, for her part, is confused at Davus's actions, and Chremes thinks himself clever for eavesdropping upon this important conversation:

> Davus: Hey! What's this nonsense! Here you, Mysis, where does this baby come from? Who brought it here?
> Mysis: Are you in your right mind? Asking me that?
> Davus: Who else am I supposed to ask? There's no one else here.
> Chremes: I wonder where it does come from.
> Davus: Are you going to answer my question?
> Mysis: Ow!
> Davus: Come over here to the right.
> Mysis: You're crazy: Didn't you yourself—?
> Davus: Just answer my questions. If you utter a single word more. Abusing me are you? Where does it come from? Tell me straight!
> Mysis: It's from our house ...
> Chremes: This is the Andrian woman's maid, unless I'm mistaken. (*Andr.* 748–758 [Barsby])

The scene continues as Davus manipulates Chremes while also confusing Mysis. The comical contrast in this scenario derives from Davus simultaneously occupying two roles: (1) the incredulous servant (for Chremes) and (2) the devoted servant (for Pamphilus). Terence highlights this as Davus jumps back and forth between characters, eliciting confusion and frustration from Mysis.

Finally, *Andria* illuminates Terence's use of incongruity in characterization, particularly in the characters of Simo and Davus. From the outset, these two characters are at odds with one another as Simo wants to prevent Pamphilus's marriage, while Davus desires to aid Pamphilus without crossing Simo. This generates a competition of scheming between the two, with Simo being overly suspicious and Davus overly clever. The conflict reaches a comical pitch in the third act when Simo confesses to Davus that the plan to marry off Pamphilus was just a scheme to reign in Pamphilus—there was no wedding. However, he withheld this information because he was suspicious that Davus would try to trick him and help Pamphilus. Unfortunately, Davus, in his own scheming, recommended that Pamphilus agree to the wedding, leading Simo to change his mind and pursue the actual marriage. There is much comedic incongruity here informing both characters. Simo, in confession of his own intelligent scheme, has still incorrectly judged the character of Davus. Davus, for his part, has undone his own plans for Pamphilus by being too tricky.

Altogether, the comedic playwrights of Greece and Rome demonstrate the enduring value of incongruity. Whether through farcical and exaggerated plays that wove in comical wordplay or restrained, more realistic narratives, Aristophanes, Menander, Plautus, and Terence relied on incongruity as a technique to generate laughter for their audiences. Throughout the entire corpus of Greco-Roman comedy, one can see incongruity flowing through its fabric as a means to achieve the comical.

Incongruity and Material Culture

In addition to the texts of antiquity, it is instructive to analyze the material culture of the Greco-Roman world to trace the use of incongruity in ancient humor. Notably, there are several examples of such humor, evidenced visually as well as in ancient artifacts.

In the ancient world, there are numerous illustrations of visual humor, particularly in depictions of the gods that appear to offer a farcical take on an otherwise serious subject. This is evident, for instance, in a relief found at Aquileia of Jupiter mid-thunderstrike. This particular carving depicts Jupiter striking a man with two thunderbolts. Such a portrait is not funny in itself, per se, as such depictions of Jupiter are known elsewhere.[51] However, in this case the relief is odd, for Jupiter is not striking just any man—he has hurled thunderbolts at an individual for defecating in the wrong place. The artist of this scene has depicted the bolt-smitten man mid-act, with toga up, genitals exposed, and falling forward as Jupiter casts a second bolt at him.[52] The contrast between an otherwise powerful, energetic god killing a man for defecation is striking and likely comical. Indeed, as John R. Clarke notes: "The relief gets its humor from the unlikely event that Jupiter would take offense at a mere act of elimination and hurl not one, but two thunderbolts at the offender."[53]

A similarly comical contrast is present in visual representations of Hercules's encounter with Ophale. In this story, Hercules acts as the slave of Ophale for a year. Notably, this tale is found throughout antiquity with Hercules depicted in female garb.[54] For example, in a painting from Pompeii, the artist has rendered Hercules in female clothing trying to spin wool, sitting apart from his club and lion's skin.[55] The portrait strikes a contrast between Hercules's expected manly depictions by placing him in the role of a female slave. Such incongruity would certainly have struck ancient audiences as humorous.[56] Indeed, this particular scene appears to have captured the imagination of Roman audiences, for artists and writers reproduced and recounted this scene elsewhere.[57]

Artists of Greco-Roman antiquity were not only interested in crafting humorous portraits; they also appear to have created "trick vases" or

---

51. E.g., a similar image is found on Trajan's Column. See Filippo Coarelli, *The Column of Trajan* (Colombo, 2000), 68, pl. 24.

52. John R. Clarke, *Looking at Laughter: Humor, Power, and Transgression in Roman Visual Culture, 100 B.C.–A.D. 250* (University of California Press, 2007), 61.

53. Clarke, *Looking at Laughter*, 61.

54. The story raises interesting questions about the performative and essential nature of gender, for Hercules's manliness does not entirely vanish in the encounter. So Sarah Lindheim, "Hercules Cross-Dressed; Hercules Undressed: Unmasking the Construction of the Propertian *Amator* in Elegy 4.9," *American Journal of Philology* 119 (1998): 43–66, who attempts to account for the manner in which seemingly conflicted statements about gender work together.

55. Clarke, *Looking at Laughter*, 178, fig. 85.

56. Clarke, *Looking at Laughter*, 177, labels this the "most transparently comic painting of Hercules in Omphale's thrall."

57. See, for instance, Clark, *Looking at Laughter*, 173–74, fig. 83, who cites the "mass-made Arretine cups" that depict a similar scene between Hercules and Omphale.

"practical joke pottery."[58] Notable examples of this include "dirty trick vases," which artisans designed to spill their contents onto hapless partygoers—in effect, an exaggerated ancient dribble-glass.[59] These cups had holes in their sides and feet with walls that one could plug with a stopper, which in turn possibly had a string attached to a pain in the stopper that one could release upon an unwitting drinker.[60] Still other trick vases generated humor, though not necessarily at the expense of someone else. For instance, artisans crafted some cups to look like several while being only one cup, while they wrought others with false bottoms in order to appear more voluminous than they actually were.[61] Such craftsmanship generated juxtaposition between expectations and reality that many likely perceived as humorous.

Incongruity, Humor, and the Ancient Witnesses: Summary

The classical sources I have explored above demonstrate that incongruity, while not the only source of humor in the ancient world, was a key element for many thinkers and dramatists. Undoubtedly, some figures focused on it more than others. Yet it is clear by its inclusion across such a wide range of authors and eras that incongruity was present in humorous discourse. Such observations find further grounding in modern humor theories that have pursued an empirical accounting of the causes of humor.

Incongruity and the General Theory of Verbal Humor

Though Greco-Roman comedians utilized incongruity as a comedic engine and philosophers and rhetoricians reflected upon the relationship between incongruity and humor, the connections between the two became a primary way of explicating humor during the Renaissance. Writers of

---

58. Philip Young, "Fighting in the Shade: What the Ancient Greeks Knew About Humor," *Soundings* 74 (1991): 300. I have used Young's term *practical joke pottery* above. On such vases see also Karl Kilinksi II, "Boeotian Trick Vases," *AJA* 85 (1986): 153–58; Joseph Veach Noble, "Some Trick Greek Vases," *Proceedings of the Philosophical Society* 112 (1968): 371–78; G. A. S. Snijder, "Eine zaubervase im Allard Pierson Museum zu Amsterdam," *Mnemosyne* 5 (1997): 40–52.

59. Michael Vickers, "A Dirty Trick Vase," *AJA* 79 (1975): 282; Vickers, "Another Dirty Trick Vase," *AJA* 84 (1980): 183–84.

60. Vickers, "Dirty Trick Vase," 282.

61. Young, "Fighting in the Shade," 300.

the era anticipated many of the conclusions at which modern scholars would arrive in their analyses of humor.[62] For instance, Baldesar Castiglione in *The Book of the Courtier* (1528 CE) underscores the importance of incongruity for humor: "I know no way of explaining it otherwise; but if you think about it, you will realize that invariably what causes laughter is something that is incongruous and yet not really unpleasing."[63] Shortly thereafter, Laurent Joubert wrote his *Treatise on Laughter* (1579 CE) wherein he highlighted, among other sources of humor, incongruous situations engendering comedic effects: "Such is the case if an old man plays in the streets as would a child, or, if an extremely well-known and imposing person, after drinking much wine, dresses up in a strange manner; or if a fool imitates a wise man in dress."[64]

Such observations continued into the late Enlightenment and early Modern periods, even as discussions surrounding humor grew more nuanced. For instance, Francis Hutcheson observed in his essay "Reflections upon Laughter" (1725 CE) that "generally the cause of laughter is the bringing together of images which have contrary additional ideas as well as some resemblance in the principal idea; this contrast ... seems to be the very spirit of burlesque; and the greatest part of our raillery and jest is founded upon it."[65] Notably, key philosophers of the period also weighed in on the discussion of humor.

Immanuel Kant (1724–1804), in his *Critique of Judgment*, offered what scholars often perceive as a classical formulation of the modern incongruity-theory of humor: "Laughter is an affection arising from the sudden transformation of a strained expectation into nothing."[66] Arthur Schopenhauer (1788–1860), too, commented on the correlation between incongruity and humor: "The cause of laughter in every case is simply

---

62. Cristina Larkin-Galiñanes, "An Overview of Humor Theory," in *The Routledge Handbook of Language and Humor*, ed. Salvatore Attardo (Routledge, 2017), 13.

63. Bernard Castiglione as quoted in Jorge Figueroa-Dorrego and Cristina Larkin-Galiñanes, ed., *A Source Book of Literary and Philosophical Writings about Humour and Laughter: The Seventy-Five Essential Texts from Antiquity to Modern Times* (Edwin Mellen, 2009), 224.

64. Laurent Joubert as quoted in Figueroa-Dorrego and Larkin-Galiñanes, *Source Book of Literary and Philosophical Writings*, 261.

65. Franches Hutcheson as quoted in Figueroa-Dorrego and Larkin-Galiñanes, *Source Book of Literary and Philosophical Writings*, 398.

66. Immanuel Kant as quoted in Figueroa-Dorrego and Larkin-Galiñanes, *Source Book of Literary and Philosophical Writings*, 433.

the sudden perception of the incongruity between a concept and the real objects which have been thought through it in some relation, and laughter itself is just the expression of this incongruity."[67] Such observations made by thinkers of the Renaissance, Enlightenment, and early modern periods were prescient, for they hit upon a method of exploring humor that scholars would come to regard highly in the twentieth century as they pursued more empirical methods of studying humor.[68] One of the most fruitful developments in incongruity-based humor has been the creation of the General Theory of Verbal Humor (GTVH). This method, developed in the late 1980s by humor theorists Raskin and Attardo, has become one of the most prevalent linguistic theories of humor.

Raskin and the Semantic Script Theory of Humor

The GTVH's roots lie first and foremost in Raskin's script semantic theory of humor (hereafter SSTH). With this theory, Raskin laid the groundwork for a strictly linguistic approach to determining the necessary conditions for detecting humor. Foundational to Raskin's work was the notion of a "script":

> The script is a large chunk of semantic information surrounding the word or evoked by it. The script is a cognitive structure internalized by the native speaker and represents the native speaker's knowledge of a small part of the world.[69]

Scripts act as a kind of "common sense" determined by "certain routines, standard procedures, basic situations, etc., for instance, the knowledge of what people do in certain situations, how they do it, in what order, etc."[70] However, scripts carry inherent ambiguity as scripts can evoke a wide array of possible meanings. For example, the script DOCTOR can, on the one hand, evoke a picture of an altruistic, hard-working individual concerned with the health and well-being of her patients. On the other hand,

---

67. Arthur Schopenhauer as quoted in Morreall, *Taking Laughter Seriously*, 52.
68. For an excellent treatment regarding key developments in humor scholarship in its transition from the Renaissance to early Modernity, see Figueroa-Dorrego and Larkin-Galiñanes, *Source Book of Literary and Philosophical Writings*, 179–221.
69. Raskin, *Semantic Mechanisms of Humor*, 81.
70. Raskin, *Semantic Mechanisms of Humor*, 81

based on the cumulative negative experience many people have had as patients, the same script can also evoke the portrait of a callous, uncaring professional interested solely in status and monetary gain. It is this inherent ambiguity that comedy often exploits and which the SSTH seeks to locate. Consequently, Raskin offered the following hypothesis:

> A text can be characterized as a single-joke-carrying text if ... (i) the text is compatible, fully or in part, with two different scripts (ii) the two scripts with which the text is compatible are opposite.[71]

Raskin's theory depended on the presence of "script opposition." Significantly, the same text must not simply be compatible with more than one script; the scripts need to be opposed in one of three key binaries, each a subset of a real/unreal situation evoked by a particular text: (1) actual/nonactual, nonexisting situation; (2) normal, expected/abnormal, unexpected state of affairs; (3) possible, plausible situation/fully or partially impossible or much less plausible situation.[72]

In addition to the presence of two overlapping and opposing scripts in the same text, Raskin emphasized the importance of a "semantic script-switch trigger" or "trigger."[73] That is, in a joking-text, one should find a word or phrase that actively switches the meaning of the text from one script to another, or a "punch line." The utterance of the punch line introduces a new overlapping and opposing script that forces the person hearing the joke to rethink the text in a new light. Upon apprehending the incongruity between the two scripts that the punch line evokes, one typically has some sort of humorous response. It is helpful at this point to cite one of Raskin's joke-texts to illustrate the theory:

> "Is the doctor at home?" the patient asked in his bronchial whisper.
> "No," the doctor's young and pretty wife whispered in reply. "Come right in."[74]

---

71. Raskin, *Semantic Mechanisms of Humor*, 99

72. Raskin, *Semantic Mechanisms of Humor*, 111. Raskin regards these subsets of the real/unreal binary as being fundamental to a wide range of binaries located in his survey of jokes including, though not limited to employee/lover; senators are gentlemen/senators are not gentlemen; church/sex; going out/going away; ordinary week (life)/death; disease/money (transaction); etc. For a full list, see pp. 107–8.

73. Raskin, *Semantic Mechanisms of Humor*, 114.

74. Raskin, *Semantic Mechanisms of Humor*, 32.

This joke, concise as it is, qualifies as a joke-text by the SSTH because it plays off of the scripts of DOCTOR/LOVER. The opening language of the joke, referencing as it does a "doctor," "patient," and "bronchial whisper," conjures the script of a patient seeking medical treatment from a doctor at home.[75] However, the sentence that follows calls this script into question as the reader is told of the doctor's spouse, who whispers for the man to come inside. The statement problematizes the former understanding of the script by suggesting something besides a DOCTOR script is at play. Indeed, the text implies an entirely different scene by introducing the second scene. Upon further reflection, the recipient of the joke (ideally) realizes that the scene here is one of two lovers rather than that of a patient seeking medical help. The text is compatible with both the DOCTOR and LOVER scripts (based on an actual/nonactual binary); moreover, while these scripts overlap, they are opposed to one another. Finally, the text triggers the script-opposition by the second statement, which effectively acts as a punch line. It forces the reader to backtrack and reread the situation from the first half of the joke.[76]

The SSTH, particularly with its focus on script-opposition and script-switch triggers, was the first step toward the construction of the GTVH. However, the GTVH would incorporate key ideas from Attardo's work, which he developed just a short time later in his analysis of the different levels present in jokes.

Attardo, Raskin, and the GTVH

Following the work of Raskin and the SSTH, Attardo developed a method of examining humor that focused on levels of humor analysis.[77] Attardo and Raskin took this method and reworked it to create the GTVH. In their seminal article "Script Theory Revis(it)ed: Joke Similarity and the Joke Representation Model," Attardo and Raskin combined elements of Raskin's SSTH and Attardo's "Five-Level Model of Joke Representation."[78]

---

75. Raskin, *Semantic Mechanisms of Humor*, 32.

76. I am paraphrasing Raskin here. For his explanation of the humor, see Raskin, *Semantic Mechanisms of Humor*, 32. For a full breakdown of the joke as it is run through Raskin's method, see *Semantic Mechanisms of Humor*, 117–27.

77. Salvatore Attardo, "A Multiple-Level Analysis of Jokes," *Humor* 2 (1989): 438–39.

78. Salvatore Attardo and Victor Raskin, "Script-Theory Revis(it)ed: Joke Similarity and Joke Representational Model," *Humor* 4 (1991): 295–96. For an in-depth explanation of Attardo's model, see 309–12.

This resulted in a model that was first and foremost rooted in the notions of "script-opposition" and the "logical mechanism," with an additional set of elements that could be found in each joke including a joke's "situation," "target," "narrative strategies," and "language."

Attardo and Raskin's work in "Script Theory Revis(it)ed" represented a significant step forward in the development of the GTVH. By combining their respective models, Raskin and Attardo crafted a robust model for deciphering humor in texts. In spite of this achievement, the GTVH had limited scope as it focused on locating humor in simple jokes rather than longer texts or narratives.

Attardo, the GTVH, and Narrative

The next major development in the GTVH came in the form of Attardo's application of the method to complete narratives.[79] In the early 2000s, Attardo applied the GTVH to longer stories such as Anne Sexton's version of Cinderella as well as Oscar Wilde's "Lord Arthur Saville's Crime." By applying the GTVH in this way, Attardo demonstrated that it could succeed as an analytical method for entire stories irrespective of length. Furthermore, he developed a helpful framework within which to deploy the GTVH.

Attardo applied the GTVH in much the same way he and Raskin deployed it in their 1991 article. The primary difference came in the scope of its application: "It is, in fact, an extension of the GTVH which broadens its coverage, while not altering most of the tenets of the theory. Specifically, the GTVH is broadened to include (ideally) all humorous texts, of any length."[80] The length of narratives is an important distinction, however, and raises questions about the type of text to which one might apply the GTVH. Attardo distinguishes between two types of text: "those texts that are structurally similar to jokes ... and those which are not."[81] For those texts that are not formally analogous to jokes, they "can be most profitably analyzed as consisting of two elements: a non-humorous narrative and a humorous component, which occurs along the narrative."[82] Beyond

---

79. Attardo, *Humorous Texts*.
80. Attardo, *Humorous Texts*, 28.
81. Attardo, *Humorous Texts*, 29.
82. Attardo, *Humorous Texts*, 29. These elements are important for the study of Mark as most scholars would maintain that, humorous moments notwithstanding,

expanding the analysis of humor to long-form texts, Attardo also extended his definition of "scripts":

> A script is an organized complex of information about some entity, in the broadest sense: an object (real or imaginary), an event, an action, a quality, etc. It is a cognitive structure internalized by the speaker which provides the speaker with information on how a given entity is structured, what are its parts and components, or how an activity is done, a relationship organized, and so on to cover all possible relations between entities (including their constituents).[83]

Put another way, a script "contains information which is prototypical of the entity being described.... At the simplest level a script is equivalent to the lexical meaning of a word."[84] Additionally, Attardo follows Raskin in maintaining that scripts are "related to, and evoked by, lexical items. Therefore, each script will have a lexematic 'handle' which causes its activation." At face value, this definition may seem too broad. After all, the full understanding of a script such as a CAR includes a wide range of possibilities. However, as Attardo observes, the interpretive possibilities of a specific lexeme are immediately narrowed by the context in which they sit, thereby bringing the script into a manageable range of potential meanings.[85]

Attardo expanded the idea of punch lines to "jab lines" in order to understand how script-switch mechanisms functioned in longer-form texts. The idea of the jab line is straightforward, as it is a transposition of the notion of a punch line. But, whereas a punch line stands at the end of a joke, jab lines "may occur in any other position in the text ... [and] are humorous elements fully integrated in the narrative in which they appear."[86] Significantly, jab lines often appear multiple times throughout a text, an element Attardo labels "strands."

Attardo defines a strand as "at least three instances" of a jab line.[87] Additionally, strands may further divide into central and peripheral strands.

Mark is still primarily a serious narrative. Thus, in the present study, I proceed with the view of Mark as a serious text that deploys humor selectively, rather than being a humorous narrative that feigns a serious plot.
83. Attardo, *Humorous Texts*, 2–3.
84. Attardo, *Humorous Texts*, 3.
85. Attardo, *Humorous Texts*, 9–16.
86. Attardo, *Humorous Texts*, 82.
87. Attardo, *Humorous Texts*, 84.

Central strands are those which are extant throughout a large part of a text (i.e., 75 percent or greater), while peripheral strands are in "one (or few) instance(s) in the text."[88] Furthermore, Attardo notes the presence of "substrands ... a subset of lines that constitute a strand which share some combination of feature which is not common to the strand at large."[89] Finally, one can categorize strands as "combs" and "bridges." A comb contains three jab or punch lines in a highly constrained place within a text.[90] Bridges, on the other hand, consist of jab or punch lines located "a considerable distance from one another,"[91] with hapax bridges comprising two jab or punch lines without apparent connection to another strand in the narrative.

Attardo's work on the GTVH and narrative is more extensive than I can fully explore here. For the present study, I rely on key fundamentals of his development of the GTVH, namely, the GTVH itself, Attardo's definition of script, the mechanism of the jab line, and the various ways in which punch and jab lines congregate in strands. These elements form the backbone of my method. Additionally, in my analysis I focus on locating script-oppositions, as they are foundational to the GTVH. Finally, I accept, in broad terms, the validity of the GTVH as an approach to humor that allows for the discovery of humor across texts, cultures, and historical periods given its use in many countries across several decades.[92] As I noted above, the ability for the GTVH to accomplish this rests in part through its focus on script-oppositions as they are built upon abstractions that appear across cultures.[93]

Conclusion

The question before the present study remains a challenging one; namely, did the Markan evangelist intend for their audience to find humor in their

---

88. Attardo, *Humorous Texts*, 84.
89. Attardo, *Humorous Texts*, 84.
90. Attardo, *Humorous Texts*, 87.
91. Attardo, *Humorous Texts*, 88.
92. Attardo, *Humorous Texts*, 9.
93. Attardo and Raskin, "Script-Theory Revis(it)ed," 308, explain this in further detail: "First, at the most abstract level, the joke opposes the *real* and the *unreal*, that is, factual reality to an imagined one. This may take three possible forms, existing at lower levels of abstraction, namely, the *actual vs. nonactual*, *normal vs. abnormal*, and *possible vs. impossible*. At the lowest level of abstraction, these can be manifested by such oppositions as *good vs. bad, life vs. death, sex vs. nonsex, money vs. no-money, high-stature vs. low stature*, etc."

gospel, and, if so, how might present readers determine such moments? In the present chapter, I have articulated how this might be achievable. By using the GTVH, a linguistic method focused on abstract oppositions found across cultures and which comports with ancient understandings of incongruity as an engine for humor, it is possible to key in on certain potentially humorous moments in Mark's gospel. One can, in turn, analyze these incongruities to see whether they might have qualified as humorous in light of comparanda known from the Greco-Roman world. However, before taking this up, I must address one final issue.

Gospel scholars may raise concerns about the likelihood of an ancient *bios* containing humor. In particular, one may wonder whether this potentially serious genre would have adopted comical elements. As it happens, this tendency exists in one of the Greco-Roman world's serious genres: tragedy. Scholars have commented on the use of humor in tragic writings such as the *Iliad* and the *Aeneid*.[94] To provide but one example from each epic, in the *Iliad* one finds a cruel humor in the characterization and ill-treatment of Thersites by Odysseus, who abuses and humiliates the man, all while earning laughter from Achaean soldiers standing nearby (Homer, *Il.* 2.211–70). In the *Aeneid*, one encounters comical relief in the boat race scene where Gyas becomes so enraged with his boat pilot Menoetes that he tosses the pilot from the boat, once more eliciting laughter from onlookers (Vergil, *Aen.*5.143–148).

In addition to finding comical elements in serious writings, scholars have argued that ancient biographers themselves indulged in humor to make rhetorical points. For instance, Trevor Luke maintains that Suetonius includes two strange episodes in his biography of Vespasian (withdrawal of a praefecture and denial of shoes to sailors [*Vesp.* 8.3]) that underscore the beneficial differences of Vespasian's reign over against that of Julio-Claudian rule.[95] Humor is also potentially present in Suetonius through his dialogue, as Robert Cowan notes when examining Lucan's scatologi-

---

94. Eugene De Saint Denis, "Le Sourire de Virgile," *Latomus* 23 (1963): 446–63; Robert Lloyd, "Humor in the 'Aeneid,'" *CJ* 72 (1977): 250–77; Gary Meltzer, "The Role of Comic Perspectives in Shaping Homer's Tragic Vision," *CW* 83 (1990): 265–80; P. Miniconi, "La Joie Dans l'Eneide," *Latomus* 21 (1962): 563–71; Ernd Seidensticker, *Palintonos Harmonia: Studien zu komischen Elementen in der griechen Tragödie*, Hypomnemata 72 (Vandenhoeck & Ruprecht, 1982).

95. Trevor Luke, "Ideology and Humor in Suetonius' 'Life of Vespasian' 8," *CW* 103 (2010): 511–27.

cal humor in his biography of Lucan.[96] Mark Beck, in his examination of Plutarch's life of Antony, proffers that Plutarch employs humor in his depiction of the failed emperor with Antony representing "a failure in leadership."[97] Furthermore, Beck perceives Lucian's extensive use of chreia in *Life of Demonax* to be an excellent example of "biographical literature that does indulge humor."[98] Taken together, these examples illustrate that ancient biographers could deploy humor beyond the confines of comedic works. Moreover, many of these examples are rooted in salient incongruities.[99] All told, whether writing in a tragic work or a serious biography, ancient authors drew upon humorous scenes and dialogue as needed. In this regard, the Markan evangelist was no different, as an analysis of incongruities and script-oppositions in Mark 4:35–6:6 demonstrates.

---

96. Robert Cowan, "Lucan's Thunder-Box: Scatology, Epic, and Satire in Suetonius' 'Vita Lucani,'" *HSCP* 106 (2011): 301–13.

97. Mark Beck, "The Serio-Comic Life of Antony," in *A Versatile Gentleman: Consistency in Plutarch's Writing*, ed. Jan Opsomer, Geert Roskam, and Frances B. Titchener, Plutarchea Hypomnemata (Leuven University Press, 2016), 137–46.

98. Beck, "Serio-Comic Life," 137.

99. For instance, Luke, "Ideology and Humor," 511–12, detects humor in Suetonius's account through the juxtaposition of Vespasian tending to the rebuilding of Rome only to be offended by a man's bad smell and weighing in on a request for shoes. Beck, "Serio-Comic Life," 145, underscores the incongruity present in Plutarch's depictions of Antony. He argues that Antony, with his perceived tendency to be dominated by wives and lovers, dawn slave-garb, and engage in generally carnivalesque behavior, is depicted by Plutarch "as a comic actor for the first part of his *Life*. We witness those laughing at Antony, but we do not laugh with him." Cowan, "Lucan's Thunder Box," 302, avers that a comical moment is observable in an anecdote wherein the poet Lucan, upon flatulating in a public bathroom, is supposed to have quoted a line from Nero: "you might suppose it thundered 'neath the earth.'" The humor here comes from the "incongruous parallelism between a low, socially deprecated bodily function and what is at least an awesome and sublime act of nature, if not a divine signal from the supreme deity" (302).

3
Script-Oppositions in Mark 4:35–6:6

Introduction

Mark 4:35–6:6 comprises a critical, engaging block of material in the Markan narrative.[1] These chapters illuminate vital elements of the gospel, focusing as they do on some of Jesus's most powerful miracles. Additionally, in these chapters the evangelist broaches the possibility of a gentile mission through Jesus's work in the Decapolis. Yet the narrative also raises questions, particularly regarding the disciples' relationship to Jesus, peoples' reactions to Jesus, and, perhaps most shockingly, Jesus's status as a powerful wonder-worker. Indeed, this section of Mark begins with the question "Who is this, that even the winds and sea obey him?" (4:41), yet ends with the startling observation that Jesus could only heal a handful of people (6:6). In addition to this startling contrast, other curiosities emerge. Throughout 4:35–6:6, Jesus sleeps as his boat is sinking, struggles to gain control of a mighty demon, fails to recognize a woman with a medical condition, and possibly fails to prevent a young girl's death. The juxtaposition between Jesus's abilities at the beginning of this collection of miracle stories and his standing at the end is striking. At first glance, such features read as highly incongruous and suggest that the miracle-cycle may contain humor. Scholars have taken note for, as I observed in chapter 1, they have drawn on passages in these chapters to comment on Markan humor. As such, Mark 4:35–6:6 stands as an excellent site for beginning to query

---

1. On the possibility that the evangelist has taken over a set of traditions that were possibly collected before appearing in the gospel, see Paul Achtemeier, "The Origen and Function of the Pre-Markan Miracle Catenae," *JBL* 91 (1972): 198–221; Achtemeier, "Toward the Isolation of Pre-Markan Miracle Catenae," *JBL* 89 (1970): 265–91.

whether or not the Markan evangelist may have used humor in their retelling of Jesus's life.

In order to determine whether humor may be extant in these texts, I will investigate the text along three separate axes:

1. I will apply the GTVH and tease out potential script-oppositions in the the text along with their potential respective jab lines.
2. I will examine potential incongruities in light of ancient cultural expectations, paying particular attention to their use in texts considered humorous or prone to humor because of their genre (i.e., comedy, satire, novels).[2]
3. I will consider possible humor-limiters to particular script-oppositions that foreclose the possibility of humor or soften/shift hermeneutical choices for an imagined audience.

In the present chapter, I will take up the first two tasks. I will examine each pericope in Mark 4:35–6:6. This will include a brief description of the script-oppositions found in each story, followed by an analysis of relevant comedic cotexts and an examination of each pericope and its respective potential script-oppositions.[3] While I may offer passing remarks on how such script-oppositions may be functioning within the text were they humorous, I will withhold full consideration of this point and take up the third axis of the current method in chapter 4.

Stilling the Storm (Mark 4:35–41)

The first pericope in 4:35–6:6 relates the story of Jesus crossing the Sea of Galilee with his disciples. This sea-crossing turns dangerous when, in

---

2. The current argument is not reliant on these sources in a temporal manner. I am not seeking to demonstrate direct dependence between comedic texts and the Gospel of Mark. Rather, I am pointing to script-oppositions present in the text that were used as potential elements for humor in Greco-Roman literature more broadly. The majority of texts that I use as touchpoints predate the gospels (e.g., Aristophanes, Plautus, Terence, Menander, etc.), with a handful being contemporary to or a little later than the gospel (e.g., Martial, Lucian, etc.).

3. Because of space limitations, I do not analyze every script-opposition in depth vis-a-vis ancient comedic possibilities. Also, occasionally I have pushed discussion of a prevalent script-opposition to a subsequent section if the discussion is more critical to that pericope.

the middle of the night, a storm rises and threatens to drown everyone aboard their respective vessels. Curiously, when the disciples turn to Jesus for help, they find him fast asleep. He, in turn, finds them terrified after answering their petition for help. This action-packed pericope, succinct as it is, carries a number of potential script-oppositions: ASLEEP/ALERT, ROMAN IMPERIUM/JESUS'S IMPERIUM, APPROPRIATE/INAPPROPRIATE FEAR or APPROPRIATE/INAPPROPRIATE RESPONSE TO JESUS, and KNOWLEDGE/IGNORANCE OF JESUS'S IDENTITY. These script-oppositions find interesting contact points in the comedic use of sleep, imperial satire, and cowardice in Greco-Roman literature.

Comedic Themes in Ancient Sources

Sleep

The act of sleeping provided fodder for ancient comedians.[4] Aristophanes's *Equites* and *Nubes* exploit sleep as a comical action that provides cover for a slave to steal from his master, and the playwright links sleep to the laziness of Strepsiades's household.[5] Furthermore, in both instances, sleeping is comically, albeit crudely, linked to flatulence. In *Equites*, a dialogue between two slaves reveals that one of them has been able to steal from Paphlagon because "Paphlagon's snoring [ῥέγκεται] and farting so loud, he didn't even notice when I grabbed his holy oracle" (*Eq.* 115–117 [Henderson]). Similarly, in the opening of *Nubes*, Strepsiades laments that his slaves and son are lazy, for they sleep too late into the morning:

> I did hear a cock crow quite awhile back, but the slaves are snoring [ῥέγκουσιν].... And this fine young man won't rouse himself before daybreak either, but farts away wrapped up in five woolen coverlets. All right then, let's all get under the covers and snore [ῥέγκωμεν]!" (*Nub.* 5–11 [Henderson])

---

4. Silvia Montiglio, *The Spell of Hypnos: Sleep and Sleeplessness in Ancient Greek Literature* (Tauris, 2016), offers an extensive analysis of sleep and its place in Greek literature. On the examples used here, see also Jon Carman, "Jesus Asleep on the Job? Analyzing an Incongruity in Mark 4:35–41," in *Biblical Humor and Performance: Audience Experiences That Make Meaning*, ed. Peter Perry, Biblical Performance Criticism 20 (Cascade, 2023), 99–117.

5. Aristophanes is exemplary of Old Comedy, writing in fifth/fourth century BCE Athens.

The exploitation of sleep for comic effect is also noticeable in the opening scene of *Vespae*. The play begins with a scene depicting two slaves, Sosias and Xanthias, who are supposed to be standing guard alongside their master Loathecleon. However, both men struggle to stay awake:

> Sosias: Hey Xanthias, you damned jinx, what's the matter with you?
> Xanthias: I'm learning how to relieve the night watch
> Sosias: Then your ribs will have a bad grudge against you. Don't you realize what a monster we've got in our custody?
> Xanthias: Certainly; that's why I want to absent me from solicitude awhile.
> Sosias: Take your own chances then. Why should I care? Something pleasant is beginning to drop over my eyeballs too.
> Xanthias: Whoa there, are you losing your mind, or having a corybantic fit?
> Sosias: No, Sabazius has put me under a sleep spell. (*Vesp*. 1–9 [Henderson])

In just a matter of a few lines, Aristophanes flexes the script of sleep in several ways to comedic effect. First, there exists the inherent incongruity regarding watchmen who not only have fallen asleep but continue to do so. Indeed, Sosias, who initially wakes the sleeping Xanthias, falls asleep himself just a few lines later. Second, Aristophanes depicts sleep as a way to cut oneself off from the world and its responsibilities, a fact Xanthias admits when Sosias confronts him. Finally, Sosias potentially draws laughter from an audience through his inability to control himself while asleep.[6]

In addition to mocking an overly lazy son, *Nubes* makes resourceful use of sleep to comedic effect. The play opens with Strepsiades unable to sleep even as his slaves doze past the cock of the crow and his son Phidippides farts under his blankets (*Nub*. 1–10). This restlessness finds humorous extension later in the play after Strepsiades has encountered Socrates and is attempting to gain entry to the Thinkery as a pupil. After protracted etymological lessons, Socrates commands Strepsiades to lie down on a

---

6. It is somewhat unclear here how best to understand Sosias's actions. Yet as noted by E. Kerr Borthwick, "Observations on the Opening Scene of Aristophanes' Wasps," *ClQ* 42 (1992): 274, even if the action is as simple as Sosias snapping himself awake, the action reads comically: "I assume therefore that the lines of conversation are punctuated by this pair of none-too-vigilant warders imbibing copiously and drowsing off to sleep."

bed and to think through one of his many pressing worries (*Nub*. 695). In the process, Strepsiades is supposed to remain awake and alert. Thus, the chorus of clouds exhorts Strepsiades to remain awake and watchful: "Now think and contemplate ... and let sweet-spirited sleep be remoted from your eyes" (*Nub*. 701–705 [Henderson]). Socrates, too, checks in on Strepsiades to make sure he has not fallen asleep: "Now then, I'll begin by observing what this one's been up to. You there, are you asleep?" (*Nub*. 731 [Henderson]). As it happens, Strepsiades has managed to avoid sleep but for comical reasons: bed bugs are "draining my lifeblood, yanking my balls, poking my arsehole, and altogether killing me" (*Nub*. 710–715 [Henderson]), among other reasons. These examples demonstrate just a small range of comical possibilities open to the notion of sleep. In particular, sleep could be juxtaposed against wakefulness or alertness necessary for standing guard and rational thought.

In addition to Greek comedies, there is the possibility that sleep could be used in humorous ways by Jewish authors. This is particularly true for Jonah, a tale which some scholars have interpreted as being humorous in both its Hebrew and Greek forms.[7] The Greek version of Jonah is particularly interesting as it inserts the additional detail that Jonah was "snoring" (ῥέγκειν): "and Jonah went down into the hollow of the ship and fell asleep and snored. And the captain came to him and said to him, 'Why are you snoring?'" (Jonah 1:5b–6a). The use of ῥέγκειν is significant, for it translates the otherwise serious Hebrew רדם ("to fall into a heavy sleep") into a Greek term at home in the world of Aristophanic farce.[8]

Imperium

Greek and Roman writers frequently targeted state authority in the form of satire. While I will explore this in greater length below, presently it is

---

7. See, for example, Will Kynes, "Beat Your Parodies into Swords, and Your Parodied Books into Spears: A New Paradigm for Parody in the Hebrew Bible," *BibInt* 19 (2011): 276–310; Judson Mather, "The Comic Art of the Book of Jonah," *Soundings* 65 (1982): 280–91; John A. Miles, "Laughing at the Bible: Jonah as Parody," *JQR* 65 (1975): 168–81; Brent Strawn, "On Vomiting: Leviticus, Jonah, Ea(r)Rth," *CBQ* 74 (2012): 445–64.

8. Constantin Răchită, "Why Does Jonah Snore in the LXX Translation (Jonah 1:5–6)? From the Theological Sobriety of the Patristic Exegesis to the Facetiousness of a Hellenizing Translation," *Vulgata in Dialogue* 1 (2017): 71–82.

critical to note one example. In Lucan's retelling of Julius Caesar's attempt to cross the Adriatic, there is a possible satirical edge to his writing.[9] In his account of this towering imperial figure, Lucan appears to mock the character of Caesar. For instance, in the face of an approaching storm Caesar launches into a longwinded speech:

> "Despise the angry sea," he cried, "and spread your sail to the raging wind.... Burst through the heart of the storm, relying on my protection. Yonder trouble concerns the sky and sea, but not our bark; for Caesar treads the deck, and her freight shall insure her against the waves." (*Phar.* 5.577–586 [Duff])

Later, when buffeted by the storm, Caesar rages furiously against the elements as it becomes clear that he may fail in his endeavor to cross the sea:

> "What trouble the gods take," he cried, "to work my ruin, assailing me on my little boat with such a mighty storm! If the glory of my death, denied to battle-field, has been granted to the deep, I shall not shrink from meeting whatever end Heaven appoints for me. Although the date, hastened by destiny, cuts short a great career, my achievements are sufficient: I have conquered the Northern peoples; by fear alone I have quelled the Roman forces opposed to me; Rome has seen me take precedence by Magnus; by appeal to the people I won the consulship denied to me by force of arms; no Roman office will be found missing from my record; and none other than Fortune, who shares with me the secret of my ambition, shall ever know that, though I go down to the Stygian gates loaded with honours, dictator as well as consul, nevertheless I am dying a private citizen. I ask no burial of the gods; let them leave my mutilated corpse amid the waves; I can dispense with grave and funeral pyre, provided I am feared for ever and my appearance is dreaded by every land." (*Phar.* 5.654–671 [Duff])

Caesar's intuition regarding the failure of his journey is prescient for he fails to reach the opposite shore: "As he spoke thus, a tenth wave ... upbore him and his battered craft; nor did the billow hurl him back again ... but bore him onwards till it lay him on the land" (*Phar.* 5.671–675 [Duff]). Lucan's depiction of Caesar and his imperium is potentially comical as

---

9. Lucan wrote in the mid-first century CE.

Lucan depicts the Roman dictator as a braggart who declaims against the cosmos even as they thwart his plans.[10]

Cowardice

The Greco-Roman world highly valued courage—in battle, in rhetoric, in everyday life. Conversely, cowardice was despised. As one might expect, Greco-Roman comedic writers found much humor that could be wrung out of this particular trait. This is evident, for instance, in the description that Theophrastus provides regarding cowards, a point which is particularly important as his work on characters would prove influential for New Comedy and its widespread deployment of stock characters.[11] Theophrastus describes a coward thus:

> The Coward is the sort who, when at sea, says that the cliffs are pirate ships. When a wave hits, he asks whether anyone on board has not been initiated. Of the helmsman he first pops up and asks whether he is halfway, and how he thinks the heavens look, and says to the man sitting beside him that his fear is the result of some dream. He strips off his shirt and hands it to his slave; he begs to be put ashore. When he is on military service and the infantry is attacking he calls to everyone and orders them to stand near him first and reconnoiter, and says that their task is to discern which ones are the enemy. When he hears a tumult and sees men falling, he says to those beside him that in his haste he forgot to take his sword, and runs to his tent, sends his attendant out and orders him to spy out the enemy's location, he hides the sword under his pillow, then wastes a long time pretending to look for it. (5) When from his tent he sees one of his friends brought in wounded, he runs up to him, bids him be brave, picks him up and carries him; then he takes care of him, sponges him off, sits at his side shooing the flies off his wound—anything rather than fight the enemy. When the trumpeter sounds the charge, he sits in his tent and says "Go to hell! He won't let a man get any sleep with his endless signaling!" (6) Drenched in blood from another man's

---

10. So Roger Aus, *The Stilling of the Storm: Studies in Early Palestinian Judaic Traditions*, International Studies in Formative Christianity and Judaism (Global Publications, 2000), 68: "Caesar was extremely confident that his fortune or destiny would enable him to cross the Adriatic Sea even during a ferocious windstorm of the stormy winter season. His lack of success in this endeavor contrasts him to Jesus, the Son of God, who calmed the Sea of Galilee while crossing it during a ferocious windstorm."

11. Theophrastus was active in Athens during the fourth–third centuries BCE.

wound, he meets the man returning from battle and tells the story as if he'd been in danger: "I saved one of our friends." Then he leads the members of his tribe inside to view him lying there, while he tells each one that he personally brought him into the tent with his own hands. (*Char.* 25 [Rusten and Cunningham])

Through his description of cowardice, Theophrastus underscores the comical actions of such an individual, highlighting their absurd fear and incongruity in deeds and intentions. Notably, one finds this trait occasionally among the gods.

Aristophanes sketches a comical portrait of Dionysus in his play *Ranae*. Among the god's many laughable attributes, one finds Dionysus's fear contrasted against the bravery of Hercules. The playwright augments this juxtaposition by the fact that Dionysus has dawned the iconic garb of Hercules, touring the underworld in a lion's skin with club in hand. In doing so, Dionysus unwittingly stumbles upon and elicits confrontations from Hercules's many enemies, displaying his cowardice in the process. Dionysus's encounter with Aecus, keeper of the hell-hound Cerberus that Hercules stole from Hades, is particularly comical. Upon running into the disguised Dionysus, Aecus threatens to torture him with the monsters of the underworld. Dionysus responds in a fantastically cowardly manner—he soils himself:

> Dionysus: My butt runneth over; let us pray.
> Xanthias: Stand up right now, you clown, before somebody sees you!
> Dionysus: But I feel faint. Please, give me a wet sponge for my heart.
> Xanthias: Here, take this and apply it. Where is it? Ye golden gods, is that where you keep your heart?
> Dionysus: Yes, it got scared and sneaked down to my colon.
> Xanthias: You're the worst coward in heaven and earth!
> Dionysus: Who me, a coward? Me, who asked you for a sponge something no other man would have dared?
> Xanthias: Well, what would he have done?
> Dionysus: If he were a coward, he'd have lain there in his own stink. But I got up, and wiped myself too.
> Xanthias: Poseidon, what bravery!
> Dionysus: Damn right. (*Ran.* 479–493 [Henderson])

The image of cowardice, be it in persons or gods, was a comical sight for ancient audiences and a trope playwrights wielded often.

Analysis of Mark 4:35–41

The first sea-crossing in the Markan Gospel relates a gripping tale.[12] The story follows on the heels of a series of parables, acting as a transition from teaching material to several powerful acts that will culminate in Jesus's near-powerless station at Nazareth (6:1-6). The narrative is dramatic, striking a contrastive portrait between the serene teacher and his petrified disciples, ending on the odd note that, after escaping danger the disciples "became greatly afraid" (ἐφοβήθησαν φόβον μέγαν). Notably, there are several possible script-oppositions in the text. Table 3.1 articulates their presence as signaled by potential jab lines:

Table 3.1. Vectors of Humor in Mark 4:35–41

Script-Oppositions	Mark 4:35–41
ASLEEP/ALERT	4:38
ROMAN IMPERIUM/JESUS'S IMPERIUM	4:39, 41
APPROPRIATE/INAPPROPRIATE FEAR OR APPROPRIATE/INAPPROPRIATE RESPONSE TO JESUS	4:41
KNOWLEDGE/IGNORANCE OF JESUS'S IDENTITY	4:41

The first curious feature of the story is the report by the evangelist that Jesus was "sleeping in the stern upon a cushion" (4:38).[13] Jesus's activity appears strange, a point the narrative underscores, for it immediately follows the statement that a great windstorm had arisen, whipping up waves that were "falling upon the boat, with the result that already the boat had begun to be filled" (4:38). The evangelist presents the audience with a sharp contrast between a chaotic environment and a man completely at rest. The disciples' statement in 4:38 buttresses the oddity of this behavior: "Teacher, does it not worry you that we are perishing?" It is important to

---

12. The current analysis draws from previous work I have done on this topic: Carman, "Jesus Asleep on the Job?," 99–117.

13. Notably, Jesus's strange behavior overlaps with similarly odd behavior from an individual who decides to write poetry amid a shipwreck as told in the *Satyricon*. For more on this point and the similarities between the Markan storm account and the *Satyricon*'s comical take on a ship wreck at sea, see Carman, "Jesus Asleep on the Job?," 99–117.

underscore just how odd this portrait might appear to the gospel audience. The evangelist has presented the audience with a highly incongruous picture in this compressed narrative and commented on it through the character of the disciples: how is it that Jesus can be asleep on the disciples' boat even as they are in the process of sinking? He is so sleepy that he cannot even be roused though they are all on the brink of death.

At first glance, the image of Jesus asleep during a storm that is already in the process of drowning the disciples is highly incongruous.[14] In this case, there is potentially a script-opposition of ASLEEP/ALERT present. The disciples act as one might expect in such a moment, while Jesus exhibits behavior that borders the absurd. The incongruity of Jesus's actions come into sharper focus when one considers the ubiquity of seastorms in antiquity and the fear they aroused—a reality attested to in Jewish, Greek, and Roman sources.

Throughout the Hebrew Bible, water and the sea frequently stand as images of chaos. The pressing dangers of the sea were especially evident in voyages where sailors undertook travel at great risk. The temperamental nature of the sea and the fear it could engender are evident in texts such as Ps 107:23, 25–29:

> Some went down to the sea in ships, doing business on the mighty waters.... He commanded and raised the stormy wind, which lifted up the waves of the sea. They mounted up to heaven, they went down to the depths, their courage melted away in their calamity, they reeled and staggered like drunkards, and were at their wits' end. (NRSV)[15]

Such fears are front and center in the story of Jonah. This book portrays a chaotic scene where Jonah is asleep in a ship below deck, while sailors are above trying to keep the ship afloat during a storm that threatens to drown them all: "But the Lord hurled a great wind upon the sea, and such

---

14. It is critical to note that the evangelist seems to intentionally cast Jesus in a strange light in these situations, only to normalize the narrative later. For more on this pattern, see especially the discussion in chapter 4, where I explore the comical effects of this pattern at greater length, including the disruption of this pattern in 6:1–6.

15. Scholars have suggested Ps 107 as a background text that may have shaped the present form of the Markan story (e.g., Adela Yarbro Collins, *Mark: A Commentary*, Hermeneia [Fortress, 2008], 258). I shall return to this point below when considering what intertextual references might be most accessible to a Markan audience.

a mighty storm came upon the sea that the ship threatened to break up. Then the mariners were afraid, and each cried to his god" (Jonah 1:5).

Profound anxiety regarding the sea and sea travel is evident in Greek and Roman sources as well. Tales about seafaring and shipwreck abound in Greco-Roman sources, undoubtedly reflecting the perilous realities these civilizations faced as people who crossed the Mediterranean with great frequency.[16] Indeed, storms play a central, driving role in the plots of foundational epics such as the *Odyssey* and the *Aeneid*, and continue as a trope all the way through the novels of the first centuries CE. Hesiod notes in his observations on the season for sailing that "it is a terrible thing to die among the waves ... a terrible thing to encounter grief among the waves" (*Op.* 687–693 [Most]). Ovid provides a window into this fear through his recounting of a storm at sea:

> Wretched me! What vast mountains of water heave themselves aloft! Now, now, you think, they will touch the highest stars. What mighty abysses settle beneath us as the flood yawns apart! Now, now you think they will touch black Tartarus. Wherever I gaze there is naught but sea and air—sea swollen with billows, air athreat with clouds...We are surely lost, there is no hope of safety; as I speak, the waters overwhelm my face. The billows will crush this life of mine, and lips that pray in vain I shall drink in the destroying water." (*Tristia* 19–36 [Wheeler])

In addition to the general anxiety of perishing, there was the added fear that a person would not be properly buried.[17] Should someone not receive proper burial, they "ran the risk of becoming a ghost, who would then be manipulated by magicians."[18] Interestingly, not only does the evangelist remark on the disciples' fear; the evangelist also plays up the details of the narrative to reinforce the dread of the situation.

There are three significant details in the storm-stilling account that augment the fear of the disciples and suggest that Jesus should not be sleeping so easily: (1) the fact that the storm occurs at night (4:35);

---

16. Peter Bolt, *Jesus' Defeat of Death: Persuading Mark's Early Readers* (Cambridge University Press, 2008), 131–42, and Geyer, *Fear, Anomaly, and Uncertainty*, 97–110, offer a helpful treatment of the scary elements present in this passage, as well as tracking attitudes Greco-Roman sources maintained with respect to sea-faring.

17. Peter Bolt, "Mark 16:1–8: The Empty Tomb of a Hero?," *TynBul* 47 (1996): 27–37.

18. Bolt, *Jesus' Defeat of Death*, 136.

(2) the description of the storm (4:37); and (3) the evangelist's use of θάλασσα. In 4:35, the evangelist remarks that Jesus and the disciples set sail "when it had become evening" (ὀψίας γενομένης). While this statement functions as a temporal marker setting apart the prior scene from the following action, many scholars have noted the importance such a detail plays in establishing a portentous setting for the chaos that will ensue on the lake.[19] The dangers of the night are well-documented in Jewish and Greco-Roman sources. For instance, in the Hebrew Bible, darkness is associated with cataclysmic danger (e.g., Ps 91:5; Job 27:20; 34:25, 30) and the demonic (Isa 34:14). Indeed, early Jewish and rabbinic demonological traditions drew from the latter reference, as evidenced in the legends that grew up around the figure Lilith, the night-demon that purportedly consumed children.[20] Greek writers, too, maintained a fear of the night. In Hesiod, the night (νύξ) was associated with a host of terrible elements:

> Night bore loathsome Doom and black Fate and Death, and she bore Sleep, and she gave birth to the tribe of Dreams. Second, then, gloomy Night bore blame and painful Distress. (*Theog.* 211–214 [Most])

Such imagery finds expression elsewhere in both cosmological and orphic writings, with the result that the night became a part of what Geyer terms the "anomalous frightful" in the Greco-Roman world.[21] Significantly, the Markan Gospel bolsters this understanding of darkness just a couple of chapters later for, in another nighttime seastorm (6:45–52), the disciples mistake Jesus for a "ghost" or "phantom" (φάντασμα), striking fear into the heart of his followers in the process (6:50).[22] In addition to references to the night, 4:37 reveals that the storm is actually a "storm of great wind" (λαῖλαψ μεγάλη ἀνέμου) that takes place upon the "sea" (θάλασσα). By

---

19. See, for instance, John R. Donahue and Daniel J. Harrington, *The Gospel of Mark*, SP 2 (Liturgical, 2005), 157; Robert A. Guelich, *Mark 1–8:26*, WBC 34a (Word, 1989), 264; Ludgar Schenke, *Die Wundererzählungen des Markusevangeliums* (Katholisches Bibelwerk, 1974), 27.

20. Geyer, *Fear, Anomaly, and Uncertainty*, 98.

21. Geyer, *Fear, Anomaly, and Uncertainty*, 99. For a more detailed analysis of night imagery in Jewish and Greco-Roman sources and their connection to the "anomalous frightful," see pp. 97–100.

22. For an interpretation of this particular scene as comical, see Combs, "Ghost on the Water?," 345–58.

using the term *sea*, the evangelist's rendition of the narrative joins up more readily with traditions about storms on the Mediterranean or great bodies of water, opposed to being a squall on the much smaller Galilean lake.[23] The audience is left with the startling image of a handful of people alone on their modest vessel, overwhelmed in darkness upon a great sea even as a hurricane bears down on them.

Taken together, the construction of the narrative, together with its descriptive details underscoring the spooky setting and imminent threat to life, raises the possibility that, at a surface-level reading or performance, the script-opposition ASLEEP/ALERT is operative, activated by the potential jab line "he was in the stern sleeping upon a cushion" (αὐτὸς ἦν ἐν τῇ πρύμνῃ ἐπὶ τὸ προσκεφάλαιον καθεύδων, 4:38). That is, the evangelist, through the statement of Jesus's being asleep, has crafted a scenario with particular expectations: people should be scared at this moment. However, when the narrative focus shifts to Jesus, one instead finds him sleeping and unaware of the possibility of death. This juxtaposition generates an incongruity that may well rise to the level of amusement. To further establish this point, it is paramount to consider the range of meaning activated in the script of SLEEPING.[24]

When considering the best way to interpret Jesus's sleep in Mark 4, it is key to bear in mind other locations in the gospel where sleep occurs. In addition to Mark 4:38, the evangelist references καθεύδω in 4:27, 5:39, 13:36, 14:37, 40–41. Of the eight instances, five are unambiguously negative. For example, in 13:36 Jesus warns the disciples through a parable that they should not fall asleep lest their master return and catch them unawares. This precedes the emotional scene in the garden where the disciples fall asleep three times even as Jesus has enlisted their aid for prayerful support (14:37–41). The evangelist juxtaposes this action by calls to remain awake and alert for whatever may come (13:35–37; 14:34, 37–38). Such an understanding of sleep is not surprising, as sources from antiquity frequently viewed sleep similarly.

Individuals in the ancient world held a wide range of views regarding sleep; however, this activity could and often did connote negative characteristics. For instance, Proverbs links the stupor of sleep to that

---

23. Note, for instance, Luke 8:22–25 and its use of λίμνη instead.
24. The wide range of allusions sought to explain Jesus's sleeping is indicative of just how strange this scene is, underscoring the ambiguity of the action.

of drunkenness:[25] "And you will lie down like one in the heart of the sea and like a captain in many waves" (Prov 23:34 LXX). Philosophers such as Plato and Aristotle, while not dismissing the inevitability of sleep, understood this period of human (in)activity to be a time of inhibition for the mind (e.g., Aristotle, *De. anim.* 429a7; Plato, *Tim.* 71e4–6).[26] Physicians such as Galen could reinforce this view by similarly reasoning that sleep inhibited higher cognitive functions where "the mind entered a condition similar to death" (*Symp. caus.* 1.8).[27] Roman discourse elsewhere echoed such sentiments, likening sleep to death and coupling it with drunkenness and other "deplorable things such as drowsiness, laziness, and ignorance."[28] Such examples underscore the ambivalence surrounding the script of sleep both within Mark as well as the Greco-Roman world more broadly. While sleep was natural and many perceived it as an avenue for divine communication through dreams, people often correlated sleep to drunkenness, laziness, lack of alertness, and other vices. Consequently, the evangelist's use of sleep is potentially ambiguous, possibly to be taken in a negative or, at the very least, an odd sense. Such a point gains greater clarity in the broader context of possible intertextual allusions scholars often draw upon to explain Jesus's behavior.

Scholars frequently turn to Jonah in order to make sense of this narrative.[29] There are few stories in the Hebrew Bible that depict a voyage at sea coupled with a furious storm, so Jonah stands as a natural point of connection when considering intertextual possibilities.[30] In addition to the obviously similar contours Jonah and Mark share, both stories saliently depict their main characters as being asleep amid a terrible storm. Notably, the connection between these stories enhances the possibility that aspects

---

25. Robert Anderson, "'A Man Asleep in a Storm at Sea' as a Biblical Motif," *Proceedings: Eastern Great Lakes and Midwest Biblical Societies* 6 (1986): 35.

26. Leslie Dossey, "Watchful Greeks and Lazy Romans: Disciplining Sleep in Late Antiquity," *JECS* 21 (2013): 209–39.

27. Dossey, "Watchful Greeks and Lazy Romans," 214.

28. Laura Nissin, "Sleeping Culture in Roman Literary Sources," *Arctos* 49 (2015): 95–133.

29. On this topic, see the work of Aus, *Stilling the Storm*, 1–88, who offers an extended reading of this narrative against both Hebrew Bible and early Jewish and rabbinic traditions.

30. Indeed, such a link is already present in the Q tradition, where Jesus speaks of death and resurrection as the "sign of Jonah" (Matt 12:38–42 // Luke 11:29–32).

of the narrative may be comical.³¹ If Jonah has indeed influenced the Markan pericope, as seems likely, this bolsters the possibility that Jesus's actions are humorous. The evangelist allusively links Jesus, not only to Jonah, but possibly to the LXX Jonah who comically fell asleep and sawed logs even as a thunderous storm cleaved the timber of his ship.³²

Another possible allusion behind Mark 4 is that of Odysseus and his occasional tendency to sleep during storms at sea. Dennis MacDonald has put forth the argument that such scenes play into the formation of the Markan tradition.³³ He notes the parallels between Mark 4:35–41 and *Od.* 10.1–69 where, while Odysseus sleeps, his jealous crew has unbound the sack of winds Aeolus has awarded Odysseus. Their actions let lose a fierce storm that drives them back to Aeolus's island. Additionally, *Od.* 13.73–90 recounts how Odysseus, in his final journey home, falls asleep once more until he arrives in Ithaca. While it is possible that the *Odyssey* is a point of reference for the Markan text, it serves to underscore the strangeness of Jesus's actions, for the narrative does not typically correlate sleep and storms. Notably, this is true of type-scene approaches to Mark 4 generally.

Occasionally, scholars interpret Mark 4 within the broader context of seastorm type-scenes. While there are points of contact between the present passage and such scenes, consistently lacking in other narratives is the presence of persons sleeping even as the ship is sinking.³⁴ Pamela Thimmes's study on this type-scene is indicative of the rarity of such an action for, after canvassing Greek, Roman, and biblical sources, she does

---

31. Yarbro Collins, *Mark*, suggests as much when considering the reaction of the disciples, "the question of the disciples may owe something to the humor and realism of the Jonah story" (260).

32. See the discussion above regarding sleep and comedic sources.

33. Dennis Macdonald, *The Gospels and Homer: Imitations of Greek Epic in Mark and Luke-Acts*, The New Testament and Greek Literature 1 (Rowman & Littlefield, 2015), 207: "It would appear that Mark created his narrative eclectically by imitating both the Book of Jonah and the *Odyssey.*"

34. See, e.g. Anderson, "Man Asleep in a Storm"; Pamela Thimmes, "The Biblical Sea-Storm Type-Scene: A Proposal," *Proceedings: Eastern Great Lakes and Midwest Biblical Societies* 10 (1990): 107–22; Thimmes, *Studies in the Biblical Sea-Storm Type Scene: Convention and Invention* (Mellen Research University Press, 1992). Anderson's study includes a wide variety of stories, but only four touch on falling asleep in the midst of a storm or on a ship: Moses (as a baby), Jonah, Jesus, and the drunk of Prov 23:34 (35). Of these scenes, only Prov 23:34 has direct significance, a point to which I will return below.

not include sleeping as a key motif in any of the primary sources.[35] Thus, it may be said that, while sleeping is known in other seastorm stories, it is not common, nor does it generally present with storms at sea.

The final allusion I consider here concerns the wide-spread motif of the sleeping god in the ancient Near East and Greco-Roman world who required that supplicants rouse them from their slumber.[36] Passages such as Pss 7:7, 35:23, 59:5–6; 77:65–66 correspond to a broader tradition in the ancient Near East wherein "the motif of divine sleep was often bound together with that of divine rest or leisure…. The ability to sleep undisturbed was the symbol of the deity's absolute dominance."[37] Scholars have suggested that the present passage represents the evangelist's use of this motif with "the image of the sleeping Jesus modeled after that of the sleeping divine king."[38] Psalm 43:24–27 is indicative of such a motif:

> Wake! Why are you sleeping, O Lord? Rise and do not push us away forever. Why do you turn your face away? Have you forgotten our poverty and our suffering? For Our life has been forced down into dust, our stomach joined to the ground. Rise, O Lord! Aid us and redeem us for the sake of your name.

It may well be the case that, beyond a surface reading of the text, the evangelist has sought to allude to such a tradition. The Hebrew Bible well attests the *chaoskempf*, and the activity of Jesus and his followers in Mark 4 does envisage a powerful, theophanic moment wherein Jesus sleeps amid chaotic forces only to rise and conquer them with a word. Yet if this is the primary intertextual touchstone for the evangelist, it must be admitted that this represents a more esoteric point and one which rank-and-file Markan audience members might not catch in the moment.

---

35. Thimmes, *Biblical Sea-Storm Type-Scene*, does not include sleep as a part of her chart comparing "conventional motifs." Thimmes does state regarding Jesus that he "is said to be asleep in the stern, a position not uncommon for central characters in sea-storm type-scenes" (137). I am less convinced on the commonality of this action as the only other character who does this is found in Jonah 1:5.

36. Several scholars note the possibility of such a connection. So Bernard Batto, "The Sleeping God: An Ancient Near Eastern Motif of Divine Sovereignty," *Bib* 68 (1987): 153–77; Yarbro Collins, *Mark*, 260; Marcus, *Mark*, 336–37; Michael Whitenton, *Hearing Kyriotic Sonship: A Cognitive and Rhetorical Approach to the Characterization of Mark's Jesus*, BibInt 148 (Brill, 2017), 179.

37. Batto, "Sleeping God," 164.

38. Batto, "Sleeping God," 175.

Immediately following the notice that Jesus sleeps even as the waves have already begun to overtake the boat, the evangelist states that "having been woken, he rebuked the wind and said to the sea, 'Be still! Quiet!' And the wind ceased and there was a great calm" (4:39). Notably, this impressive statement potentially reads as a jab line that activates the script-opposition of ROMAN IMPERIUM/JESUS'S IMPERIUM. Scholars have pointed out the connection between royal power in the ancient world and command over the forces of the sea, a theme that appears to be at play in Mark 4:35–41.[39] For example, according to Herodotus, Xerxes ordered that the Hellespont be "scourged with three hundred lashes" (*Hist.* 7.34 [Godley]) and that he commanded the people to admonish the waters: "Thou bitter water ... our master punishes thee, because thou didst wrong him.... Xerxes the king will pass over thee....' Thus he commanded that the sea should be punished" (*Hist.* 7.35 [Godley]). Roman rulers echoed such attitudes. Augustus, in a self-commissioned testament of his achievements, notes in Res gestae divi Augusti his conquest of the sea. Augustus speaks of wars he "undertook throughout the world, on sea and land" (Res gest. divi Aug. 1.3 [Shipley]), "successful operations on land and sea" (Res gest. divi Aug. 1.4 [Shipley]), and that he "freed the sea from pirates" (Res gest. divi Aug. 1.25 [Shipley]). Augustus's dominion, as he perceived it, was such that it stretched even to the lawless, chaotic realm of the sea. More significantly, there are possible parallels between Mark 4:35–41 and stories of Julius Caesar.

Roger Aus and Mark Strelan have argued for strong contact points between this pericope and accounts of Julius Caesar's failed crossing of the Ionian and/or Adriatic Sea as recounted by Lucan, Plutarch, Appian, and Cassius Dio.[40] These accounts relate the attempt of their powerful protagonists to cross a body of water, only to encounter resistance due to tempestuous weather. Critical differences between these narratives include the manner in which the storm is addressed and the outcome of the journey—Caesar rages against the hurricane even as he fails to cross the sea, whereas Jesus wakes from deep slumber, quells the storm with a

---

39. Yabro Collins, *Mark*, 261; Gabriella Gelardini, *Christus Militans: Studien zur politisch-militärischen Semantik im Markusevangelium vor dem Hintergrund des ersten jüdisch-römischen Krieges*, NovTSup 165 (Brill, 2016), 153–58; Herman Hendrickx, *The Miracles Stories*, Studies in the Synoptic Gospels (Chapman, 1987), 184.

40. Aus, *Stilling of the Storm*, 56–88; Mark Strelan, "A Greater than Caesar: Storm Stories in Lucan and Mark," *ZNW* 91 (2000): 166–79.

word, and arrives on the other side. Thus, it is possible that the evangelist has initiated a script-opposition of ROMAN IMPERIUM/JESUS'S IMPERIUM in verse 39 that recurs in verse 41 when the journey is complete.

Bruce Longenecker has raised an intriguing point regarding juxtapositions between Jesus and Roman imperium. Through his work on the material culture of Pompeii, Longenecker has suggested a possible point of comparison/contrast between a fresco in Pompeii and the Markan account.[41] In the Pompeian fresco, Venus (possibly representing the mother of Rome and/or Rome itself) is positioned in a boat, carefully guiding it to shore amid a storm. Such symbolism could have connected "Venus ... to the Roman project of eradicating chaos and establishing order."[42] If the evangelist had such a portrait or image in mind when crafting the account of 4:35–41, it quite possibly would have acted as an anti or counter-imperial image, depicting Jesus as savior over chaos rather than Rome.[43]

Upon Jesus coming to the disciples' aid, one encounters the last script-opposition present in Mark 4:35–41, this time regarding fear and misunderstanding. Rather than thank Jesus for his intercession, the disciples become "greatly afraid" (4:41). Notably, fear occurs at two critical junctures in the pericope, before and after the typhoon on the lake. In the first instance, fear on the disciples' part is present when they wake and confront Jesus with the statement: "Teacher, does it not worry you that we are perishing?" (4:38). While scholars sometimes characterize the disciples negatively for this, such fear was characteristic of seastorm type-scenes and entirely within keeping for someone in such a dire situation.[44]

---

41. Bruce W. Longenecker, *In Stone and Story: Early Christianity in the Roman World* (Baker Academic, 2020), 66–67.

42. Longenecker, *In Stone and Story*, 67.

43. Longenecker, *In Stone and Story*, 67.

44. Scholars often collapse the fear of the disciples with Jesus's rebuke moments later. Yet arguably fear could have been a natural response to such a situation, a fact that writers in the first century reflect: "The popular entertainment literature of the first century [shows] an abundance of sea-storm stories in which the hero shows his character during a sudden threat to life. In the first century, such stories serve as metaphors, the sea representing the uncertainty of life in the sublunar region, the sector of the cosmos where one found famine, disease, war, and death." Wendy Cotter, "Cosmology and the Jesus Miracles," in *Whose Historical Jesus*, ed. William Arnal and Michel Desjardins, Studies in Christianity and Judaism 7 (Wilfrid Laurier University Press, 1997), 118–31, as quoted in Bolt, *Jesus' Defeat of Death*, 139.

The deeper problem for the evangelist appears to be the reaction to Jesus's saving actions after the fact. That is, the fear and lack of faith *after* Jesus's clear intentions and ability to save his disciples is what elicits condemnation, rather than the simple presence of fear in a life-threatening situation.[45] Such an interpretation of the disciples' fear finds support in 6:45–52.

In the evangelist's second sea-crossing-storm account, the audience encounters a very similar episode. In this pericope, Jesus enjoins the disciples to cross the sea on their own. As fate would have it, another powerful storm occurs and threatens to sink their boat yet again. Jesus, seeing them in distress, initially plans to "pass by them," but instead joins them in the ship and exhorts them to have courage (6:48–50). The fear of the disciples and their condemnation by Jesus raise significant points for understanding fear in 4:35–41. The initial fear of the disciples earns them no rebuke. Indeed, Jesus sees them in their distress and comforts them even after they have mistaken him for a φάντασμα (6:49) ("Have courage! It is I, do not fear!," 6:50). It is only after Jesus has come aboard with them and the wind has died down that they find condemnation. At this point, the evangelist characterizes them as being "exceedingly astonished among themselves, for they did not comprehend regarding the loaves; but their hearts were hardened" (6:51b–52).

When one compares the two seastorm scenes in Mark, it appears that there is a two-step development in the disciples' fear: (1) initially the disciples are rightly afraid given their life-threatening circumstances; (2) then, after experiencing Jesus's extraordinary power, rather than be at peace, they are more afraid than before. Though this second stage of fear in 4:35–41 is sometimes read as theophanic or epiphanic fear and carrying a positive valence, such an interpretation downplays the condemnation of the disciples by Jesus (4:40) and the narrator (6:51–52).[46] Instead, the second stage of fear more likely represents the disciples' failure to understand God's soteriological actions in their midst. What is more, it is possible that this is a jab

---

45. Edwin Broadhead, *Teaching with Authority: Miracles and Christology in the Gospel of Mark*, JSNTSup 74 (JSOT Press, 1992), 94, also notes ambivalence regarding fear and its role in the present passage. Indeed, he notes a two-stage development, interpreting the initial fear of the disciples as a failure on their part, followed by a more positive appraisal in the second instance, which represents epiphanic fear.

46. Broadhead, *Teaching with Authority*: "While this term [φόβος] may continue the negative image of the disciples, it possibly presents the fear which marks those who experience the power or presence of God" (94).

line eliciting a script-opposition of APPROPRIATE/INAPPROPRIATE FEAR or APPROPRIATE/INAPPROPRIATE RESPONSE TO JESUS. In 4:40–41, the audience expects that the disciples should be grateful now that the storm has given way to a calm sea. Indeed, as Geyer observes, similar soteriological actions by God in Ps 107:23–28, a passage often seen as a background to Mark 4:35–41, includes deliverance from a seastorm, which elicits peace and praise.[47] Yet Jesus rebukes them, demonstrating their continued fear. Furthermore, in response to an accusation of cowardice the disciples "became afraid with a great fear and said to one another 'Who is this that even the wind and sea obey him?'" (4:41). The picture here is potentially humorous. Having just been deemed cowards, the disciples do not even have the courage to directly defend themselves. The men who were swift to rouse Jesus and rebuke him for sleeping are now even more afraid and turn to one another in a conference of murmurs, confirming Jesus's statement and acting strangely in response to the person who just delivered them from harm.

Notably, additional character traits often coexisted with cowardice. As Geyer notes, both superstition and faithlessness could accompany this characteristic:

> The companion character to this [coward], Δεισιδαιμονία, has similar traits.... The main feature of this character is a compulsive trait: any accident or a strange, one-time event calls for cultic purification, oracular response, or expiation. The third character, Ἀπιστία, is that of obsessive mistrust.... The critical aspect here is not just a lack of trust during strange and unusual situations, but chronic mistrust where one would normally trust.[48]

In the Markan account, one sometimes finds these traits clustered together.[49] In the present passage, the disciples demonstrate both cowardice and mistrust. At a critical juncture where they should offer thanks and trust to the power that has delivered them, they instead manifest opposing, negative traits. In this way, they end up looking more like stock, comedic characters than stout-hearted followers of the teacher they roused to help them in the first place.

---

47. Geyer, *Fear, Anomaly, and Uncertainty*, 106.
48. Geyer, *Fear, Anomaly, and Uncertainty*, 108.
49. Note especially the storm scene in Mark 6:45–52 where all three traits are found together.

Finally, there is also likely another script-opposition in 4:41b activated by the potential jab line "who is this that even the wind and sea obey him?" The opposing scripts here lie in the question of mistaken identity, particularly by those who should seem to know who Jesus is.[50] Indeed, immediately before this story, the evangelist states that Jesus has provided access to the hidden meaning of his parables, signaling the disciples' privileged standing as an inner-circle who should correctly apprehend Jesus's identity (4:33–34).[51] Rather than gaining insight into Jesus's character through his actions upon the sea, however, the disciples are instead baffled about his identity and are even openly afraid of him. This understanding of Jesus's identity directly opposes his true identity as the Son of God, an appellation delivered in the opening lines of the gospel (1:[1], 11).[52] Thus, 4:41b quite possibly activates a script-opposition of KNOWLEDGE/ IGNORANCE OF JESUS'S IDENTITY, a script-opposition that will find further extension in the coming stories.

The Man with Demonic Affliction (Mark 5:1–20)

The second pericope in Mark 4:35–6:6 relates the striking tale of one of Jesus's most momentous spiritual power encounters. This extended story of demonic possession is dramatic and unfolds in an exciting manner. As it does so, it potentially utilizes several script-oppositions: SUCCESSFUL/FAILED EXORCIST, ROMAN IMPERIUM/JESUS'S IMPERIUM, CIVILIZED/ BARBARIAN, APPROPRIATE/INAPPROPRIATE FEAR or APPROPRIATE/INAPPROPRIATE RESPONSE TO JESUS, and WORSHIP/OPPOSITION. Ancient comedic treatments of madness and demonic possession, imperial satire, cowardice, and barbarians illuminate these script-oppositions.

---

50. So Robert Stacy, "Fear in the Gospel of Mark" (PhD diss, The Southern Baptist Theological Seminary, 1979), 197, in tracing the role of fear in Mark makes a similar observation: "Therefore, Mark employed the motif of fear (v.41) in order to point out the disciples' failure to grasp the true identity of Jesus on the basis of his miraculous power alone."

51. Jordash Kiffiak, *Responses in the Miracle Stories of the Gospels: Between Artistry and Inherited Tradition*, WUNT 2/429 (Mohr Siebeck, 2017), 143, maintains that the disciples should be in a position to better understand the nature of the miracle before them than the crowds as they have been entrusted with understanding Jesus's teaching.

52. Timothy Dwyer, *The Motif of Wonder in the Gospel of Mark*, JSNTSup 128 (Sheffield Academic, 1996), 110.

Comedic Themes in Ancient Sources

Madness and Possession

While it may strike the contemporary reader as strange or in poor taste, deriving humor from madness and demonic possession was not uncommon practice in ancient texts. This is likely rooted in the incongruous behavior a person thought to hold such a disposition maintained. Plutarch relates the story of one such person, Nicias.[53] This leading citizen of Engyium engendered the wrath of his fellow citizens when attempting to persuade the city to join the cause of the Romans, rather than the Carthaginians. Upon learning that the city would soon arrest him and deliver him to Carthage, Nicias fell upon the ground amid an assembly, moved his head about while speaking in strange tones, and finally

> tore off his mantle, rent his tunic, and leaping up half naked, ran towards the exit, crying out that he was pursued by the Mothers.... He ran out to the gate of the city, freely using all the cries and gestures that would become a man possessed and crazed. (*Marc.* 20.5–6 [Perrin])

Plutarch's account of Nicias reflects the startling behavior of a person considered to be mad and possessed. Such behavior provided fodder for comedic playwrights. Plautus's writings illustrate this tendency.[54]

In the comedy *Menaechmi* about estranged twin brothers, Plautus crafts incongruous scenarios wherein one brother is mistaken for the other to great comical effect. One of the stranger scenes in the play concerns the mix-up of Menaechmus and his brother Sosicles by Menaechmus's wife and father-in-law. In the fifth act of *Menaechmi*, the unfortunate Sosicles stumbles into his twin's wife while holding the mantle Menaechmus stole from her to give his mistress. A fight ensues between the *matrona* and Sosicles, with the former accusing him of cheating on her and the latter being thoroughly confused as to why she is telling him her personal business in addition to being cross with him. The *matrona* sends for her father who becomes upset upon learning that Menaechmus is stealing from his daughter only to give them to a mistress. In the resultant argument, Sosi-

---

53. Plutarch wrote during the late first and early second centuries CE.
54. Plautus, one of the exemplars of Latin New Comedy, was active during the third and early second centuries BCE.

cles is accused of being insane, prompting him to embrace the allegation in an attempt to be left alone (*Men.* 831–833). This leads to an exchange where Sosicles feigns divine possession while the *matrona* and *senex* attempt to bind him:

> Sosicles: Look, Apollo tells me through a divine utterance to burn out that woman's eyes with flaming torches
> Wife: I'm Dead! My dear father, he's threatening to burn out my eyes.
> Old Man: Hey there, my daughter!
> Wife: What is it? What are we doing?
> Old Man: What if I summon slaves here? I'll go and fetch people to lift him up from here and tie him up at home before he makes more trouble. (*Men.* 841–845 [de Melo])

Sosicles's behavior escalates at the threat of being arrested:

> Sosicles: This is your command [Apollo], that I should smash his limbs, bones, and joints to pieces with his own walking stick.
> Old Man: You'll get a beating if you touch me or come any closer to me.
> Sosicles: I'll do what you tell me: I'll take a double-edged ax and hew away this old man's flesh, bit by bit, down to the bone. (*Men.* 854–860 [de Melo])

Following more severe threats, Sosicles proceeds to fall onto the ground, leading the *senex* to seek medical help, thereby allowing Sosicles his opening to escape:

> Sosicles: But who is that dragging me off the chariot by the hair? The power over you and Apollo's behest is failing.
> Old Man: Goodness! A bitter and harsh illness…I'll go and fetch the doctor as quickly as possible.
> Sosicles: Have they left my sight now, please? They force me to act crazy even though I am healthy. (*Men.* 870–877 [de Melo])

This episode plays off of the symptoms of divine possession. Sosicles, initially accused of being out of his mind because he does not know who he is (i.e., he *is not* his estranged twin brother), embraces this behavior. In a dramatic performance, Sosicles feigns to hear the voice of Apollos and, driven by divine power, threatens everyone around him until he secures his escape. This scene offers a striking example of how ancient comic playwrights could wield divine possession to comical effect.

Notably, Plautus is not the only ancient writer to do this, for Lucian treats this topic as well. In his satirical account of perceived superstitions, *Philopseudes*, Lucian touches on the question of exorcism in a comical manner.[55] In the extended dialogue between the character, Tychiades, and his myriad superstitious interlocutors, Ion sets forth an account of a famous exorcist:[56]

> Everyone knows about the Syrian from Palestine, the adept in it, how many he takes in hand who fall down in the light of the moon and roll their eyes and fill their mouths with foam; nevertheless, he restores them to health and sends them away normal in mind, delivering them from their straits for a large fee. When he stands beside them as they lie there and asks: 'Whence came you into his body?' the patient himself is silent, but the spirit answers in Greek or in the language of whatever foreign country he comes from, telling how and whence he entered into the man; whereupon, by adjuring the spirit and if he does not obey him, threatening him, he drives him out. Indeed, I actually saw one coming out, black and smoky in colour. (*Philops*. 16 [Harmon])

Lucian's account is meant to be a satirical take on the phenomenon of possession. He is not concerned for persons who might actually be afflicted with illness. Rather, Ion's speech is meant to be patently ridiculous, a fact which Tychiades's response reflects:

> "It is nothing much," I remarked, "for you, Ion, to see that kind of sight, when even the 'forms' that the father of your school, Plato, points out are plain to you, a hazy object of vision to the rest of us, whose eyes are weak." (*Philops*. 16 [Harmon])

Lucian derives a different comedy from possession than Plautus. His humor is rooted in a thoroughgoing skepticism aimed at the beliefs of persons, who, in his opinion, ascribe impossible explanations to straightforward physical afflictions.

---

55. Lucian, a prolific writer and satirist, was active during the second century CE.

56. The question of Lucian's dependence on Christian traditions here is beyond the scope of the present study, nor does it affect the interpretation of the text. Whether Lucian is lampooning the Christian exorcistic traditions or some other exorcist, the fact remains that persons in the ancient world could and did find ways to view such activity as humorous.

Finally, there is one further narrative concerning humor and the demonic worth considering here: Tobit.[57] The book of Tobit relates the story of the pious protagonist Tobit, his son Tobias, and the demonically afflicted Sarah. While the story maintains many comical elements, it is quite possible that the author intends for Sarah's condition to be humorous.[58] This unlucky bride-to-be, in spite of her faithfulness to God, cannot prevent the demon Asmodeus from killing all of her suitors—seven in all—because he is in love with her (Tob 3:8; 6:15). The solution to this problem, as the angel Raphael prescribes, is to lay the innards of a fish on burning incense, the terrible smell of which will drive Asmodeous away (Tob 6:18). Comically (and happily), this strategy succeeds, and Asmodeus flees at the awful smell of burning fish (Tob 8:3).

These examples demonstrate that humor could be deployed when considering the phenomenon of possession, be it of divine or demonic origin.

Imperium

As noted above, ancient comedic writers lampooned many ideas, political power included. Though not targeted perennially or with the same consistency in different eras, Greek and Roman humorists and satirists did take aim at political institutions. This is evident, for instance, in the works of Aristophanes and Seneca.

Aristophanes crafts fantastical scenarios throughout his comedies, occasionally venturing into overtly political critiques.[59] This is particularly true regarding the rise of Cleon, a fifth century BCE Athenian

---

57. Tobit was likely written during the third or second century BCE.

58. On comedy and its use in Tobit, see D. A. Bertrand, "Le Chevreau d'Anna: La Significatio Du l'anecdotique Dans Le Livre de Tobit," *RHPR* 68 (1988): 269–74; David McCracken, "Narration and Comedy in the Book of Tobit," *JBL* 114 (1995): 401–18; Anathea Portier-Young, "Alleviation of Suffering in the Book of Tobit: Comedy, Community, and Happy Endings," *CBQ* 63 (2001): 35–54.

59. For further political readings of Aristophanes, see Paul Ludwig, "The Portrait of the Artist in Politics: Justice and Self-Interest in Aristophanes' Acharnians," *The American Political Science Review* 101 (2007): 479–92; Ian Worthington, "Aristophanes' Knights and the Abortive Peace Proposals of 425 B.C.," *L'Antiquité Classique* 56 (1987): 56–67; John Zumbrunnen, "Elite Domination and the Clever Citizen: Aristophanes' 'Archarnians' and 'Knights,'" *Political Theory* 32 (2004): 656–77; Zumbrunnen, "Fantasy, Irony, and Economic Justice in Aristophanes' 'Assemblywomen and Wealth,'" *The American Political Science Review* 100 (2006): 319–33.

whom Aristophanes regarded as a dangerous demagogue. The playwright attacks him directly in both *Equites* and *Vespae*, where he depicts Cleon as "a corrupt politician who used his power to blackmail … allies and prominent Athenians and took every opportunity to embezzle public funds."[60] In the guise of the slave-tanner Paphlagon, Aristophanes excoriates Cleon (Paphlagon) for his corruption and public policies. Aristophanes indicts him through the character of the Sausage Seller as both Paphlagon and Sausage Seller compete for the position of Demos's (Athens) steward:

> Paphlagon: Isn't it awful to hear him say these things about me, Demos, just because I cherish you?
> Demos: Shut up, shut up, you, and stop your sleazy mud-slinging! You've been getting away with hoodwinking me for far too long already.
> Sausage Seller: He's utter scum, my precious Demos, and a champion evildoer. While you're gaping into space, he breaks the choicest stalks off the audits of outgoing officials and gulps them down, and with both hands sops the gravy from the people's treasury.
> Paphlagon: You won't get the last laugh; I'll convict you of stealing thirty thousand drachmas! (*Eq.* 820–826 [Henderson])

Aristophanes did not limit his political critiques only to specific individuals. The playwright also took aim at what he considered to be problematic, militant foreign policy; namely, he was a staunch critic of the Peloponnesian War.[61] This is clearly (and comically) evident in *Lysistrata*, where the women of Athens organize a sex-strike in order to end the war. In an extended exchange with an Athenian magistrate, Lysistrata addresses her husband's assertion that war is the business of men:

> How could he be right, you sorry fool, when we were forbidden to offer advice even when your policy was wrong? But then, when we began to hear you in the streets openly crying, "There isn't a man left in the land," and someone else saying, "God knows, there isn't, not a one," after that we women decided to lose no more time, and to band together to save Greece. What was the point of waiting any longer? So, if you're ready to listen in your turn as we give you good advice, and to shut up as we had to, we can put you back on the right track.… Now hitch up your clothes

---

60. T. A. Dorey, "Aristophanes and Cleon," *Greece & Rome* 3 (1956): 132–39.
61. Worthington, "Aristophanes' Knights," 56–67.

and start sewing; chew some beans while you work. War shall be the business of womenfolk! (*Lys.* 521–528; 538 [Henderson])

In this dialogue, Lysistrata and her female companions offer a critique of both civic authority generally and an incessantly aggressive military policy in particular. Significantly, the use of humor as a tool to critique civic and/or imperial authority continued into the Roman era.[62]

Seneca, a dedicated letter-writer and poet of the early Roman Empire, offered a sharp appraisal of Claudius and deleterious Roman imperium upon the emperor's death in *Apocolocyntosis* ("pumpkinification").[63] In his satirical eulogizing of Claudius, Seneca depicts the late emperor as attempting to attain the status of a god, only to be unrecognized by the divine pantheon and rebuked by Augustus himself. Claudius is ultimately banished to the underworld, where he is doomed to toil eternally as a clerk for a freedman. Among Claudius's many faults, Seneca highlights his violent predilection for assassination. While standing court before the gods of Olympus, Augustus rises and objects to Claudius's apotheosis, particularly on the grounds of his violence:

> This man you see, who for so many years has been masquerading under my name, has done me the favour of murdering two Julias, great-granddaughters of mine, L. Silanus—see, Jupiter, whether he had a case against him.... Come tell me, blessed Claudius, why of all those you killed, both men and women, without a hearing, why did you not hear their side of the case first, before putting them to death? (*Apol.* 10 [Heseltine])

Seneca's treatment of Claudius reflects sharp displeasure with the way the emperor wielded his imperium, especially his killing of individuals on a

---

62. A qualification is important here. Overly political targets dwindled as comedy shifted into Middle then New Comedy, a trend evidenced by Terence and Plautus. Yet in spite of the shift to more domestic comedies, some Roman writers did adopt satirical methods for treating certain political figures. This was especially true of Seneca and Juvenal.

63. Timothy Robinson, "In the Court of Time: The Reckoning of a Monster in the 'Apocolocyntosis' of Seneca," *Arethusa* 38 (2005): 225, notes that Seneca's satire holds up Nero and Claudius as "images [which] are reflected in the mirror of *imperium*: Claudius as an utter travesty and Nero as model ruler." Although "there is panegyric to Nero in Seneca's satire ... it must also be acknowledged that there is satire in the panegyric" (254).

whim, without due process. Claudius, in his prolific violence, flouted what Seneca perceived to be proper strictures of Roman imperium, leading the satirist to critique such political power in a denunciation of the Roman emperor.

Cowardice

As noted above, cowardice was a theme comedic playwrights frequently utilized. They often depicted soldiers as cowardly, reveling in the obvious contrast. The notion of a scared or domesticated soldier provided an easy target for its inherent contradictions. Menander's *Perikeiromone* exemplifies this trope with the soldier Polemon bearing little resemblance to the ideal military man.[64] For instance, his slave characterizes him as a blubbering fool for grief he exhibits over losing his love, Glykera:

> Our swaggering soldier of an hour ago.... Now lies upon his couch in tears. Just now I found some lunch being fixed for them, his friends Have mustered there together, just to help Him soldier through this business with less pain. (*Perik*. 172–177 [Arnott])

Furthermore, in pleading with Pataikos to resolve the conflict between he and Glykera, Polemon descends into a discussion of her possession and dresses. While the speech references her beauty, the scenario borders on absurdity as Polemon gets lost in unnecessary details:

> Polemon: It's so vital, Pataikos. All success in this attempt Depends on it! You see, if I have ever At all wronged her ... if I don't keep on trying My best, in every way ... if you could see her things ...
> Pataikos: No need for that!
> Polemon: Just look, Pataikos, please—You'll pity me the more!
> Pataikos: In heaven's name!
> Polemon: Do Come here—such dresses! How she looks when she Slips one of these on! Perhaps you won't have seen ...
> Pataikos: I have.
> Polemon: Of course her height's remarkable—but why Should I now introduce her height? I'm crazy, Going on about irrelevances!
> Pataikos: No, Heavens, no!

---

64. Menander, an Athenian playwright, was active during the fourth century BCE.

Polemon: No? Yet, Pataikos, you should see Them. Walk this way! (*Perik.* 513–525 [Arnott])

Polemon hardly resembles a Corinthian soldier. In place of bravery and a stolid presence, he unravels into fits of crying and distracted behavior. The reduction of his idealized, manly state provides fertile ground for comedy.

Barbarians

Humor in the ancient Mediterranean often utilized social and ethnic difference as a source of comedy, with playwrights ethnocentrically targeting the way foreign persons spoke, in addition to their music, food, and clothing.[65] Aristophanes was no stranger to leaning on stereotypes of so-called barbarian peoples in order to earn a laugh. The comic playwright explicitly noted the distinction between "Hellas" and "barbarian" ("Ελλησι καὶ τοῖς βαρβάροισι [*Ran.* 720]) and drew at different times upon these categories. One sees this, for instance, in *Thesmphoriazousai* through the depiction of a Scythian archer wherein Aristophanes portrays the foreign character as deficient of speech, lustful, and violent.

Menander, at times, made use of foreignness as a device in his comedies. In *Samia*, Menander utilizes the Adonis festival as a central point in his play. The celebration of the death of Adonis came late into Athenian life, and many of the city's inhabitants regarded it as a foreign religious rite.[66] Menander exploited this event for its stereotyped understanding as a ritual that facilitated unbridled licentiousness.[67] Ultimately, comedic

---

65. Timothy Long, *Barbarians in Greek Comedy* (Southern Illinois University Press, 1986), 69–75, treats several of these topics. Importantly, as Long observes, the category of barbarian was not universally negative. The ancients could and did speak positively of certain aspects of so-called barbarian society. Food, in particular, seems to have been an arena in which non-Greeks succeeded over against their Greek counterparts. See also Raymond Coon, *The Foreigner in Hellenistic Comedy* (PhD diss, The University of Chicago, 1920). The question of Greek identity and its relationship to non-Greek peoples is complicated by the question of Hellenic identity more broadly and shifting attitudes towards non-Hellenic persons from the fifth century BCE onwards. However, in broad strokes, the dichotomy of Greek/non-Greek or Greek/Barbarian held through antiquity with Romans similarly finding the customs and behaviors of non-Romans a source of humor.

66. Long, *Barbarians in Greek Comedy*, 22.

67. Long, *Barbarians in Greek Comedy*, 25.

playwrights exploited one-dimensional stereotypes of cultures beyond their own to generate humor.

Analysis of Mark 5:1–20

Upon quieting the raging sea, Jesus and the disciples safely make it to the opposite shore. However, as they will quickly learn, they are not free from danger for it is here where Jesus confronts the most powerful demonic force in the gospel, save for Satan himself (1:12).[68] Jesus ultimately demonstrates that he is the "stronger one" (1:7) able to bind the "strong man" (3:27) by driving out the demons that plague the unfortunate man.

Many scholars have noted the literary qualities of the narrative, its logical difficulties notwithstanding. Eugene Boring aptly represents this view, labeling the pericope "the longest, most detailed, and most vivid of the Synoptic miracle stories."[69] In this narrative, the evangelist portrays a man hellbent on his own destruction because of the unclean spirits that have overtaken him (5:3–5).

The pericope of the man with unclean spirits contains a high volume of curious elements. Though some commentators read the text in a strictly serious manner, others have noted a comic tone in the text, stating that "the humor ... is thoroughly evident" as the pericope maintains "un humour blasphématoire" and has qualities of "burlesque comedy."[70] However, scholars have not attempted to systematically interpret the humor in the pericope or its rhetorical function.[71] A close reading of the text reveals several potential script-oppositions at work in the passage: SUCCESSFUL/FAILED EXORCIST, ROMAN IMPERIUM/JESUS'S IMPERIUM, CIVILIZED/BARBARIAN, and APPROPRIATE/INAPPROPRIATE RESPONSE TO JESUS. These

---

68. I adopt the position here connecting this story to the region of Gerasa.

69. Eugene Boring, *Mark: A Commentary*, NTL (Westminster John Knox, 2006), 149.

70. For those who read the text in a serious manner, see, e.g., Richard Deibart, *Mark*, Interpretation Bible Studies (Geneva, 1999), 49; William Lane, *The Gospel according to Mark*, NICNT (Eerdmans, 1974); Vincent Taylor, *The Gospel according to St. Mark*, 2nd ed. (Macmillan, 1966). For the quoted authors who read a comic tone, see, respectively, Tolbert, *Sowing the Gospel*, 167; LaMarche, *Evangile de Marc*, 145; and Marcus, *Mark*, 350.

71. If the rhetorical function of humor is treated at all in the narrative, it is usually with respect to the reaction to Jesus's miracle. See, for example, Camery-Hoggatt, *Irony in Mark's Gospel*, 135–37.

script-oppositions potentially form the bedrock of humor in Mark 5:1–20, with additional layers found in such script-oppositions as WORSHIP/OPPOSITION, seen below in table 3.2.

Table 3.2. Vectors of Humor in Mark 5:1–20

Script-Oppositions	Mark 5:1–5	Mark 5:6–13	Mark 5:14–17	Mark 5:18–20
SUCCESSFUL/FAILED EXORCIST		5:6, 7, 8, 13		
ROMAN IMPERIUM/JESUS'S IMPERIUM		5:10, 11, 13		
CIVILIZED/BARBARIAN			5:17	5:18
APPROPRIATE/INAPPROPRIATE FEAR or APPROPRIATE/INAPPROPRIATE RESPONSE TO JESUS			5:17	
WORSHIP/OPPOSITION		5:6		

Setting the Stage (Mark 5:1–5)

The narrative begins in 5:1 with Jesus stepping off the boat after calming the turbulent storm just hours before. Immediately after Jesus disembarks, he is met by a man "with an unclean spirit" who has come from the tombs (5:2). The evangelist follows this introduction with a vivid description of the man in 5:3–5, where they note that the afflicted man has been living in the tombs (5:3) and unable to be bound by shackles or chains (5:3–4). Not only does the man possess preternatural strength, but "day and night, in the tombs and in the mountains he was screaming out and cutting himself with stones" (5:5). The picture is tragic. The man is, as Boring observes, "a picture of death, of one already banished from the land of the living."[72] In this opening scene, nothing appears overtly comical. Yet there is one narrative feature that requires comment. The evangelist utilizes appropriate language to characterize the man. That is, they have crafted a believable portrait of a man afflicted by spirits.

Similar maladies, in varying forms, were known in the ancient world. The notion of persons losing rational capacity, especially due to divine or demonic affliction, is attested in Jewish and Greco-Roman sources. In the

---

72. Boring, *Mark*, 150.

Hebrew Bible, for instance, one finds examples of such a condition in the characters of Saul, Jehu, and Nebuchadnezzar.[73] Nebuchadnezzar stands as a particularly striking example, ultimately separating himself from society for an extended period of time (Dan 4:33).[74] Such characters present in Greco-Roman texts with figures like Ajax, Cassandra, Dionysus, Orestes, and Phaedra representing different forms of such conditions, be it because of Dionysiac frenzy or prophetic ecstasy.[75] The evangelist takes up this motif in the use of the EXORCISM script.

The evangelist depicts affliction in the context of an exorcism scene but does so in a specific way, particularly with respect to the wider Markan narrative. The description of the man's power in 5:1–5 loads the script of EXORCISM with remarkable tension, for this is not a typical demonic encounter. Rather, this is *the* demonic encounter wherein Jesus will clash with the most powerful, maleficent spirit in his ministry.[76] Yet while the man with spirits might be potent, the audience should have no reason to fear (1:25; 7:29; 9:25). In the initial exorcism at Capernaum, which the present pericope parallels, Jesus casts out the unclean spirit with no special ritual or struggle. Using a simple phrase ("Shut up and go out from him!," 1:23), Jesus forces the demon to abandon his corporeal host (1:26). However, it is key to observe that the EXORCISM script did not always entail success.[77] Indeed, there existed in the ancient world not only a script of EXORCISM, but a script-opposition of SUCCESSFUL/FAILED EXORCIST bound up in this phe-

---

73. Madalina Vartejanu-Joubert, "Representations of Madmen and Madness in Jewish Sources from the Pre-exilic to the Roman-Byzantine Period," in *The Routledge History of Madness and Mental Health*, ed. Greg Eghigian, The Routledge Histories (Routledge, 2017), 19–41.

74. On the subject of Nebuchadnezzar's condition, see Matthias Henze, *The Madness of King Nebuchadnezzar: The Ancient Near Eastern Origins and Early History of Interpretation of Daniel 4*, JSJSup 61 (Brill, 1999).

75. Lillian Feder, *Madness in Literature* (Princeton University Press, 1990), 35–97; Chiara Thumiger, "Ancient Greek and Roman Traditions," in Eghigian, *Routledge History of Madness and Mental Health*, 42–61. See also Ruth Padel, *Whom Gods Destroy: Elements of Greek and Tragic Madness* (Princeton University Press, 1995).

76. Extended accounts of possession occur at 1:23–28, 7:24–30, and 9:14–29. While these are also dramatic encounters, they do not underscore the threat and/or power of the demonic force with the same intensity (though the account in ch. 9 comes close, insofar as the disciples are incapable of exorcizing the demon).

77. The Sons of Sceva pericope in Acts 19:11–20 offers a striking example of an exorcism gone awry.

nomenon. Furthermore, it should be said that even an average interaction with the man (i.e., walking through standard rituals elsewhere associated with exorcists) reads as veering toward the trajectory of FAILED EXORCIST for Jesus, as everywhere else he has so much command over demonic forces. That is to say, the Evangelist's sharpening of the EXORCIST script as it concerns Jesus is one of complete dominance. Nowhere else in Mark does Jesus struggle when he encounters demonic forces, even in the case of the demon that thwarted the disciples (9:14–29). This is paramount for it is precisely this script-opposition (i.e., SUCCESSFUL/FAILED EXORCIST), which stands as the central, potentially comical strand running through 5:13.

Jesus and the Man with Spirits (Mark 5:6–13)

The incongruity begins in the second scene with the opening statement in 5:6 that, upon seeing Jesus, the man with spirits rushed up and "bowed down to him" (προσεκύνησεν αὐτῷ). At first glance, this appears to be an act of surrender or obeisance. However, there is some ambiguity on this point. The language is potentially unclear as the only other time the evangelist uses προσκυνέω, it is with reference to the soldiers mocking Jesus (15:19). Furthermore, as the text unfolds, it becomes clear that the demons afflicting the man resist Jesus at every turn.[78] Thus, the phrase could read as a jab line that activates a one-off script-opposition of WORSHIP/OPPOSITION as the action comports with both obeisance and resistance to Jesus's presence.[79] However, if this is the case, it only becomes clear as the text unfolds. Notably, this may also read as the first jab line of the central strand that revolves around the EXORCISM script, playing off of the script-opposition of SUCCESSFUL/FAILED EXORCIST as it potentially adumbrates the demonic forces' resistance.[80]

---

78. Camery-Hoggatt, *Irony in Mark's Gospel*, 137, underscores the ambivalence of the demoniac's presentation: "The fact that he prostrates himself before Jesus and that he cries out 'with a loud voice' (v. 6) presents a mixed image.... There are elements here which appear to be threatening, even spectral—the blurting out of Jesus' name and title, the claim to be Legion, "'for we are many.'"

79. On the possibility of using the action of falling down in a comedic sense, see Jared Ludlow, "Are Weeping and Falling Down Funny? Exaggeration in Ancient Novelistic Texts," in *Reading and Teaching Ancient Fiction: Jewish, Christian, and Greco-Roman Narratives*, ed. Sara Johnson, Christine Shea, and Rubén Dupertuis, WRGWSup 11 (Atlanta: SBL Press, 2018), 165–77.

80. To be sure, that demons might act out against Jesus is not surprising, even in the Markan narrative. In 1:24 and 3:11, these malevolent beings cry out Jesus's name,

The next potential jab line occurs in 5:7, where the man cries out: "What have we to do with one another, Jesus, Son of the Most High God? I adjure you by God, do not torture me!" The language of adjuration is striking, for here the evangelist has used specific exorcistic terminology. Indeed, this statement has puzzled many scholars because of the blatant incongruity it presents.[81] The use of ὁρκίζω with an appeal to a helping power was common among ancient exorcists. Josephus uses the term in reference to a powerful exorcism conducted by Eleazar in Vespasian's court: "and, when the man at once fell down, [he] adjured [ὥρκου] the demon never to come back into him" (*A.J.* 8.2.5 [Marcus]). More significantly, both Acts and the Greek Magical Papyri use ὁρκίζω in conjunction with a similar formula. In the "sons of Sceva" episode of Acts 19:11–20, itinerant exorcists are said to declare "I adjure [ὁρκίζω] by Jesus whom Paul preaches" (Acts 19:13). Similarly, the Greek Magical Papyri testify to an identical formulation "I adjure [ὁρκίζω] you by God" (*PGM* 4.3045). Consequently, the evangelist's audience almost certainly would have noticed something strange in hearing the words commonly attributed to an exorcist being put on the lips of the one being exorcized.[82] By crafting the story thus, the evangelist switches the place of Jesus and the unclean spirits. This potentially generates script-oppositions of EXORCIST as EXORCIZED and EXORCIZED as EXORCIST, with a completely absurd inversion of what one should expect in exorcistic narratives. This,

---

possibly in an attempt to name Jesus and gain power over him. What is more, in 3:11 the spirits are said to "lay prostrate" before Jesus, perhaps an ironic gesture as in 5:6. The difference between these actions, which may read as similar examples of script-opposition is the degree to which they are qualified by the ensuing narrative. If the script-opposition of SUCCESSFUL/FAILED EXORCIST is activated in these instances, it is immediately quelled by the obedience of the unclean spirits just moments later. Mark 5, on the other hand, is much more ambiguous as the demon will continually resist Jesus's attempts to control him.

81. To note just a handful of commentators, Boring, *Mark*, 151, terms this a "reverse exorcism"; Donahue and Harrington, *Mark*, 165, state that "ironically the demoniac himself acts like an exorcist"; Robert Gundry, *Mark: A Commentary on His Apology for the Cross* (Eerdmans, 1993), 250, remarks that the demon attempts "to exorcise Jesus out of exorcising it'"; Marcus, *Mark*, 344, suggests that the phrase constitutes "deliberate parody."

82. For more on this formulation, see Burrow, "Bargaining with Jesus," 234–51. Burrow tracks the irony in this passage and notes of this phrase that "Now, the situational irony of the demons' statement becomes clear: although the reader expects Jesus to adjure the demons out of the man, it is the demons that adjure Jesus" (242).

in turn, is interposed onto the script the Markan audience would usually anticipate.

The oddness of this rhetorical move should not be underestimated. Ancient discussions of rhetoric stressed the importance of crafting believable speech for characters. Rhetorica Ad Herennium notes that "Dialogue consists in assigning to some person language which as set forth conforms with his character" (Rhet. Her. 4.52.65 [Caplan]). Indeed, in hypothetical dialogues one is supposed to imagine what a person would say based on their character, and "then one must add what they will say" (Rhet. Her. 4.52.65 [Caplan]). Quintilian notes, regarding a character's speech, that "we use them (1) to display inner thoughts of our opponents as though they were talking to themselves.... (2) to introduce conversations between ourselves and others, or others among themselves, in a credible manner, and (3) to provide appropriate characters for words of advice, reproach, complaint, praise, or pity" (*Inst.* 9.2.30–31 [Russell]). The progymnasmata dwell at length on the issue of speech-in-character under the labels προσωποποιία (Theon, *Prog.* 115-118) and ἠθοποιία (Pseudo-Hermogenes, *Prog.* 20-22; Apthonius, *Prog.* 34R, 44-45, 35R; Nicolaus, *Prog.* 63-67). Theon defines προσωποποιία as "the introduction of a person to whom words are attributed that are suitable to the speaker and have an indisputable application to the subjects discussed" (*Prog.* 115 [Kennedy]). Pseudo-Hermogenes and Apthonius speak of ἠθοποιία as the imitation of the character of a person being represented in speech, while Nicolaus the Sophist declares it to be "speech suiting the proposed situation" (*Prog.* 63 [Kennedy]). Amid all of this, the progymnasmata stress the importance of consistency between a person's speech and character, with Theon noting that "we become masters of this [προσωποποιία] if we ... give what is appropriate to each subject, aiming at what fits the speaker and his manner of speech and the time and his lot in life and each of the things mentioned above" (*Prog.* 116 [Kennedy]). The evangelist has violated this elemental tenet of rhetoric, and one must pursue the question of why, especially when elsewhere the evangelist is capable of crafting believable speech for the characters.

In switching the position of the exorcist and the man with unclean spirits, the evangelist stresses demonic resistance, in turn raising questions about Jesus's capacity as an exorcist. Consequently, this potentially constitutes the second jab line in the strand of the script-opposition related to SUCCESSFUL/FAILED EXORCIST, for now there is not only mocking but a direct attempt to control Jesus. The evangelist augments this in the first half of the statement, which likely signals a naming of Jesus in an attempt to overpower him.[83] The audience is left somewhat confused and possibly amused by this puzzling interaction. Jesus, the wonder-worker successful in every other exorcism, has encountered an opponent in the man with spirits and now finds himself in the position of the demon rather than the exorcist.[84]

In 5:8, the narrative shifts abruptly, letting the audience know that prior to this adjuration by the demoniac, Jesus had actually been repeatedly telling (ἔλεγεν) the spirits to leave the man's body. This narrative backtracking presses the script-opposition of SUCCESSFUL/FAILED EXORCIST to its breaking-point, for it strongly suggests that Jesus has been struggling throughout this power encounter.[85] Indeed, this third potential jab line makes explicit what the previous two possible jab lines of mocking and adjuration have intimated—perhaps Jesus is not the wonder-worker who can easily cast out any demon after all. Additionally, the script of the struggling EXORCIST is so opposed to Jesus's normal status that it likely

---

83. The pronouncement, "What is there between you and me?," is a strong statement. If, as some have suggested, there is a connection to a similar formulation in Josh 22:24, Judg 11:12, or 2 Sam 16:10, it potentially amplifies the combative nature of the statement, becoming a formula of dissociation addressed to a potential aggressor. R. T. France, *The Gospel of Mark: A Commentary on the Greek Text*, NIGTC (Eerdmans, 2002), 104. Indeed, Lane, *Mark*, 183, regards this as a direct threat. This is compounded by the widely held view that Legion's naming of Jesus is generally seen as an attempt to gain control over him. This was a common practice among exorcists demonstrable in later magical papyri. John Hull, *Hellenistic Magic and the Synoptic Tradition*, SBT 28 (SCM, 1964), 67.

84. Bas van Iersel, *Mark: A Reader-Response Commentary*, trans. W. H. Bisscheroux, JSNTSup 164 (Sheffield Academic, 1998), 198, in his focus on the audience's reaction to the text suggests that an audience would be "embarrassed" by this interaction. Rudolf Bultmann, *The History of the Synoptic Tradition*, trans. John Marsh (Harper & Row, 1963), 210, views the story as originally having been comical, possibly at the expense of Jesus.

85. Some scholars see in this aside evidence that Jesus has taken control of the situation because he was the first to speak (e.g., Boring, *Mark*, 151; Marcus, *Mark*, 351). Similarly, Donahue and Harrington, *Mark*, 165, resolve the ambiguity by suggesting that ἔλεγεν be read as inchoative rather than iterative. Such readings, to my mind, remain unconvincing. The evangelist appears comfortable with the notion that Jesus, powerful though he is, sometimes has limits to his power or must work in a process (e.g., 8:22–26).

functions as a script-opposition.[86] The evangelist reinforces this with the possible jab line of 5:9 where Jesus, resorting to a common apotropaic ritual, must ask the demonic force its name. Functionally, by the time the audience reaches verse 9 in the story, Jesus resembles a typical or struggling exorcist. Vanished is the exorcist who casts out the demons of Capernaum with one command and no protracted exchange (1:26; 3:11). In his stead stands a man adjured by a demon, asking its name in an attempt to wrest power back.

In the second half of 5:9, the spirits give their name as "Legion." This title is key, for it primes the narrative for the development of a potential satirical substrand riffing on the script-opposition of ROMAN IMPERIUM/ JESUS'S IMPERIUM.[87] That the spirits are named Legion is fitting as it conjures up the might of the Roman military, possibly explaining the spirits' ability to resist Jesus. Yet the evangelist will not let the image stand. Immediately, having just given their portentous name, the unclean spirits begin to beg that Jesus not banish them from the region.[88] The action is jarring, for it switches the script-opposition of SUCCESSFUL/FAILED EXORCIST that has potentially been at play thus far.[89] The evangelist now reverts back to the script of Jesus as a successful exorcist by signaling the

---

86. I do not mean to say that this is the only function of such irony in the text, only that the parodic nature of this pericope can be taken as comical.

87. While not all see Mark's discourse here as overtly political, several scholars have underscored the political overtones of the present pericope. Derrett, "Contributions to the Study of the Gerasene Demoniac," 2–17 has drawn attention to terms like λεγιών (v. 9), ἀποστείλῃ (v. 10), ἀγέλη (vv. 11, 13), ἐπιτρέπω (v.13), and ὁρμάω (v.13), all of which are direct references to military activity. See further Carter, "Cross-Gendered Romans," 139–55; Horsley, *Hearing the Whole Story*, 141–49; Leander, *Discourses of Empire*, 201–19; Ched Myers, *Binding the Strong Man: A Political Reading of Mark's Gospel* (Orbis, 1988), 190–93.

88. It is not particularly important that one knows exactly how many soldiers made up a legion at this point in Rome's imperial history. The point seems to be that the man is possessed by a powerful, multiplicity of unclean spirits which the evangelist confirms through the sign of the pigs. Nor does there need to be a one-to-one correspondence between the number of demons and pigs. If a plurality of unclean spirits could occupy one host as in the case of the man, surely some of them could have buddied up and shared a porcine host.

89. One could argue that a script-opposition of EXORCIST/EXORCIZED is in place here alongside the image of Jesus as a struggling exorcist. Indeed, it is quite possible that there is an intentional elision of both script-oppositions activated by the same jab lines.

spirits' submission. Moreover, this statement potentially acts as a jab line that activates a new substrand based on the satirical script-opposition of ROMAN IMPERIUM/JESUS'S IMPERIUM. Here, the audience, having witnessed the great power of these spirits, watches as this mighty Roman demonic horde begs for their very existence. Such bargaining is hardly commensurate with a powerful cohort of demons who, only moments before, seemed so powerful. The juxtaposition is potentially comical and the spirits' behavior will only grow increasingly incongruous relative to their prior stature.[90]

In 5:11, the audience learns that there happens to be a large herd of pigs nearby. This narrative detail is a coincidental, metanarrative disruption, a feature frequently seen in comedic plots. The once-mighty spirits now turn to Jesus in 5:12 and beg again. This time they entreat him to send them into pigs, rather than simply to remain in the region. Their plea reinforces the switch back to the expected script of Jesus as the successful exorcist, but it is also possibly the second jab line in the substrand of ROMAN IMPERIUM/JESUS'S IMPERIUM. The terrifying Legion is now utterly reduced, pleading for their lives. The image of Roman military power abiding in pigs is an odd picture indeed.

If the portrait of the legion of spirits were not incongruous enough, the evangelist pushes the satirical script-opposition of ROMAN IMPERIUM/JESUS'S IMPERIUM one step further. In 5:13, the evangelist states that Jesus permitted the demons to inhabit the pigs. This acquiescence on Jesus's part seems odd. Why does Jesus give these demons any quarter?[91] Is this a script switch once more to Jesus the SUCCESSFUL/FAILED EXORCIST? This is possible, as such bargaining was not unknown in ancient stories of exorcisms.[92] However, whatever the case, the moment passes.

---

90. Attardo, *Humorous Texts*, 99, defines coincidences as "statistically highly improbable events taking place in circumstances that do not explain away the statistical unlikelihood" and, though typically avoided in more serious narratives, are commonplace in comical stories. That there is a *large* herd of pigs great enough to house the entire host of demons plaguing the man fits Attardo's definition well.

91. Van Iersel, *Mark*, 200, aptly states: "The reader sees no reason why Jesus should give the demons safe shelter."

92. See, for example, b. Pesah. 112b, where the demon Igrath originally had 180,000 demons that were given free rein to wreak havoc. However, in an encounter with R. Ḥanina b. Dosa, she finds herself restricted and must negotiate a compromise: "'I beg you ... leave me a little room.' So he left her the nights of Sabbaths and the nights of Wednesdays."

Upon entering the swine, the spirits do not leave in peace. Instead, the entire herd of pigs (about two thousand) rushes headlong into the sea and drowns. Several elements of this verse must be noted. First, this final statement is possibly another jab line in the central strand regarding the script-opposition SUCCESSFUL/FAILED EXORCIST, portraying, if only for a moment, Jesus as a more typical exorcist than elsewhere in the gospel. Second, it is simultaneously potentially the third jab line in the substrand relating the script-opposition of ROMAN IMPERIUM/JESUS'S IMPERIUM. In a strikingly absurd portrait of Roman imperial power, the evangelist reduces the Legion to a submissive, inept force tricked into its own destruction. Third, the number of pigs is both potentially a humorous coincidence and comically hyperbolic.[93] Fourth, some scholars have suggested that the evangelist has foregrounded a potential underlying tension of Jews/gentiles in the Markan audience by linking unclean spirits to unclean animals, introducing a possible script-opposition of CIVILIZED/BARBARIAN as the destruction of the pigs could be seen as humorous from a halakhic perspective.[94] Members of the Markan audience who maintained a halakhic perspective on food could possibly have found pigs unclean and their destruction a happy coincidence, refracting this through a CIVILIZED/BARBARIAN script-opposition.

Fearing the Miraculous (Mark 5:14–17)

In the third scene, the evangelist provides an unusually detailed account of the peoples' response to the miraculous exorcism. In 5:14, the pig herders report the news of this event in the city and the country. People rush to the scene to find the formerly violent man "sitting, having been clothed, with his full senses" (καθήμενον ἱματισμένον καὶ σωφρονοῦντα). He could not be more different than the man described in 5:3–5. Yet rather than be amazed, the people become afraid, and, after learning about the destruction of the pigs (5:16), they beg Jesus to leave the area (5:17). The reaction

---

93. Boring, *Mark*, 152, observes that even a herd of three hundred pigs was considered by ancient Greco-Roman standards to have been extraordinary. For there to be two thousand is incredible.

94. Gundry, *Mark*, 262, notes that "because of their revulsion against pigs, a Jewish audience would find humorous satisfaction in the drowning of the herd as well as in the self-banishment of the unclean spirits." See too Donald Juel, *Master of Surprise: Mark Interpreted* (Fortress, 1994), 69; Marcus, *Mark*, 347.

is surprising, and there are possibly two instances of script-oppositions at play regarding the peoples' response to Jesus. On the one hand, the evangelist underscores a script-opposition of APPROPRIATE/INAPPROPRIATE FEAR in 5:14, emphasizing the people's fear in the presence of the former demon-plagued man when he is clearly not a threat to anyone.[95] On the other hand, also present in the narrative is the script-opposition of APPROPRIATE/INAPPROPRIATE RESPONSE TO JESUS. In the exorcism at Capernaum (1:21–28), which the present pericope parallels, the reaction to Jesus's power is one of positive marvel (1:27). The reaction here, however, is a surprising response to Jesus's salvific work and likely a further script-opposition, for now the people cower rather than stand in awe.[96] Scholars have suggested that in narrating the story this way, the evangelist utilizes this script-opposition while layering in the script-opposition of CIVILIZED/BARBARIAN by highlighting the halakhic/nonhalakhic distinction. They argue that this generates a picture of the residents in the Decapolis as people incapable of apprehending the significance of Jesus's work—possibly amusing at their expense. This reading finds support in their characterization mirroring that of the demons where they, like the unclean spirits, are drawn to Jesus (5:14–15), fear him (5:15), and finally beg him to go out of the region (5:17).[97]

---

95. Camery-Hoggatt, *Irony in Mark's Gospel*, 135, sees ironic reaction as the primary form of irony in the story of the man plagued by unclean spirits.

96. Many scholars see in the response of the people here a failure on their part to truly grasp what Jesus has done. Even if their reaction is justified (i.e., who *would not* be frightened by a power more capable than the man that could not be bound?), it is still generally perceived as a failure. So Boring, *Mark*, 153; Yabro Collins, *Mark*, 272, views this as epiphanic fear but also states that the "local people ... try to control or ward off the suprahuman power of Jesus by asking him to leave the district"; Donahue and Harrington, *Mark*, 167, maintain a more positive outlook but state that the people are "both in awe and suspicious of the power of Jesus."

97. Marcus, *Mark*, 353. It should be noted that this possibly mirrors the two-step development of fear in the previous pericope, albeit in the opposite direction. In 4:35–41, the disciples' initial, rational fear gives way to an irrational cowardice of Jesus. In 5:1–20, as will be seen below, the people in the region are depicted initially as irrationally afraid of Jesus but come to understand his true character upon hearing the preaching of the man.

Jesus Commissions the Man Formerly with Spirits (5:18–20)

The narrative closes with one of the more peculiar scenes in the Gospel of Mark, along with a potentially dynamic use of script-opposition. In 5:18, as Jesus is preparing to leave, the former demon-plagued man implores that he might accompany him. Jesus instead instructs him to report what has been done for him by the Lord (5:19). The man then goes throughout the whole Decapolis declaring what has happened to him, with all those hearing responding in awe (5:20). The brief conclusion is significant, for it potentially plays off of the CIVILIZED/BARBARIAN distinction of the previous verses. First, the man's actions in 5:18 should be understood as a discipleship scene, for here, as in 3:14 where the disciples are appointed to "be with" (μετ' αὐτου) Jesus as the man wishes "to be with him" (μετ' αὐτοῦ ᾖ) also.[98] Furthermore, contrary to the disciples' call, the man approaches Jesus himself. Second, Jesus's command to go and tell about what has happened to the man is highly unusual in the gospel where Jesus otherwise frequently tells people to remain quiet about his acts of power. The man becomes the first missionary sanctioned by Jesus in the Markan narrative. The result of all his proclamation is that those in the gentile territory "marveled" (ἐθαύμαζον), this time reacting with unequivocal awe to Jesus's work. Having initially portrayed the people of the Decapolis as ignorant in 5:13–17, the evangelist switches the script. They portray the formerly violent man terrorized by a host of unclean spirits as an upstanding example of discipleship, and his audiences as receptive to his work. This effectively transmutes the people of the Decapolis from BARBARIAN to CIVILIZED.

Doctors, Power, and Death (5:21–43)

The third pericope in Mark 4:35–6:6 relates two stories of Jesus's power, interwoven into an intricate, dramatic, and extended narrative wherein Jesus inadvertently heals one woman while possibly raising another from death.[99] The script-oppositions present in these stories are potentially

---

98. So Tolbert, *Sowing the Gospel*, 168.
99. The current analysis draws from work I have done on this topic elsewhere: Jon Carman, "Ancient Quackery: The Sick Woman and the Cost of Incompetence," in *Looking Both Ways: At the Intersection of the Academy and the Church; Essays in Honor of Joseph Grana II*. Edited by William Curtis Holtzen and J. Blair Wilgus (Claremont, 2021), 31–46.

fewer than in the previous pericope and are, at times, deployed in a more intricate manner. They consist of the following: DOCTOR/INJURER, KNOWLEDGE/IGNORANCE, DEATH/SLEEP, and APPROPRIATE/INAPPROPRIATE RESPONSE TO JESUS. These potential script-oppositions find illumination in parallels from ancient comedic treatments of doctors and illness, professional incompetence, and sleep.

Comedic Themes in Ancient Sources

Doctors, Illness, and Stupidity

Healers and physicians played a critical role in the Greco-Roman world, as disease was a constant threat to local populations. However, their status in society was ambiguous. While many might view them as a boon, suspicion of doctors flourished. Writing in the first century CE, Pliny the Elder represents this perspective well when, in summing up his genealogy of medicine, he remarks:

> There is no doubt that all these, in their hunt for popularity by means of some novelty, did not hesitate to buy it with our lives. Hence those wretched, quarrelsome consultations at the bedside of the patient, no consultant agreeing with another lest he should appear to acknowledge a superior.... Medicine changes everyday, being furbished up again and again, and we are swept along on the puffs of the clever brains of Greece. (*Nat.* 29.11 [Jones])

While Pliny refracted his view of medicine through a general suspicion of Greek culture, he also lamented its nonstandardized nature, lack of success, experimentation with the lives of patients, and intrusion into privacy (*Nat.* 29.1–21).[100] In addition to these problems, Pliny underscored the immorality of charging money for delivering someone from disease or death:

---

100. Pliny is not alone in his distrust of Hellenistic medicine. In the Republican era, Cato delivers a withering critique of Greek doctors: "I shall speak about those Greek fellows in their proper place, son Marcus, and point out the result of my enquiries at Athens.... When that race gives us its literature it will corrupt all things, and even all the more if it sends hither its physicians. They have conspired together to murder all foreigners with their physic, but this very thing they do for a fee, to gain credit and to destroy us easily.... I have forbidden you to have dealings with physicians (Cato as quoted in Pliny, *Nat.* 29.7 [Jones]).

"Let me not even bring charges against their avarice, their greedy bargains made with those whose fate lies in the balance, the prices charged for anodynes, the earnest-money paid for death" (*Nat.* 29.21 [Jones]). Notably, the ambivalent standing of doctors made for good satire and comedy.

Martial, the late first- and early second-century CE Roman poet, offered several stinging observations of physicians in his satirical *Epigrams*. Regarding their proclivity to injure, he notes: "Daiulus used to be a doctor till recently; now he's an undertaker. What the undertaker does, the doctor used to" (*Epigr.* 1.47 [Ker]). Martial bolsters this link when remarking upon a doctor-turned-gladiator: "You are a gladiator now, you were formerly an eye-doctor. You did as a doctor what you do as a gladiator" (*Epigr.* 8.74 [Ker]). Finally, regarding the question of greed, though Martial does not touch often on this topic, he appears to have characterized one doctor Herodes in such a manner: "Doctor Herodes had purloined a ladle from a patient. When caught he said: 'You fool, why are you drinking then?'" (*Epigr.* 9.96 [Ker]).[101] In this epigram, Martial comically depicts Herodes as greedy to the point of thieving.[102] When the patient confronts him, the doctor humorously tries to turn the accusation back against the patient, inquiring as to why the patient has been drinking (presumably against doctor's orders).

Plautus too openly mocked the issue of physician competence. This is most evident in Plautus's famous scene concerning madness (*Men.* 820–1000). In this play, Plautus crafts a scene in which one twin brother, Sosicles, feigns madness in order to escape the wrath of his twin brother's wife and father. Unfortunately for Menaechmus, Sosicles's twin, he arrives at the same time as the doctor, while Sosicles has already fled the scene (*Men.* 885–900). An exchange ensues wherein a supposed expert physician subjects the reasonable Menaechmus to diagnosis, all while being completely wrong.

> Doctor: Hello, Menaechmus. Please, why are you exposing your arm? Don't you know how much worse you're making your illness now?
> Menaechmus: Why don't you hang yourself?
> Doctor: Do you feel anything?
> Menaechmus: Why shouldn't I? (*Men.* 910–913 [De Melo])
> Doctor: Tell me this: are your eyes ever apt to become hard?

---

101. John Spaeth, "Martial Looks at His World," *CJ* 24 (1929): 361–73.
102. Yabro Collins, *Mark*, 281.

> Menaechmus: What? Do you think I'm a lobster, you disgraceful creature?
> Doctor: Tell me, do your intestines ever rumble, as far as you know?
> Menaechmus: When I'm full, they don't rumble at all: when I'm hungry, they do.
> Doctor: On this issue he didn't answer like a madman. Do you sleep through till dawn? Do you sleep easily when you go to bed?
> Menaechmus: I sleep through if I've paid everyone I owe money to. May Jupiter and all the gods ruin you, questioner!
> Doctor: Now he's beginning to have a fit. Be careful on account of those words. (*Men.* 923–934 [de Melo])

The scene ends with the doctor concluding that the very unsick Menaechmus is a danger and must be bound and treated:

> Doctor: I'll make you drink hellebore for some twenty days.
> Menaechmus: But I shall hang you up and jab you with cattle prods for thirty days.
> Doctor: (to Menaechmus' father-in-law) Go, fetch men to take him to me.
> Old Man: How many does it take?
> Doctor: Considering how … I can see him acting, four, no less.
> Old Man: They'll be here in a moment. You watch over him, doctor.
> Doctor: No, I'll go home so that what needs to be prepared is prepared. You tell your slaves to bring him here to me. (*Men.* 950–955 [de Melo])

In this extended encounter between doctor and patient, Plautus characterizes the physician as being completely oblivious to the reality that the man he has diagnosed with madness is, in fact, fine (being the wrong brother, of course).[103] So egregious is his error that he almost ends up committing Menaechmus to house arrest. All told, it stands as a comical depiction of an incompetent physician.

Such examples demonstrate that physicians in the ancient world sometimes occupied an ambivalent social space. On the one hand, they were needed and sought after for cures. On the other hand, people also perceived physicians as inept, obsessed with novelty, prone to experiment on patients, and even avaricious. Ancient writers, rooted in the dark

---

103. Lydia Baumbach, "Quacks Then as Now? An Examination of Medical Practice, Theory, and Superstition in Plautus," *Acta Classica* 26 (1983): 99–104.

humor that supposedly beneficent healers were, ironically, sometimes greedy butchers, lampooned such traits.

The critique of doctors one sees in some ancient writers touches upon a further script-opposition, namely, that of KNOWLEDGE/IGNORANCE. Ancient comic writers found humor in the juxtaposition between persons who ought to have been wise or knowledgeable, only to be found ignorant or foolish.[104] This script-opposition is strikingly evident in the scene of the doctor above. Not only does Plautus ridicule the doctor for his capacity to harm Menaechmus, he directly mocks the doctor's ignorance. The man society deems capable of assessing the mad man's condition is actually inept. Aristophanes and Lucian offer similar comical juxtapositions.

Aristophanes offers his audience an absurd portrait of Socrates in *Nubes*. In this comedy, Aristophanes lampoons the lauded intellectual, paying special attention to the excellent so-called science being conducted in the Thinkery. For instance, under Socrates's auspices, the Thinkery teaches people that "the sky is a barbeque lid" (*Nub*. 96 [Henderson]), a gnat's hindquarters function as a trumpet (*Nub*. 165), the study of astronomy should be conducted by pointing one's buttocks toward the sky (*Nub*. 193–195), meteorological phenomena can only be investigated while in a floating basket (*Nub*. 225–230), one's thoughts get sucked into the earth when on land (*Nub*. 231–234), and the clouds shapeshift based on what they perceive on the ground (*Nub*. 347–355)—these and other such scientific conclusions all fall under Socrates's wisdom. Indeed, so outlandish is Aristophanes's caricature of Socrates and his school that Plato, in his *Apologia*, engages this characterization:

> So, as if they were making the charge, I must read out their affidavit: "Socrates is guilty and wastes his time searching what's below the ground and in the heavens, and makes the weaker argument the stronger one and teaches others these same things." It's something like this: for you too have seen them in Aristophanes' comedy, someone called Socrates swinging around there claiming that he's treading on air and burbling a lot of other nonsense. (*Apol*. 19bc [Emelyn-Jones and Preddy])

---

104. See, e.g., the exploration of this comedic theme in the ancient joke-book Philogelos (Carman, "Ancient Quackery," 31–46).

Lucian, similarly to Aristophanes, held none too high a view of many philosophers.[105] At the very least, he did not consider them invincible to ignorance. Lucian delivers this attitude forcefully and comically in *Philopseudes*, the satirical story of one Tychiades, who acts as a skeptic against various forms of superstition. Throughout the narrative, Tychiades repeatedly encounters different philosophers who try to persuade him of the reality of supernatural activity.[106] The last straw for Tychiades occurs when the Pythagorean, Arignotus, appears at Eucrates's symposium. Tychiades expects this man to be a bastion of wisdom against the inferior beliefs of the philosophers he has hitherto encountered: "As I caught sight of him, I drew a breath of relief, thinking: 'There now, a broadaxe has come to hand to use against their lies. The wise man will stop their mouths when they tell such prodigious yarns" (*Philosp.* 29 [Harmon]). Unfortunately, Tychiades's hopes run aground, as this formidable Pythagorean is also a purveyor of the supernatural: "What is it you say?' said Arignotus, with a sour look at me. 'Do you think that none of these things happen, although everybody, I may say, sees them?'" (*Philops.* 30 [Harmon]). Upon Tychiades's reply that he has never seen supernatural forces at work, Arignotus launches into an elaborate story of how he himself drove out a *daimon* haunting the house of one Eubatides (*Philops.* 31). Tychiades laments that this man, too, should maintain such folly: "What is this, Arignotus? Were you, Truth's only hope, just like the rest—full of moonshine and vain imaginings? Indeed the saying has come true: our pot of gold has turned out to be

---

105. Lucian is widely seen as targeting philosophical schools in his many satirical writings. As George Bragues, "The Market for Philosophers: An Interpretation of Lucian's Satire on Philosophy," *The Independent Review* 9 (2004): 230, observes: "Lucian is typically classified as a satirist who specialized in the comedic-dialogue form to deride foibles and pretensions of the leading figures and symbols of Greek-Roman civilization. In this view, philosophy features in Lucian's work only as one of the chief targets of his satire." On the philosophical schools as represented in *Philopseudes*, see Daniel Ogden, "The Love of Wisdom and the Love of Lies: The Philosophers and Philosophical Voices of Lucian's Philopseudes," in *Philosophical Presences in the Ancient Novel*, ed. J. R. Morgan and Meriel Jones, Ancient Narrative Supplementum 10 (Barkhuis, 2007), 177–203.

106. Daniel Ogden, "The Apprentice's Sorcerer: Pancrates and His Powers in Context (Lucian, Philopseudes 33–36)," *Acta Classica* 47 (2004): 102, sums up the narrative well, stating that "credulous symposiasts have attempted to tell him [Tychiades] of the efficacy of magic and the reality of supernatural intervention in human life by telling him fantastic stories, supposedly of their own experience."

nothing but coals" (*Philops.* 32 [Harmon]). Thus does Lucian depict the champion of wisdom, Arignotus. Rather than being a reasonable thinker who is not prone to supernaturalism, Arignotus is as deceived as those around him. Consequently, he, along with the other philosophers present, cuts a comical figure as one acting against type—the wise person playing the fool.

These depictions illustrate how ripe for humor the script-opposition of KNOWLEDGE/IGNORANCE could be for ancient comedic writers. Not only was misunderstanding a basic plot conceit for many ancient comedies, but it could find focus through the lens of specific individuals for whom wisdom and knowledge were expected—doctors should be able to diagnose correctly, philosophers should be capable of discerning truth from fiction, politicians should be effective at civic management, et cetera.[107] Unsurprisingly, ancient humorists turned these expectations upside down, depicting the converse in order to create a comical juxtaposition.

Sleep

The notion that someone might be asleep, rather than dead, was an issue of some concern in the Greco-Roman world.[108] With imperfect methods to determine whether or not a person had perished, there was always a threat that a person might be in a deep slumber, trance, or coma, opposed to being dead. This theme is extant in resurrection/resuscitation accounts.[109] For example, in Apuleius's compilation of various writings and speeches, he relays a brief episode regarding the physician Asclepiades (*Flor.* 19).[110] One day, as the doctor is traveling back to the city from his estate, he happens upon a large funeral. Driven to know more about the situation, Asclepiades examines the dead man. Upon close review of his body, Asclepiades realizes the man is not dead and, through great remonstrations, persuades the family to call off the funeral and restores the man back to full health. In yet another account of miraculous resurrection/resuscitation, Philostratus similarly recounts a story of

---

107. On the tendency to use misunderstanding as a primary plot device, see the discussion in chapter 2 regarding New Comedy and incongruity.
108. On this point, see the discussion above regarding Jesus's slumber during the storm.
109. Yabro Collins, *Mark*, 277–79.
110. Apuleius was active during the second century CE.

Apollonius rescuing a woman from the brink of death (*Vit. Apoll.* 4.45). During a funerary procession for the woman on the eve of her wedding, Philostratus states that Apollonius "woke the girl up" (ἀφυπνίζω) and that "he may have seen a spark of life in her which the doctors had not noticed … or he may have revived and restored her life when it was extinguished, but the explanation of this has proved unfathomable" (*Vit. Apoll.* 4.45 [Jones]). These accounts illustrate the ambiguity that could at times pervade the event of death in the Greco-Roman world and reveal the potency for portraying heroic figures who were perceptive enough and/or capable of rescuing such persons from an untimely demise. Notably, the hair's breadth that separated someone in a sleep-like state from death could be exploited to comical effect.

To begin with, while Apuleius's story regarding Asclepiades conveys a serious episode, it is by no means clear that humor is absent from the narrative (that this is the same Apuleius who famously wrote the comical *Metamorphoses* makes this reading more plausible). In particular, the close of the story appears to tilt in a humorous direction (*Flor.* 19). Upon realizing that the seeming-dead man is about to be burned alive, Asclepiades shouts in protest, attempting to disrupt the process. Yet rather than respond with gratitude, the man's relatives take some convincing:

> Meanwhile mutterings arose: some said that a medical man deserved belief, some even mocked the art of medicine. Finally, though all the relatives objected too, either because they already had a legacy, or as yet had no trust in him, even so Asclepiades with painful difficulty obtained a brief delay for the deceased, and, having thus wrested him from the hands of the undertakers, brought him home like one restored from the underworld, and immediately used certain medicines to revive the life hiding in the recesses of the body. (*Flor.* 19 [Jones])

In the response of the family, one finds mutterings, wholesale skepticism of medicine, and even the mocking of doctors. Their response, while appropriate from the perspective of the mourners, may read as comical, for their mockery of Asclepiades and doctors generally is dangerous—the man is not dead! Apuleius's description of their reaction and even designation of them as undertakers is so ironic as to be humorous in its presentation. Notably, the incongruity of persons acting and carrying on as though a person were dead, when, in fact, they actually lived could be a source of humor. One sees this in the comical novel *Metamorphoses* by

Apuleius. At the outset of the story, the plight of an unfortunate Socrates is relayed to the audience wherein the narrator discloses that, though still very much alive, Socrates's family and city-state have written him off for dead:

> At your home you already have been lamented and ritually addressed as dead, guardians have been appointed for your children by decree of the provincial judge, and your wife, after performing all the funeral services, disfiguring herself with long mourning and grief, and nearly weeping her eyes into uselessness, is being pressed by her parents to gladden the family's misfortunes with the joys of a new marriage. (*Metam.* 1.6 [Hanson])

Through this unfortunate circumstance, Apuleius derives humor from the juxtaposition of persons carrying on with funerary and legal customs for a dead Socrates, who is, in fact, alive.

Analysis of Mark 5:21–43

The collection of miraculous narratives continues in 5:21–43 with Jesus performing two profound miracles for two individuals in the grips of disease and death. In addition to this story maintaining a heightened, suspenseful pathos, the narrative possibly holds comical elements, a point that some scholars have already noted.[111] Indeed, there are at least four script-oppositions possibly present in the text: DOCTOR/INJURER, KNOWLEDGE/IGNORANCE, DEATH/SLEEP, and APPROPRIATE/INAPPROPRIATE RESPONSE TO JESUS. These script-oppositions are located throughout the narrative,

---

111. Culpepper, "Humor and Wit," 333, has remarked that there is a joke at the expense of doctors in 5:25–26, while Shepherd, *Markan Sandwich Stories*, 169, suggests that "comedy is interjected along the way in both stories, not only in the amusing … questions which Jesus asks (5:30, 39) but also in the very picture of Jesus himself searching for the person who touched him." Hatton, "Comic Ambiguity," 91–123, has offered the most extensive treatment of humor in the text that I am aware of. Hatton argues that the intercalated narratives center on comedic ambiguity, playing off of whether or not Jairus's daughter is actually dead and whether or not the bleeding woman actually touched (with sexual overtones) Jesus. The present analysis differs markedly from Hatton's work, particularly in attempting to place the humor of the present pericope in a more comprehensive framework regarding the miracle stories that proceed and follow the text. Furthermore, I view the evangelist's depiction of Jesus in this narrative as part of a broader rhetorical strategy. For more on this last point, see especially the explanation in chapter 4.

offering color and, occasionally, perplexity to this long tale that interweaves the stories of Jairus's daughter and the woman of faith.

Table 3.3. Vectors of Humor in Mark 5:21–43

Script-Oppositions	Mark 5:21–24a	Mark 5:24b–34	Mark 5:35–43
DOCTOR/INJURER		5:26	
KNOWLEDGE/IGNORANCE		5:30, 31, 32	
DEATH/SLEEP			5:35, 38, 39, 42
APPROPRIATE/INAPPROPRIATE RESPONSE TO JESUS			5:40

Setting the Stage (Mark 5:21–24)

The pericope of Jairus, the woman of faith, and Jairus's daughter begins similarly to that of the Gerasene demoniac. Once again, the opening verses depict a tragic situation and set the stage for the subsequent dramatic story. Indeed, the narrative action mirrors that of 5:1–5, for, in the current pericope, once again Jesus crosses the lake and disembarks only to be immediately met by a man who falls at his feet (5:21–23). Yet this time Jesus does not meet a demon-possessed man. Instead, Jesus finds himself engaged by a desperate father, Jairus the synagogue leader: "My little daughter is at the brink of death, please come with me in order that you place your hands on her that she might be saved and live" (5:23). Jesus immediately goes with Jairus, intent on healing the daughter. But as the story unfolds, the evangelist complicates the plot by noting the actions of a new character: an anonymous woman, herself deeply afflicted by disease and in search of a cure.

The Woman of Faith (Mark 5:25–34)

In 5:25–34, the narrative shifts into high dramatic gear. In this intercalated tale, Jesus pauses his journey to help Jairus as the narrative, in unusual fashion, narrows to the perspective of an anonymous woman seeking a cure for an illness.[112] This story, much like the pericope of the man afflicted

---

112. There has been much discussion regarding the combination of stories pres-

by unclean spirits, starkly contrasts the pathos of the woman's condition with a high degree of incongruous elements. These include the evangelist's wry statement about the doctors who help the woman (5:25) and a potentially farcical exchange between Jesus and his disciples (5:30–32).

The first potential script-opposition that the audience encounters in the passage rests in the evangelist's statement regarding physicians. In 5:25–26, the evangelist describes the condition of a woman who has had an incurable disease for twelve years.[113] After describing her illness in 5:25, the evangelist states that she had "suffered greatly under many doctors and spent everything that belonged to her and she had not been helped in any way, but rather had grown worse." This characterization of doctors, especially when given in contrast to the woman's condition, can read as a critique by the evangelist. The woman who is profoundly suffering has sought healers for help. Yet rather than find a cure, she ends up worse off both monetarily and physically. All told, these healers have arguably robbed her.

---

ent in the narrative and the best way to understand their relationship to one another. For more on Markan intercalations, also known as "sandwich stories," see further Dean Deppe, *The Theological Intentions of Mark's Literary Devices: Markan Intercalations, Frames, Allusionary Repetitions, Narrative Surprises, and Three Types of Mirroring* (Wipf & Stock, 2015); James Edwards, "Markan Sandwiches: The Significance of Interpolations in Markan Narratives," *NovT* 31 (1989): 193–216; Shepherd, *Markan Sandwich Stories*, 139–71; Shepherd, "The Narrative Function of Markan Intercalations," *NTS* 41 (1995): 522–40.

113. There is considerable discussion regarding the woman's exact malady and, more significantly, whether it makes the woman ritually impure. Settling this issue in one particular direction is not necessary for the present study as it does not affect the script-oppositions considered in the pericope, though I am persuaded by those who do not foreground purity issues in the present narrative. I am convinced that the story is concerned with the act of healing more so than being freed from purity conventions. For more on this issue, see Shaye Cohen, "Menstruants and the Sacred in Judaism and Christianity," in *Women's History and Ancient History*, ed. Sarah Pomeroy (University of North Carolina Press, 1991), 273–98; Mary D'Angelo, "Power, Knowledge and the Bodies of Women in Mark 5:21–43," in *The Woman with the Blood Flow (Mark 5:23–34)*, ed. Barbara Baert, Art and Religion 2 (Peeters, 2014), 81–106; J. D. Derrett, "Mark's Technique: The Hemorrhaging Woman and Jairus' Daughter," *Bib* 63 (1982): 474–505; Susan Haber, "A Woman's Touch: Feminist Encounters with the Hemorrhaging Woman in Mark 5:24–34," *JSNT* 26 (2003): 171–92; Hisako Kinukawa, *Women and Jesus in Mark: A Japanese Feminist Perspective*, The Bible and Liberation (Orbis, 1994), 29–50.

It is possible that there is a script-opposition in the text. First, the evangelist activates the script of DOCTOR through the use of the term ἰατρός ("doctor, physician, healer"). This script, while it likely could be nuanced in various ways in the ancient world, would have evoked an understanding of someone who had been trained to help patients. This, in turn, is the basic script the evangelist possibly subverts through incongruity. As the audience learns, these healers are no healers at all. Rather, they take the woman's money and leave her worse off than before. One, therefore, encounters a second, directly opposing script brought into contrast with the first. In this depiction of doctors, the evangelist has possibly crafted a script-opposition of DOCTOR/INJURER. The evangelist activates the script-opposition with a possible jab line at the very end of verse 26: "she had not been helped in any way, but rather had grown worse." If this is indeed what the evangelist intends, then this trigger switches the script from doctor to injurer and leads the audience to rethink the previous details of suffering and the cost of medical treatment, aspects which in themselves are not inherently incompatible with medical help. Notably, the language is concise, making for a pithy, forceful turn in the text.

After describing the woman's condition, the evangelist relates her thoughts and activity even as a crowd jostles Jesus and the disciples en route to Jairus's home. The woman thinks to herself that, if she might just touch Jesus's garment, she will be healed (5:28). Consequently, she reaches out and, upon brushing his outer cloak, immediately she is cured. Yet furtive as she considers her touch to be, Jesus becomes aware that "power had gone out of him" (5:30). This precipitates a scene where, in a series of three possible jab lines, the evangelist wields the script of Jesus's knowledge by introducing a script-opposition of KNOWLEDGE/IGNORANCE.

In response to feeling power leave his body, Jesus states in 5:30: "Who touched my clothing?" The statement is odd for at least two reasons: (1) earlier in the narrative, the evangelist depicts Jesus as having preternatural knowledge bordering on omniscience (e.g., in Mark 2:6–7, Jesus is able to detect the inner thoughts of religious leaders scandalized by his healing of the paralytic's sins). Oddly, Jesus no longer has this ability, though he can detect when salvific power flows out of his body.[114] (2) At a more

---

114. There is some question regarding whether or not Jesus actually knows who touched him. This is due to the inflection found in περιεβλέπετο ἰδεῖν τὴν τοῦτο ποιήσασαν, which allows for the reading that Jesus was looking for the woman who

3. Script-Oppositions in Mark 4:35–6:6

literal level, it is strange for Jesus to inquire in this manner when he is surrounded by a large crowd that is "pressing in" (συνθλίβω) upon him (5:24). Indeed, who has not touched Jesus in this jostling throng? Consequently, 5:30 potentially acts as a possible jab line that activates the script-opposition of KNOWLEDGE/IGNORANCE.

Replying to Jesus's query, the disciples state the obvious question: "You see the crowd pressing upon you and you say: 'Who touched me'?" (5:31). The disciples' inquiry is significant, for it openly identifies the oddness of Jesus's statement, capturing the inherent incongruity of a man squeezed by a crowd asking who has touched him.[115] Though scholars sometimes take this statement as further negative characterization of the disciples, reading a mocking or derisive tone into the retort, the narrative does not require such an interpretation.[116] Indeed, Shepherd observes that there is a "truly comical nature of the story. It is really very funny that Jesus says 'who touched me?'"[117] Shepherd presumably grounds his humorous interpretation here on the sharp incongruity present in the text. Consequently, this statement potentially acts as the second jab line in the script-opposition of KNOWLEDGE/IGNORANCE. At a surface level, it is strange that any person would ask such a question in a crowd; at a deeper level, it is stranger still that Jesus, the man capable of reading the hearts of the scribes (2:8), the

---

did this. I agree with those such as Boring, *Mark*, 160; Yabro Collins, *Mark*, 283; and Lane, *Mark*, 193 n. 50, who see in the statement the perspective of the narrator rather than Jesus's knowledge of the woman.

115. Guelich, *Mark*, 298, remarks that "the press of the crowd ... made contact with him unavoidable and his question ridiculous," while Shepherd, *Markan Sandwich Stories*, 148 n.1, states that this question makes "Jesus ... the comedian in this scene."

116. e.g., Yabro Collins, *Mark*, 283, observes that, apropos of the woman, the disciples have less understanding and "less trust"; Donahue and Harrington, *Mark*, 175, regard this moment as "another instance of progressive misunderstanding by the disciples"; Lane, *Mark*, 193, describes the disciples as "impatient"; Marcus, *Mark*, 368, remarks that the disciples ask a "dense and somewhat sarcastic question." Yet not everyone is convinced that the characterization here is negative. Rather, the narrative itself makes the question completely understandable. So Broadhead, *Teaching with Authority*, 298, who notes that the "disciples respond to Jesus' question with amazement" (105); Guelich, *Mark*, states that the disciples offer an "obvious response"; Hatton, "Comic Ambiguity," 109, argues that the disciples' statement is not a point of negative characterization but a narrative technique reinforcing the ambiguity of whether or not Jesus was touched; Shepherd, *Markan Sandwich Stories*, 148 n. 1, maintains that "ignorance is no reason to disparage the disciples here."

117. Shepherd, *Markan Sandwich Stories*, 148 n.1.

Pharisees (3:5), and the disciples (8:17), should fail to know whom he has healed.[118]

The evangelist concludes this exchange between the disciples and Jesus with one final potential jab line in 5:32, stating that Jesus continued "looking around to see the one who had done this." The actions of Jesus here heighten the incongruity, for he will not let the issue drop. Indeed, rather than keep moving to save the ailing daughter of Jairus, Jesus insists on figuring out who touched him. This final statement, if a jab line, reinforces the script-opposition of KNOWLEDGE/IGNORANCE.

The Raising of Jairus's Daughter (Mark 5:35–43)

The discussion between Jesus and his disciples ends with the uplifting dialogue in which Jesus bids the woman, now free from her affliction, to go in peace and freedom from her illness (5:34). Yet no sooner has he said this than tragic news breaks: the girl has died (5:35). Servants of the synagogue leader arrive and inform Jairus to no longer bother Jesus, for the girl has passed on. Jesus issues a startling reply to this news: "Do not fear, only have faith" (5:35) and, taking along Peter, James, and John, proceeds once more to the house.

Upon arriving at Jairus's home, Jesus and his handful of disciples encounter a sorrowful, if expected, scene, for there is great commotion in the household. Mourners have gathered to cry and wail (5:38). Into this scene, Jesus enters and makes a seemingly bizarre statement: "Why are you making such an uproar and crying? Your child has not died but only sleeps" (5:39). So strange are Jesus's words—offensive even—that the mourners gathered in Jairus's household openly laugh at the idea (5:40).[119] For such jeering laughter (καταγελάω), Jesus casts them all out before proceeding to the girl. Upon seeing her, he performs a ritual and raises her from her death or near-death state (5:40–42).

This scene is remarkable, not only because of Jesus's impressive healing touch. Rather, the scene is also noteworthy for the ambiguity surrounding the girl's condition, Jesus's odd statement about her, and the mourners'

---

118. Marcus, *Mark*, 359.
119. On this point, see especially Dietmar Neufeld, *Mockery and Secretism in the Social World of Mark's Gospel*, LNTS 503 (Bloomsbury, 2014), 160–67, who helpfully articulates the social dynamics of mourning and the ways in which Jesus's statement might be heard.

response as this is the only mention of laughter in the entire gospel. When the narrative begins, there is seemingly no doubt about the condition of the girl. She has been pronounced dead, and the presence and activity of the emotional crowd further emphasize this reality. It is against this backdrop that Jesus offers an alternative explanation for the girl's behavior—she is asleep. Additionally, Jesus observes that their behavior does not make any sense in light of his explanation. This interjection complicates the narrative, for Jesus himself has introduced a script-opposition by proposing an alternative, oppositional understanding of the girl's behavior (DEATH/SLEEP). Significantly, this elicits the kind of response one would expect from such an incongruous statement: scornful laughter. While the crowd's laughter is clearly a kind of "laughing-down" or "laughing-at" with respect to Jesus, the juxtaposition between death and sleep produces the reaction.[120] Indeed, scholars have taken note of this detail. Shepherd maintains that this functions as a "comic explanation of the child's demise."[121] Similarly, Hatton has made the script-opposition of DEATH/SLEEP a central point in his argument regarding the likely use of humor in this narrative: "This ambiguity of death/sleep, the uncertainty in the writing, is comedy. For it is comedy that posits the vacillation of the possibilities and the unanswerability of the question by intercalating it in an ungraspable narrative."[122]

Jesus's statement, it must be underscored, is a fascinating interposition of an opposing script that throws the entire narrative into ambiguity. The audience is now confronted with the question of which script is correct: sleep or death? Is Jesus acting strangely or are those around him? What is more, as noted in the previous pericopes, the plasticity of Jesus's characterization is something of an open question. At times, he appears very human, whereas elsewhere he seems other-worldly. While this ambiguity exists, it is likely that the narrative supports the position and perspective of Jesus, opposed to the mourners, for immediately after their jeering Jesus is able to wake the girl. However one might explain what Jesus means by "sleep," his seemingly nonsensical statement turns out to be correct.[123] This, in turn, throws a potentially humorous light on

---

120. Halliwell, *Greek Laughter*, 475.
121. Shepherd, *Markan Sandwich Stories*, 163.
122. Hatton, "Comic Ambiguity," 106.
123. The question of whether or not Jairus's daughter actually died is difficult to resolve. Scholars have addressed this interpretive difficulty in various ways. For those who view the girl as actually having died, arguments of metaphorical language and/

the surrounding narrative, for Jesus's skepticism of the mourners in verse 39 can be read throughout the entire story. Consequently, in addition to verse 39, possible jab lines emerge in verses 35, 38, and 42 where people are now perceived to be acting strangely in light of the reality that the girl is not actually dead.[124] This leads to another script-opposition of APPROPRIATE/INAPPROPRIATE RESPONSE TO JESUS in 5:40. Rather than agree with the new perspective proposed by Jesus, the crowd of mourners jeer

---

or proper perspective are often employed. Boring, *Mark*, 162, notes that the girl is indeed dead and Jesus "was expressing resurrection faith in the later Christian language"; Yabro Collins, *Mark*, 285, observes that this "introduces an element of ambiguity into the narrative" but that the "narrative rhetoric of the story ... makes clear that the girl is really dead"; Donahue and Harrington, *Mark*, 177, argue that this is a form of "Markan irony" and "both the OT and early Christianity used 'sleep' as a euphemism for death"; Guelich, *Mark*, 302, maintains that the statement's intelligibility is related to perspective: "Jesus viewed her death, which was real, in light of the approaching miracle"; Lane, *Mark*, 196–97, states that Jesus's remark is "ambiguous ... [but] Jesus' statement means that in spite of the girl's real death, she has not been delivered over to the realm of death with all of its consequences"; Marcus, *Mark*, 371, views this language as a typical Jewish metaphor for death. Yet it is possible to view the girl as quite literally just being asleep. Hatton, "Comic Ambiguity," 106, does not argue one way or the other but underscores the importance of sleep as an interpretive option: "Is the girl dead or asleep? It is unclear. If she is dead, Jesus is wrong because he tells the people she is asleep. The point, however, is that it is unanswerable. Mark does not make the point that she was dead, and he does not make the point that she was asleep. The narrative demands neither, and indeed, the text demands that it be ambiguous. The thrust is *whether* she was dead or asleep. The focus is on *whether*.... The ambiguous comedy of the story reflects the ambiguous comedy of the text and vice versa. The focus of the outer story is 'was she or wasn't she?' The comedy in/of the drama takes place above the story, away from the apparent miracle in the story to the text, the ambiguity, the self-referentiality, and the unexpected. This is comedy, this joking nod toward apparent seriousness in the story." Whether the girl is literally dead or Jesus is using euphemistic language, there is likely still humor at play here given the clear irony. As Camery-Hogatt, *Irony in Mark's Gospel*, 139–40, notes: "Jesus' words here may perhaps be understood as a subtle peirastic irony. Of course the girl was 'dead,' the whole movement of the story depends upon it. Jesus is not rejecting that notion, but rather is superimposing upon it a secondary–or, as Mark sees it, a new primary–frame of reference. Death is not final, not ultimate." Adopting such a view, the humor does not derive from a literal reading of sleep; rather, Mark interposes a miraculous frame on top of the ordinary experience of death. If this is the case, humor can still be generated from the circumstance as the script-opposition of DEATH/SLEEP is still present.

124. The jab lines occur at 5:35, 38, 39, and 42.

and mock his statement. While their response is understandable from an ordinary perspective, their failure to grasp the deeper reality results in them responding exactly the wrong way to Jesus: scorn rather than faith. Consequently, they become the immediate and primary target of both script-oppositions, while other actors in the narrative become implicit targets of the DEATH/SLEEP script-opposition (they are responding normally, if inadequately, to the perceived reality of the girl's death). That the evangelist would exploit the ambiguity of DEATH/SLEEP, while perhaps unexpected to contemporary readers, is not altogether surprising given the challenge of determining death in the ancient world as noted above. Moreover, this could act as a creative, salutary way to relativize death in light of the reality of resurrection.

Jesus and the Absence of Power (Mark 6:1–6)

The fourth and final pericope of Mark 4:35–6:6 relates the story of Jesus's return home and near powerlessness. In a remarkable moment, the healer and wonderworker, who has calmed a raging sea, quieted a furious demonic force, healed an incurable disease, and likely reversed death, finds himself able to do only a few miraculous works. This intriguing story, short as it is, potentially contains several script-oppositions: APPROPRIATE/INAPPROPRIATE RESPONSE TO JESUS, JEW/GENTILE, WONDERWORKER/LOCAL, SUCCESSFUL/FAILED HEALER, and KNOWLEDGE/IGNORANCE. These script-oppositions find illumination in ancient comedic treatments of misunderstanding and mistaken identity.

Comedic Themes in Ancient Sources

Mistaken Identity

The challenge of mistaken identity acted as one of the primary engines of humor by the time of New Comedy.[125] Though many examples of this exist, I will consider one play from Plautus and Terence as representatives of this trend in ancient comedy.

---

125. I have noted several examples of mistaken identity and humor above, though I have not drawn attention to them until now. With respect to the frequency of this trope, one need only look at Terence's extant works, most of which contain mistaken identity as a central plot point/comedic device.

Plautus made broad use of identity and misunderstanding to great comic effect. One of the best examples of this occurs in *Menaechmi*, already noted above for its scenes of possession and medical quackery.[126] As I noted previously, the entirety of *Menaechmi*'s comedy hinges on the case of mistaken identity. Identical twin-brothers, Sosicles and Menaechmus, are separated as children only to have their lives intersect as adults when Sosicles returns to Epidamnus as part of his ongoing quest to locate his lost twin. As the play unfolds, Sosicles finds himself mistaken for Menaechmus by the latter's mistress, wife, father-in-law, and doctor, while Menaechmus must reckon with the fallout of these encounters after the fact. The simple device of mistaken identity provides consistent comical fodder. This is evident in an exchange between Sosicles and Erotium, Menaechmus's mistress:

> Sosicles: Who is this woman talking to?
> Erotium: To you of course.
> Sosicles: What business have I ever had with you or have I now?
> Erotium: Because out of all men Venus wanted me to hold you alone in esteem, and not undeservedly so: you alone let me flourish through your generosity.
> Sosicles: This woman is definitely either mad or drunk, Messenio: she addresses me, a total stranger, so intimately.
> Messenio [Sosicles's slave]: didn't I tell you that it always happens like this here? Now only leaves are falling compared with what'll happen if we're here for two days.... But let me address her. Hey there, woman, I'm speaking to you.
> Erotium: What is it?
> Messenio: Where did you get to know this man?
> Erotium: In the same place where he got to know me, long ago already, in Epidamnus. (*Men.* 367–380 [de Melo])

As the conversation continues, Sosicles finds himself more confused when asked about gifts Menaechmus has stolen from his wife in order to give to Erotium.

---

126. Alison Sharrock, "Roman Comedy," in *The Edinburgh Companion to Ancient Greece and Rome*, ed. Edward Bispham, Thomas Harrison, and Brian Sparkes (Edinburgh University Press, 2010), 309–12.

Sosicles: What's that? I gave you a mantle I stole from my wife? Are you in your right mind? This woman is certainly dreaming the way horses do, while standing.
Erotium: Why do you wish to poke fun at me and to deny what's happened?
Sosicles: Tell me what I've done that I'm now denying.
Erotium: That you've given me your wife's mantle today.
Sosicles: I'm denying it even now. I for one have never had a wife, nor do I have one now, and I never put my foot here inside the city gate since I was born. I had lunch on my ship, then I came out here and met you. (394–401, [de Meleo])

Ultimately, throughout the entire play, both Sosicles and Menaechmus are caught up in comical coincidences because of their respective mistaken identities. This comes to a head in the climax of the comedy when the brothers meet and recognize one another. Notably, Terence would draw upon this technique in his own writings.

Terence's first play, *Andria*, derives its key conflict and much comedy from the problem of mistaken identity.[127] In this play, the young, love-struck Pamphilus wants to marry Glycerium. However, his father intervenes, pushing Pamphilus instead to marry Philumena, the daughter of their neighbor Chremes. Chremes, for his part, is suspicious of Pamphilus's intentions given his love for another woman. Hilarity ensues as Simo, Pamphilus's father, plots against son and neighbor to see that the wedding goes through, while Davos, Pamphilus's slave, crafts his own machinations in hopes of getting the wedding called off. Misunderstandings increase until it is serendipitously revealed that Glycerium is actually the long-lost daughter of Chremes, making her an eligible wife for Pamphilus:

Pamphilus: Davus!
Davus: Who's that?
Pamphilus: It's me.
Davus: Oh!
Pamphilus: You don't know what's happened to me.
Davus: True. But I do know what happened to me.
Pamphilus: So do I.
Davus: That's the way of the world. You know the bad that's come to me before I know the good that's befallen you.

---

127. Sharrock, "Roman Comedy," 311.

> Pamphilus: My Glycerium has found her parents.
> Davus: Congratulations ... Who?
> Pamphilus: Chremes.
> Davus: Good news!
> Pamphilus: And I can marry her immediately. (*Andr.* 966–973 [Barsby])

As the final recognition scene reveals, the entire conflict of *Andria* turns on the comedy of mistaken identity. Simo's desire is for Pamphilus to marry a daughter of Chremes, which, as it happens, Glycerium fortunately is.

Ultimately, as ancient comedians saw it, mistaken identity was a surefire way to generate a humorous plot. The inherent contradictions built into such a story-telling device provided ample means for playwrights to exploit.

Analysis of Mark 6:1–6

The evangelist caps off the narrative of powerful stories with one final, brief account of Jesus in his hometown. But, rather than relating another potent encounter, the evangelist offers a sharply contrastive vision of Jesus's abilities: the man who has squared off against nature, demons, and death, by the end of this narrative finds himself nearly bereft of power. The account is rife with stark juxtapositions as seen in the following potential script-oppositions below:

Table 3.4. Vectors of Humor in Mark 6:1–6

Script-Oppositions	Mark 6:1–6
APPROPRIATE/INAPPROPRIATE RESPONSE TO JESUS	6:3
JEW/GENTILE	6:3
WONDERWORKER/LOCAL	6:3
SUCCESSFUL/FAILED HEALER	6:5
KNOWLEDGE/IGNORANCE	6:6

Upon healing Jairus's daughter, Jesus returns to his homeland (πατρίδα) along with his disciples and begins teaching in the local synagogue (6:1–2). Initially, the townspeople appear to receive Jesus's presence and teaching, for "upon hearing him, many were astounded saying 'From where did he learn these things? And what is this wisdom that has been granted to him and such powerful works being accomplished by his hands?" (6:3) The people of Jesus's πατρίδα, at first glance, seem to marvel at the amazing deeds Jesus has wrought.[128] However, the evangelist immediately qualifies this through further elaboration: "Is this not the craftsman [τέκτων] the son of Mary and brother of James and Joses and Jude and Simon? And aren't his sisters here with us?'" (6:3).[129] This turn in the story reveals that the people's initial awe may have been more a response of confusion than veneration. What is more, their negative reaction possibly functions as a jab line for three potential script-oppositions. First, that the people would seek to domesticate Jesus by diminishing his stature and, of all things, be scandalized by Jesus's behavior may activate the script-opposition of APPROPRIATE/INAPPROPRIATE RESPONSE TO JESUS. Indeed, this is a startling reaction. Confusion around the person of Jesus is, to some extent, understandable even within the narrative framework. Yet dishonor, rejection, and being scandalized together amount to a reaction completely opposed to how individuals should respond. Furthermore, this improper response is predicated on a sharp incongruity apropos' of Jesus identity. The people regard Jesus as a craftsman and local son, rather than a wonderworker. Yet the evangelist's narrative has already demonstrated in the preceding pericopes and declared at the outset of the gospel that Jesus is no ordinary man: he is the Son of God (1:[1], 11). Consequently, 6:3 acts as a potential jab line which activates a WONDERWORKER/LOCAL script-opposition, potentially making light of the people's ignorance in their scandalizing and rejection of Jesus. Finally, scholars have also noted possible traces of a JEW/GENTILE script-opposition in the text.[130] Given that immediately after this passage the gospel will broaden its horizon to include scenes of negative appraisals of dietary and religious rites (7:1–23;

---

128. This is suggested, too, by the many ways in which this language echoes Jesus's first synagogue appearance in chapter 1:21–28. Note, e.g., the reaction of the people in 1:27: "And they all were amazed with the result that they discussed with each other saying: 'What is this? A new teaching with authority.'"

129. Whether the reading here should be τεκτων or του τεκτονος υιος και as several textual witnesses attest (ƒ 13 33vid 579 700 [P45 565 2542] it vgmss bomss), the relevant point for the present analysis is that Jesus's identity is diminished by this reference. The people of his country undercut his stature by domesticating Jesus in this way.

130. Camery-Hoggatt, *Irony in Mark's Gospel*, 143–44, adopts this reading of Jesus's rejection in 6:1–6: "we must pause here to notice the forcefulness of the rejection motif which leads to the material which follows.... In this way the reader is prepared for Jesus' abandonment of Galilee for Gentile territory."

8:11–13), remarkable gentile faith (7:24–30, 31–37), and an eschatological feast wherein gentiles participate in God's blessing (8:1–10; 14–21), some scholars have seen this closing pericope as suggesting a more receptive audience among gentiles, thereby underscoring a contrast that might function as a script-opposition.[131]

Jesus immediately perceives the import of the people's reaction, responding with a sharp statement of his own in 6:4, "A prophet is without honor in his own homeland and among his relatives and in his house." Remarkably, in a dramatic narrative turn, the evangelist notes that "he was unable to do any deed of power there, except that he healed a few sick people upon whom he laid hands, and he marveled at their unbelief" (6:5–6). These two verses, though compact, are stunning. They speak to Jesus's inability to perform miracles, Jesus's own surprise, and the profound impact of "unbelief" (ἀπιστία). Furthermore, embedded in these verses are two possible script-oppositions: (1) SUCCESSFUL/FAILED HEALER and (2) KNOWLEDGE/IGNORANCE.

The closing verses of the miracle cycle in Mark 4:35–6:6 characterize Jesus in a striking manner. While there have been questionable moments regarding Jesus's character and/or power in the previous pericopes, never has Jesus failed to deliver miraculous deeds when needed. Yet in 6:5, Jesus actually fails to heal people.[132] The evangelist states that Jesus *was not able* (οὐκ

---

131. On the issue of gentiles and their place in the salvation scheme of Mark, see Kelly Iverson, "Jews, Gentiles, and the Kingdom of God: The Parable of the Wicked Tenants in Narrative Perspective (Mark 12:1–12)," *BibInt* 20 (2012): 305–35; Brian Gamel, "Salvation in a Sentence: Mark 15:39 as Markan Soteriology," *JTI* 6 (2012): 65–78; Andrew Salzmann, "'Do You Not Still Understand?' Mark 8:21 and the Mission to the Gentiles," *BTB* 39 (2009): 129–34; Eric Wefald, "The Separate Gentile Mission in Mark: A Narrative Explanation of Markan Geography, the Two Feeding Accounts and Exorcisms," *JSNT* 60 (1995): 3–26.

132. Commentators offer various explanations for Jesus's apparent loss of power. So, for example Donahue and Harrington, *Mark*, 185–86, explain that Jesus has "not come as a magician or miracle worker who dazzles his audience with works of power that compel belief"; Lane, *Mark*, 204: "It is not Mark's intention to stress Jesus' *inability* when he states that he could perform no miracles at Nazareth. His purpose is rather to indicate that Jesus was not free to exercise his power *in these circumstances*"; Marcus, *Mark*, 380, softens the characterization of Jesus being completely powerless to simply being "checked." While it is true that the evangelist qualifies Jesus's powerlessness, the evangelist appears quite comfortable with a pliable Christology wherein Jesus's superhuman abilities are subordinated to broader theological points, if only for a few narrative moments.

ἐδύνατο) to do any work of power, though they qualify this by adding that Jesus helped some (εἰ μὴ ὀλίγοις ἀρρώστοις ἐπιθεὶς τὰς χεῖρας ἐθεράπευσεν).[133] Yet even with this additional statement, the audience feels the force of the juxtaposition. Jesus, powerful wonder-worker and healer, is depicted here as a near-normal person. He has shifted in status, if only momentarily, generating a script-opposition of SUCCESSFUL/FAILED HEALER. What is more, Jesus himself seems shocked by the circumstances, for in 6:5 he "marvels" (θαυμάζω) at the unbelief of those around him. Significantly, verse 6 may also function as a jab line that activates once more the KNOWLEDGE/IGNORANCE script-opposition found in the previous pericope. That the evangelist depicts Jesus here as wondering at people's reactions stands in stark opposition to other points in the gospel where he possesses preternatural knowledge.[134] Yet in spite of this, the audience knows Jesus's true identity as the Son of God and powerful wonder-worker.

Conclusion

In the present chapter, I have explored potential script-oppositions in Mark 4:35–6:6 and contact points with ancient comedic texts that employ similar script-oppositions with humorous intent. As one can see, this series of miracle stories potentially contains several script-oppositions, signaling the possibility that humor resides in the text. Yet it is not enough to simply note the presence of such elements. Rather, it is necessary to dig deeper into the script-oppositions and ask whether all are equally humorous or whether there is an unevenness to what audiences of Mark's Gospel may have considered comical. Furthermore, one must pursue the function of humor in these stories. It is to these issues which I now turn.

---

133. The force of this statement seems to have been felt by other gospel writers as they moderate the scene. Matthew simply states that Jesus "did not" do any work of power (Matt 13:58), while Luke omits the detail from their Nazareth rejection scene (Luke 4:16–30).

134. Yabro Collins, *Mark*, 292, observes that "there is a certain ironic contrast here with the statement in 5:20 that all marveled at the proclamation of the former demoniac."

4
Humor Effects in Mark 4:35–6:6

Introduction

In the previous chapter, I argued for the presence of a wide variety of script-oppositions extant in Mark 4:35–6:6. Additionally, I examined potentially humorous comparative texts as a means for gauging whether such script-oppositions could, in fact, be construed as comical in the ancient world. What remains to be explored is to what degree an audience might have construed these script-oppositions as comical and what their rhetorical and literary impacts upon these pericopes might be. To achieve this goal, I will first discuss preliminary results of the previous chapter's analysis. I will then discuss key parameters regarding how to best interpret the humor in script-oppositions. Finally, I will explore the potentially humorous effects of script-oppositions in Mark 4:35–6:6 through a tiered list, moving from the most obviously comical in the text to the more abstracted and/or challenging script-opposition.

Mapping Script-Oppositions in Mark 4:35–6:6

Previously, I noted several instances of potential script-oppositions in Mark 4:35–6:6. I have outlined these below in table 4.1. Several notable observations emerge when looking at this table. The high volume of script-oppositions and their recurrence are broadly commensurate with scholarship that investigates ambiguities and irony in these texts. Yet scholars have not noticed that, by looking at a broader swath of Markan text with the question of comedy in mind, it becomes clear that this tendency is not coincidental. Rather, the sustained use of incongruity in these pericopes suggests that there is a global deployment of humor throughout

4:35–6:6, opposed to just one story or another maintaining coincidental, comical details.

Table 4.1. Vectors of Humor in Mark 4:35–6:6

Script-Oppositions	Mark 4:35–41	Mark 5:1–20	Mark 5:21–43	Mark 6:1–6
ASLEEP/ALERT	4:38			
ROMAN IMPERIUM/JESUS'S IMPERIUM	4:38, 39	5:10, 12, 13		
APPROPRIATE/INAPPROPRIATE RESPONSE TO JESUS (FEAR)	4:41	5:17		
KNOWLEDGE/IGNORANCE OF JESUS'S IDENTITY	4:41	5:17	5:40	6:3
SUCCESSFUL/FAILED EXORCIST		5:6, 7, 8, 13		
CIVILIZED/BARBARIAN		5:13, 17, 18		
WORSHIP/OPPOSITION		5:6		
DOCTOR/INJURER			5:26	
KNOWLEDGE/IGNORANCE			5:30, 31, 32	6:6
DEATH/SLEEP			5:35, 38, 39, 42	
APPROPRIATE/INAPPROPRIATE RESPONSE TO JESUS (MOCKERY)			5:40	6:3
WONDERWORKER/LOCAL				6:3
JEW/GENTILE				6:3
SUCCESSFUL/FAILED HEALER				6:5

As I noted in chapter 2, after one has identified potential script-oppositions, one can then study the manner in which an author distributes these throughout a text. Attardo has crafted a helpful taxonomy for tracking such distributions of script-oppositions and their respective jab lines. Regarding a grouping of jab lines, Attardo utilizes the category of "strands." Strands occur when three or more jab lines are "formally or thematically linked."[1] With respect to narrative placement, Attardo notes two particularly helpful definitions that seek to explain the locality of jab lines, whether clustered or spread out. "Combs ... [are] a type of strand which shows the occurrence of more than 3 jab lines within a narrow space ... [and] create areas of text where there is a concentration of humor."[2] "Bridges," on the other hand, are "a type of strand in which two groups of lines (most commonly jab lines) occur at considerable distance from one another."[3] Using this taxonomy, it is possible to index the script-oppositions found in table 4.1.

Beginning with strands, there are several that run throughout 4:35–6:6 and refer to the following script-oppositions: ROMAN IMPERIUM/JESUS'S IMPERIUM, APPROPRIATE/INAPPROPRIATE RESPONSE TO JESUS (FEAR/MOCKERY), KNOWLEDGE/IGNORANCE OF JESUS'S IDENTITY, SUCCESSFUL/FAILED EXORCIST, CIVILIZED/BARBARIAN, KNOWLEDGE/IGNORANCE, and DEATH/SLEEP. Each of these script-oppositions is signaled in the text by three or more jab lines as seen below in table 4.2.

Table 4.2. Strands in Mark 4:35–6:6

Script-Opposition	Jab Lines
ROMAN IMPERIUM/JESUS'S IMPERIUM	4:38, 39; 5:10, 12, 13
APPROPRIATE/INAPPROPRIATE RESPONSE TO JESUS (FEAR/MOCKERY)	4:41; 5:17, 40; 6:3
KNOWLEDGE/IGNORANCE OF JESUS'S IDENTITY	4:41; 5:17, 40; 6:3
CIVILIZED/BARBARIAN	5:13, 17, 20
SUCCESSFUL/FAILED EXORCIST	5:6, 7, 8, 13
KNOWLEDGE/IGNORANCE	5:30, 31, 32, 6:6
DEATH/SLEEP	5:35, 38, 39, 42

---

1. Attardo, *Linguistic Theories of Humor*, 83.
2. Attardo, *Linguistic Theories of Humor*, 87–88.
3. Attardo, *Linguistic Theories of Humor*, 88.

In addition to these strands, it is helpful to introduce the notion of "threads."[4] For the purposes of the present discussion, a thread signifies a grouping of strands that combine into a larger grouping. This category allows for an analysis of the way in which script-oppositions might be combined into a higher-order incongruity for greater comical effect. Consequently, there are two major threads at work in Mark 4:35–6:6: (1) PROPER/FOOLISH RESPONSE TO JESUS, which combines the script-oppositions of APPROPRIATE/INAPPROPRIATE RESPONSE TO JESUS and KNOWLEDGE/IGNORANCE OF JESUS'S IDENTITY; and (2) WONDERWORKER/AVERAGE PERSON, which is comprised of those script-oppositions that underscore Jesus's humanity as seen in such script-oppositions as ASLEEP/ALERT, SUCCESSFUL/FAILED EXORCIST, KNOWLEDGE/IGNORANCE, DEATH/SLEEP, and SUCCESSFUL/FAILED HEALER.[5] Thus, one finds two major threads running through all the miracle stories. Notably, some strands act as combs, while both of the threads act as bridges. Taken altogether, the script-oppositions, jab lines, and their placement within Mark 4:35–6:6 may be seen in tables 4.3–4.5. Several observations emerge from this organization of script-oppositions.

Table 4.3. Threads in Mark 4:35–6:6

Thread	Jab Lines
PROPER/FOOLISH RESPONSE TO JESUS	4:41; 5:17, 40; 6:3
WONDERWORKER/AVERAGE PERSON	4:38; 5:6, 7, 8, 13 5:30, 31, 32, 35, 38, 39; 6:5, 6

---

4. This is a unique category adopted for the present study. I have created this as a tool for identifying the complex ways in which strands are often themselves taken up into larger groupings.

5. I will say more about this script-opposition when discussing the humor evident on the surface of the text. Essentially, the designation here is an attempt to collate what appears to be a pattern in each of the miracle stories, namely, the evangelist first underscores the humanity of Jesus (i.e., sleepy, struggling exorcist, unaware, and struggling healer) only to invert this by highlighting Jesus's supernatural abilities.

Table 4.4. Combs and Bridges in Mark 4:35–6:6

Combs	Bridges
SUCCESSFUL/FAILED EXORCIST	PROPER/FOOLISH RESPONSE TO JESUS
DEATH/SLEEP	WONDERWORKER/AVERAGE PERSON

Table 4.5. Script-Opposition Organization in Mark 4:35–6:6

Strands	
Script-Opposition	Jab Lines
ROMAN IMPERIUM/JESUS'S IMPERIUM	4:38, 39; 5:10, 12, 13
APPROPRIATE/INAPPROPRIATE RESPONSE TO JESUS (FEAR/MOCKERY)	4:41; 5:17, 40; 6:3
KNOWLEDGE/IGNORANCE OF JESUS'S IDENTITY	4:41; 5:17, 40; 6:3
SUCCESSFUL/FAILED EXORCIST	5:6, 7, 8, 13
CIVILIZED/BARBARIAN	5:13, 17, 20
KNOWLEDGE/IGNORANCE	5:30, 31, 32
DEATH/SLEEP	5:35, 38, 39, 42
Threads	
Strands	Jab Lines
PROPER/FOOLISH RESPONSE TO JESUS	4:41; 5:17, 40; 6:3
WONDERWORKER/AVERAGE PERSON	4:38; 5:6, 7, 8, 13 5:30, 31, 32; 6:5, 6
Combs and Bridges	
Combs	Bridges
SUCCESSFUL/FAILED EXORCIST	PROPER/FOOLISH RESPONSE TO JESUS
DEATH/SLEEP	WONDERWORKER/AVERAGE PERSON

First, regarding placement and frequency, the evangelist potentially utilizes humor in one-time jab lines, localized script-oppositions (as evidenced by combs), and globalized script-oppositions (as evidenced by bridges). Apropos of potential one-off jokes, the evangelist occasionally deploys a jab line then quickly moves on from the topic. This happens, for instance, in the DOCTOR/INJURER script-opposition of 5:26. Such script-oppositions have the potential to act as flashes of humor, dissipating as quickly as they appear.

Localized script-oppositions (combs) appear at a number of points. These consist of several jab lines making reference to the same script-opposition. This occurs in such script-oppositions as the SUCCESSFUL/FAILED EXORCIST script-opposition in Mark 5:1–20 or the DEATH/SLEEP script-opposition found in 5:21–43. These script-oppositions aggregate into strands that act as a source of humor for a longer scene than simple one-off jokes. Thus, the script-opposition of SUCCESSFUL/FAILED EXORCIST may be seen as a central strand that provides humor lasting from 5:5–5:13, while DEATH/SLEEP acts as a recurring central strand for 5:35–42. Such strands potentially function to keep humor tightly and consistently restrained within a limited narratival framework that the evangelist supplements with substrands of humor. Such strands stand in distinction to globalized script-oppositions.

At a broader level, bridges connects certain script-oppositions across several pericopes. For example, this occurs in the case of the script-opposition APPROPRIATE/INAPPROPRIATE RESPONSE TO JESUS. This script-opposition is present in every pericope, with the disciples, denizens of the Decapolis, people in Jairus's household, and Jesus's kinsfolk responding inappropriately to the work and presence of Jesus, be it from fear or disdain. Strands such as this act as bridges, presenting comedic incongruities that span large portions of the narrative and function as possibly humorous leitmotifs. The evangelist's layered use of script-oppositions reveals a potentially sophisticated understanding and employment of humor.

Second, there is some overlap regarding jab lines. Occasionally, script-oppositions activate more than one potentially humorous incongruity at any given moment. This is not particularly strange, as script-oppositions are often flexed in such a way as to generate overlap with more than one competing script. This is an important feature to keep in mind when considering the limitations of humor in the text and its performance, a point to which I will return below.

Third, while there are a number of potentially humorous moments in 4:35–6:6, two threads preponderate in the extant script-oppositions: PROPER/FOOLISH RESPONSE TO JESUS and WONDERWORKER/AVERAGE PERSON. These threads focalize the most consistent and prevalent comical points present in the text. Notably, they both center on the identity of

Jesus, drawing consideration to the tension between Jesus's human and supernatural qualities and the responses generated around Jesus as he manifests strange, divine power. Indeed, these two threads appear to be likely candidates for intentionally humorous incongruity on the part of the evangelist.

Having sketched a picture of the locality of script-oppositions in Mark 4:35–6:6 and the ways in which they combine to form sophisticated strands and threads, it is necessary to consider the bounds that might be placed on Markan humor.

Humor Limiters in Mark 4:35–6:6

The analysis I have offered so far paints a portrait of the Markan text that straddles the border of comedy. That is, at a basic level, there is potential for humor every few verses. Yet as noted earlier, I approach Mark as a serious text with humorous relief opposed to a comedic text with serious relief.[6] Furthermore, if every script-opposition I have identified were actively humorous, this would raise questions about the performance of the text. Just precisely how would a speaker move through such a narrative if people were laughing every few words? Put another way, how efficacious would it be for the evangelist to convey a serious theological message that was constantly interrupted and thrown off track by humor? Consequently, it is important to consider what limiters may be present that might bind humor in the Markan text and offer a more nuanced approach for understanding the ways in which humor might be activated in the text.[7]

---

6. I noted this approach in chapter 2. However, it is possible to further refine the spectrum of humorous communication. Villy Tsakona, "Genres of Humor," in Attardo, *Routledge Handbook of Language and Humor*, 494–98, argues for a continuum of humorous genres: (1) humor as an obligatory feature of the genre—genres produced predominantly for the amusement of the audience; (2) humor as an optional but expected feature of the genre—genres that may often include humor and may aim, among other things, at creating a humorous effect; (3) humor as an optional but unexpected feature of the genre—genres where humor may occasionally occur but it is not normally or always expected; (4) humor as an untypical feature of the genre—genres where humor hardly ever (or never) occurs such as laws, court decisions, and funeral speeches. Humorous utterances in such genres are rather unexpected than expected. Under this taxonomy, Mark would fall into category 3, being a text that utilizes humor as an option without it necessarily being untypical.

7. As is often the case in humor studies, there are many well-understood general-

Humor Competence

The first consideration regarding humor limiters involves "humor competence"—that is, the ability for humor to be apprehended.[8] While there are universals to the phenomenon of humor, the persistent study of humor has confirmed its highly subjective nature as well.[9] This is the case not only when attempting to examine humor across time and culture but within discrete places and epochs. Additionally, because humor is an act of communication, it requires both competence on the part of the performer as well as the audience in order to achieve the full effect of comedic discourse. On the one hand, a performer may attempt to make a humorous point but deliver it poorly and bomb. On the other hand, the audience maintains its own views and beliefs regarding what is appropriate for humor and what is not.[10] These and other such considerations lead to the conclusion that, in any humorous exchange, several outcomes are possible. Helpfully, Attardo outlines seven possible outcomes regarding such interactions, noting that a person may "a) not get the joke and laugh, b) get the joke, but not react, c) get the joke and smile, d) get the joke and laugh, e) get the joke and comment metalinguistically, f) get the joke and change the subject, g) not get the joke and ask for clarification, etc."[11] In addition to these possibilities, Attardo introduces the important concept of "script unavailability." Generally speaking, there are simply "some scripts that are labeled 'unavailable' for humor in a given speech community/culture/social group, etc."[12] Unfortu-

---

ized phenomena that do not yet have adequate scientific study or analysis. This is true of failing at humor as well. Though it is not hard to call to mind an example of failed humor, Nancy Bell, "Failed Humor," in Attardo, *Routledge Handbook of Language and Humor*, 368, remarks that "the systematic investigation of failed humor is a recent phenomenon, [and] virtually everything remains open to debate."

8. For a helpful treatment of the topic of failed humor see Bell, "Failed Humor," 356–70.

9. On this topic, see Annarita Guidi, "Humor Universals," in Attardo, *Routledge Handbook of Language and Humor*, 17–33.

10. In spite of the potential to misfire in humorous exchanges, Bell, "Failed Humor," 367, notes that "it seems to be a rather rare occurrence."

11. Salvatore Attardo, "The GTVH and Humorous Discourse," in *Humorous Discourse*, ed. Wladyslaw Chlopiki and Dorota Brzozowska, Humor Research 11 (de Gruyter, 2017), 93–105.

12. Attardo, "GTVH and Humorous Discourse," 99.

nately, the catalog of unavailable scripts constantly changes.[13] Yet broadly, "scripts that are associated with very high status objects within a culture/group will tend not to be available for humor."[14] This last point is salient when considering whether or not early Jesus followers felt that Jesus might act as a suitable target for humor—a point which I will explore below.

The discussion of humor competence is pertinent for the present analysis as it suggests that, although the evangelist's text may contain multiple comical script-oppositions, there can be a wide variety of responses to such humor. This better accounts for the potentially disruptive nature of such script-oppositions.[15] These humor-limiters are critical for analysis of humor in a text as they signal that there is dimensionality regarding the placement of script-oppositions in a text.

Analysis of Script-Oppositions and Humor Dimensionality

Two final points of concern regarding humor limiters and Mark 4:35–6:6 include an analysis of the number of script-oppositions in the text and the degrees to which humor may be accessible to a given audience. I consider each of these in turn.

---

13. Attardo, "GTVH and Humorous Discourse," 99.
14. Attardo, "GTVH and Humorous Discourse," 100. "High status objects" refer to those figures, institutions, etc., that are taboo apropos of humor.
15. One might raise the objection that some audiences will respond to every joke, thereby causing disruption in the telling of a narrative. While this is of no concern to a comedian, it is very much an issue for texts which, while they deploy humor, are not necessarily intended to be primarily humorous. While this is possible, it is quite unlikely. An example from the world of contemporary comedic performances illustrates this. In the filming of comedy hours or specials, comedians frequently tape more than one performance, often producing an end product that is spliced together from several performances or one version of an act performed in the same venue over several nights. This is due to the reality that, even when audiences are primed for humor, staging is set to the direction of a comedian or their director, and the comedian is in good health and good form, audiences will still often not laugh at every potential script-opposition in a given act. In short, even the most perfect setting designed to make people laugh frequently falls short of generating a response for every script-opposition. What is more, it takes very little in the way of tweaking different elements to diminish the response to script-oppositions. Comedians frequently observe that changing a room's size, lighting, or audio even in small ways are enough to noticeably reduce expected reactions from one's jokes.

When examining the statistical evidence of script-oppositions and jab lines, at first glance the numbers seem high. I have argued for the presence of fifteen script-oppositions activated by thirty-five jab lines across fifty-six verses (see table 4.1). However, closer scrutiny of the data brings this number down into more reasonable territory. This is due to the fact that several jab lines activate more than one script-opposition. For instance, the script-oppositions APPROPRIATE/INAPPROPRIATE RESPONSE TO JESUS (FEAR/MOCKERY) and KNOWLEDGE/IGNORANCE OF JESUS'S IDENTITY share the same four jab lines. When considering the ways in which the evangelist can flex the same jab line, the number of potentially comical moments becomes more commensurate with a serious narrative: twenty-two jab lines across fifty-six verses. However, the number still seems high for a serious narrative. Though it is not impossible for serious stories or plots to have moments of highly aggregated humor, it is important to determine whether any other elements might impact this analysis. It is at this juncture that humor dimensionality becomes critical.

Humor dimensionality may be viewed as a heuristic for determining tiers of humor.[16] A kind of vertical sliding-scale, dimensions of humor in a text range from the most obviously funny moments to more abstracted comical elements. At the most basic level, or first tier of humor, incongruities would violate either norms of the text itself or tenets so widely believed to be true that humorous incongruity would be readily apparent to persons reading or hearing a text. Moving further up the scale, humorous incongruities would touch on script-oppositions that would not be as obviously humorous to an audience. This could occur either by way of lacking the same background knowledge required to view particular

---

16. This is my own attempt to delineate between more and less obviously comical incongruities in texts. I have not yet come across any particular humor theorist that outlines such a model. That being said, there is precedence in attempting to create scales or tiers of humor. Ermida, *Language of Comic Narratives*, 120–27, 189–99, documents the vertical dimensions of various script-oppositions, ranging from smaller to larger incongruities, and articulates how they relate to one another and impact the unfolding of comical narratives. The aim, however, is different (i.e., she is not tracking the likelihood of humor in a serious text) and consequently cannot be utilized as a model for the present analysis. Attardo, too, is gesturing toward a similar issue when discussing humor performance. This is especially notable in his chart regarding the various factors at play in performing humor (Attardo, "GTVH and Humorous Discourse," 96).

4. Humor Effects in Mark 4:35–6:6   133

incongruities as humorous or because the target or subject would not necessarily be viewed as humorous by all in an audience. At the highest ends of a humor dimensionality register, one would expect to find the least obviously comical incongruities at play in a text. Such considerations are critical when examining incongruities in Mark, for this scale can helpfully guide modern interpreters attempting to determine where more or less obvious humor stands in 4:35–6:6. Thus, the more obvious the incongruity (provided it is not bounded by humor performance or script-availability), the more likely one of the script-oppositions in 4:35–6:6 will be humorous, and vice versa. For the present study, I will adopt a basic scale of three tiers, with tier one representing likely humorous script-oppositions and tier three representing potentially the most difficult to apprehend incongruities in the text. The script-oppositions and their placement in particular tiers are present in table 4.6 below.

When viewed from this perspective, one can detect a distinct humor profile in Mark 4:35–6:6. In this case, the threads WONDERWORKER/AVERAGE PERSON and PROPER/FOOLISH RESPONSE TO JESUS function as the primary engines of humor. These threads, in turn, operate in conjunction with occasional one-time jab lines as the most accessible tier of comedic incongruity. Moving one tier up to the second level, the script-oppositions have diminished and focus on issues such as satire, insider/outsider relationships, and a complicated use of the DEATH/SLEEP script-opposition. Ascending yet one tier higher, one reaches the most abstracted and/or riskiest forms of potential humor. At this level, the evangelist's humor potentially involves an esoteric satire on Caesar and the unraveling of the WONDERWORKER/AVERAGE PERSON thread. In addition to developing a humor profile, tracking the dimensionality of humor in Mark 4:35–6:6 reveals a significantly reduced number of jab lines on the surface level of the text: fifteen to be exact. Thus, one would expect, in the most optimal conditions, to generate a direct response from the audience only at these points. Yet given varieties in performers and audiences, this number would almost certainly drop further in live settings, thereby reducing the likelihood of performance disruption.

Having laid out the statistical data regarding script-oppositions along with their locality, frequency, and dimensionality in conjunction with potential humor limiters, it is now possible to address the rhetorical function of humor in each tier. Before turning to an examination of each tier, however, it is helpful to proceed with a general analysis of the various functions of humor.

Table 4.6. Tiers of Humor in Mark 4:35–6:6

Tier One	Tier Two	Tier Three
ASLEEP/ALERT	ROMAN IMPERIUM/ JESUS'S IMPERIUM	ROMAN IMPERIUM/ JESUS'S IMPERIUM
APPROPRIATE/INAPPROPRIATE RESPONSE TO JESUS (FEAR)	CIVILIZED/BARBARIAN	
KNOWLEDGE/IGNORANCE OF JESUS'S IDENTITY	WORSHIP/OPPOSITION	
SUCCESSFUL/FAILED EXORCIST	DEATH/SLEEP	
DOCTOR/INJURER		
KNOWLEDGE/IGNORANCE		
DEATH/SLEEP		
APPROPRIATE/INAPPROPRIATE RESPONSE TO JESUS (MOCKERY)		
SUCCESSFUL/FAILED HEALER		

Given humor's ubiquity, it is impossible to address all of its potential functions. Consequently, I will concentrate on humor's physiological, psychological, educational, and social dimensions.[17]

Physiological/Psychological

Humor studies has for some time attempted to understand the relationship between humor and physiological conditions in people. In particular, scholars have undertaken analyses of laughter that have yielded crucial

---

17. Don Nilsen, *Humor Scholarship: A Research Bibliography*, Bibliographies and Indexes in Popular Culture (Greenwood, 1993), 287–96. I have written about these categories and their role in New Testament humor elsewhere. For an analysis of humor effects in the rhetoric of Hebrews, see Jason Whitlark and Jon Carman, "Humor in Hebrews: Rhetoric of the *Ridiculus* in the Example of Esau," in *Practicing Intertextuality: Ancient Jewish and Greco-Roman Exegetical Techniques in the New Testament*, ed. Max J. Lee and B. J. Oropeza (Cascade, 2021), 246–66; and Whitlark and Carman, "Hearing Humor in the Invective against Esau: A Performance-Critical Analysis of Hebrews 12:16," in *Biblical Humor and Performance: Audience Experiences That Make Meaning*, ed. Peter Perry, Biblical Performance Criticism 20 (Cascade, 2023), 164–90.

insights into humanity's humorous proclivities.[18] To begin with, humans appear to be fundamentally hardwired for humor. Not only is the ability to laugh and smile one of the first things humans learn, developing this ability within two and sixth months of age, laughter itself is rooted in the brain "arising in subcortical, limbic, and brainstem areas and culminating in a 'laughing center' in the dorsal upper-pons."[19] Indeed, scientists have been able to elicit laughter and smiling by directly stimulating the amygdala or frontal cortex.[20] What is more, humans' ability to laugh arguably goes back to "early hominids between 4 and 2mya."[21] All told, the ability for humans to laugh appears to be an ancient trait of the species, linked as it is to fundamental, neurological structures.

There are several interesting physiological effects that stem from the experience of humor. While the oft-touted health-benefits of humor may be overstated (i.e., curing illnesses, extended life, etc.), there is evidence that suggests humor yields positive physiological benefits.[22] Indeed, "research reveals that a good sense of humor is related to muscle relaxation, control of pain and comfort, [and] positive mood states."[23] For instance, in one study, researchers showed a movie demonstrating industrial accidents to subjects while monitoring their stress levels. When the events had a humorous narration, opposed to a serious one, "the humor production group had the lowest negative affect, tension, and psychophysiological reactivity."[24] In another study, scientists explored the relationship between laughter and pain thresholds. Testing pain thresholds of subjects who watched both videos and plays, they concluded that "the results confirmed that when laughter is elicited, pain thresholds are significantly

---

18. I noted in chapter 2 that humor and laughter are not synonymous. However, unraveling the mystery of laughter goes a long way in understanding precisely how humor functions for humans given their frequent pairing.

19. Matthew Gervais and David Wilson, "The Evolution and Functions of Laughter and Humor: A Synthetic Approach," *The Quarterly Review of Biology* 80 (2005): 400. Gervais and Wilson distinguish between two types of laughter: Duchenne and non-Duchenne humor. For more on this, see pp. 395–430.

20. Barbara Wild et al., "Neural Correlates of Laughter and Humor," *Brain* 126 (2003): 2121–38.

21. Gervais and Wilson, "Evolution and Functions of Laughter and Humor," 396.

22. Robert Provine, *Laughter: A Scientific Investigation* (Penguin, 2000), 199.

23. Milicent Able, "Humor, Stress, and Coping Strategies," *Humor* 15 (2008): 365–81.

24. Provine, *Laughter*, 200.

increased, whereas when subjects watched something that does not naturally elicit laughter, pain thresholds do not change (and are often lower)."[25] The underlying cause for this seemed to be "the functional mechanism ... [of] muscular exertion involved in sustained laughter."[26] The physicality involved in laughter engendered endorphin release akin to other forms of exercise, yielding a higher pain threshold.

In addition to lowering negative affect and increasing endorphins, there is evidence to suggest that humor and laughter correlate to higher secretory immunoglobulin A (S-IgA) levels. In a study measuring the relationship between stress and daily events, Arthur and his colleagues used S-IgA as a correlating marker.[27] Through measurement of S-IgA in saliva, they determined that positive daily events yielded higher S-IgA levels.[28] Significantly, humor has the potential to act as a positive event. In several studies, scientists have "shown increase in sIgA parameters following exposure to various psychoregulatory manipulations (i.e. humor, relaxation)."[29] Consequently, humor has the potential to impact human physiology in a positive manner and can be used to therapeutic effect.

These studies illuminate the somatic nature of humor. Human beings are hardwired to produce and respond to this phenomenon. Vocal chords, facial muscles, neural networks, and brain structures all function concordantly when confronted with a humorous moment. Additionally, humor and laughter working in conjunction with one another are linked to positive physiological outcomes, lowering negative affect and tension, augmenting pain thresholds, releasing endorphins, and reducing physical stress. Similar outcomes obtain when looking at humor and psychology.

As researches have increasingly linked humor with positive health outcomes, they have also undertaken studies to measure its impact on psychological health. While they measure this in different ways, it is

---

25. R. I. M. Dunbar et al., "Social Laughter Is Correlated with an Elevated Pain Threshold," *Proceedings: Biological Sciences* 279 (2012): 1161–67.

26. Dunbar et al., "Social Laughter," 1165.

27. Arthur Stone et al., "Daily Events Are Associated with a Secretory Immune Response to an Oral Antigen in Men," *Healthy Psychology* 13 (1994): 440–46.

28. Stone et al., "Daily Events," 444–45.

29. S. Perera et al., "Increase in Salivary Lysozyme and IgA Concentrations and Secretory Rates Independent of Salivary Flow Rates Following Viewing of Humorous Videotape," *International Journal of Behavioral Medicine* 5 (1998): 118–28.

helpful to break down psychological health into three primary areas: emotional regulation (both positive and negative), stress management, and interpersonal relationship management.[30] Beginning with emotional regulation, several studies have demonstrated the potential for humor to act beneficially through the production of positive emotions and the amelioration of negative emotions. For instance, in a series of two experiments, Willibald Ruch determined that the use of clowning and humor yielded positive affect in participants.[31] Participants exposed to interactions with a clown experimenter or humorous videos reported significantly higher feelings of cheerfulness than groups who underwent serious tests.[32] Similar results are demonstrable in day-to-day situations. Researchers recruited 2500 Australians to participate in a field-test that researchers designed to gauge the efficacy of managerial humor in the workplace.[33] Over a period of ten days, participants filled out "experience sampling forms" within thirty minutes of humorous interaction with their manager. Based on these interactions and self-reporting, the authors of the study concluded "that managers' humor, when perceived by employees as positive, produces positive emotional reactions in employees."[34] In addition to producing positive emotions, researchers have linked humor to the reduction of negative emotions. Attila Szabo conducted a study involving thirty-nine university students and measured affect five minutes before and after three activities: running/jogging, watching stand-up comedy, and watching a serious documentary.[35] Participants in the study reported significant decreases in anxiety and distress upon watching twenty minutes of stand-up comedy, producing positive psychological outcomes similar to exercising.[36] Taken

---

30. Rod Martin, *The Psychology of Humor: An Integrative Approach* (Elsevier, 2007), 270.

31. Willibald Ruch, "State and Trait Cheerfulness and the Introduction of Exhilaration: A FACS Study," *European Psychologist* 2 (1997): 328–41.

32. Ruch, "State and Trait Cheerfulness," 334, 338.

33. Nilupama Wijewardena, Charmine Ej Härtel, and Ramanie Samartunge, "Using Humor and Boosting Emotions: An Affect-Based Study of Managerial Humor, Employees' Emotions and Psychological Capital," *Human Relations* 70 (2017): 1316–41.

34. Wijewardena, Härtel, and Samaratunge, "Using Humor and Boosting Emotions," 1330.

35. Attila Szabo, "The Acute Effects of Humor and Exercise on Mood and Anxiety," *Journal of Leisure Research* 35 (2003): 152–62.

36. Szabo, "Acute Effects of Humor," 152–162.

together, studies such as these demonstrate that humor has the potential, even if only for a limited time, to impact psychological states by generating positive affective states and dissipating negative affective states.[37]

Scholars also view humor as a helpful tool for dealing with psychological stress. They have conducted studies in the last few decades that increasingly confirm anecdotal evidence correlating humor's efficacy for dealing with stress. One reason for this potentially rests in humor acting as "an appraisal-focused coping strategy—where the cognitive-perceptual shifts associated with a humorous outlook permit the individual to achieve an alternate perspective and make more salubrious appraisals of an otherwise stressful situation."[38] Millicent Abel, in a study examining the relationship between college students and stress-management, reported that "the high sense of humor group appraised less stress and reported less current anxiety than a low sense of humor group despite experiencing a similar number of everyday problems."[39] Overall, those reporting higher senses of humor were able to cast stressful situations in a more positive light and weaken negative emotional states.[40] There is some evidence that this trend applies to high-stress situations as well. For instance, Michael Sliter, Aron Kale, and Zhen Yuan have shown that humor is associated with lower stress levels in firefighters, a population that regularly encounters traumatic stressors, while Smadar Bizi, Giora Keinan, and Benjamin Beit-Hellahmi have documented humor's role as a stress-reducer in soldiers undergoing combat training.[41] Notably, humor may also play a key role among populations that suffer from the stress of oppression and marginalization. When combined with a superiority-focus, humor allows a person to

> gain a sense of liberation and freedom from threat.... [Further] as a means of asserting one's superiority through playful aggression, humor

---

37. Martin, *Psychology of Humor*, 272–73.
38. Jon Roeckelein, *The Psychology of Humor: A Reference Guide and Annotated Bibliography* (Greenwood, 2002), 268.
39. Abel, "Humor, Stress, and Coping Strategies," 365.
40. Abel, "Humor, Stress, and Coping Strategies," 376.
41. Smadar Bizi, Giora Keinan, and Benjamin Beit-Hallahmi, "Humor and Coping with Stress: A Test under Real-Life Conditions," *Personality & Individual Differences* 9 (1988): 951–56; Michael Sliter, Aron Kale, and Zhen Yuan, "Is Humor the Best Medicine? The Buffering Effect of Coping Humor on Traumatic Stressors in Firefighters," *Journal of Organizational Behavior* 35 (2014): 257–72.

is a way of refusing to be overcome by the people and situations that threaten one's well-being.[42]

Researchers have documented such tendencies in American prisoners of war and Holocaust survivors.[43]

Finally, humor plays a role in bettering mental health through its capacity to facilitate interpersonal relationships. Studies have consistently demonstrated both the positive dimensions of social relationships and the negative consequences of loneliness.[44] Humor is critical in this area of mental health as it is fundamentally social in nature.[45] Indeed, research has shown that humor acts beneficially apropos of romantic pairing and friendships more broadly. Regarding romantic pairing, scholars have found correlations between relationship enjoyment and the use of affiliative humor (nonaggressive) and self-enhancing humor (coping: maintenance of positive outlook). In a study of dating relationships, Patricia Puhlick-Doris demonstrated that partners who used such humor yielded greater satisfaction in relationships than those who used maladaptive forms of humor.[46] A similar pattern is discernible for friendships. Several studies have found a correlation between affiliative and self-enhancing humor and stronger interpersonal relationships. Persons who use such humor have greater facility in making new friends, achieving intimacy, and even stress reduction by facilitating social bonding over difficult events.[47]

The studies above demonstrate the potential for humor to act beneficially for individuals. Humor not only yields positive outcomes

---

42. Martin, *Psychology of Humor*, 283.

43. Martin, *Psychology of Humor*, 287–88. The importance of humor is telling. In one anecdote from a study on American prisoners of war in Vietnam, humor was seen as so critical that prisoners would risk punishment from guards in order to tell a joke aloud to a fellow prisoner who appeared to be in need of cheering up (Martin, *Psychology of Humor*, 287).

44. Martin, *Psychology of Humor*, 298.

45. In his research, Provine has concluded that people "laughed *30 times* more when they were around others than when they were alone—laughter almost disappeared among solitary subjects not exposed to media stimulation" (Provine, *Laughter*, 45).

46. Patricia Puhlick-Doris, "The Humor Styles Questionnaire: Investigating the Role of Humor in Psychological Well-Being" (University of Western Ontario, 2004), 58–104.

47. Martin, *Psychology of Humor*, 299–303.

physiologically; rather, there appear to be several positive psychological outcomes as well, with humor potentially acting as an emotion regulator, stress-buffer, and facilitator of interpersonal relationships. While many of these studies are correlational, on the whole they suggest that humor can augment physical and mental health, especially for populations under duress—an especially helpful tool for those living in a fraught era of the Roman Empire. In addition to these positive outcomes, humor can also be useful as a pedagogical tool.

Humor and Education

In recent decades, scholars have conducted research into the intersection between humor and pedagogy. Anecdotes abound regarding humor's efficacy in this regard, with teachers and students alike praising its presence in the classroom. Notably, clinical studies have drawn similar conclusions. In particular, humor appears to engage students' attention and aid in the memory of content, make an instructor more likable, and generates a more relaxing learning atmosphere.

One of humor's most demonstrable pedagogical effects lay in its ability to gain the attention and interest of students. For example, studies of attentiveness by Jacob J. Wakshlag, Kenneth D. Day, and Dolf Zillman have revealed the efficacy of humor for gaining and maintaining the interest of children during educational programming.[48] John Banas and his colleagues, in a review of forty years of literature on humor and pedagogy, observe that "there has been a substantial amount of empirical support for humor's ability to attract and maintain attention."[49] Furthermore, there is evidence that suggests humor may play a crucial role in a person's ability to recall information. To begin with, research suggests that the use of humor in a narrative has a positive effect on an audience's memory of the performance.

In his review of literature regarding humor and memory, Keith Carlson states that "studies have generally supported the existence of a humorous

---

48. Jacob J. Wakshlag, Kenneth D. Day, and Dolf Zillman, "Selective Exposure to Educational Television Programs as a Function of Differently Paced Humorous Inserts," *Journal of Educational Psychology* 73 (1981): 27–32.

49. John Banas et al., "A Review of Humor in Educational Settings: Four Decades of Research," *Communication Education* 60 (2011): 131.

recall."[50] Additionally, broadly speaking, there are three areas of agreement regarding humor and recall: "First, the humor effect occurs in intentional and incidental memory situations.... Second, when participants are told to expect humorous material the humor effect still emerges.... Third, in free recall situations items that are recalled earlier tend to have higher humor ratings."[51] This last conclusion is especially noteworthy and has been borne out empirically as studies have demonstrated that humor, when used in educational settings, has the potential to increase recall of content.[52] Avner Ziv, in a highly influential pair of studies, has shown this correlation.[53] Ziv first enlisted 161 students to participate in a semester long experiment in control and experimental groups. The first group received no humor in their course instruction, while the latter did. This procedure was replicated once more, with 132 students participating in two groups. In both studies, the experimental groups outperformed the control groups on the final exam of the semester, though both groups had the same instructor.[54] Additionally, research has emphasized the importance of the relevance of humor to whatever content it may be enhancing. That is, for humor to be most effective in bolstering memory, it should be "closely tied to the ... content."[55]

Several studies have identified correlations between humor and likability of the person generating the humor. This holds consistently

---

50. Keith Carlson, "The Impact of Humor on Memory: Is the Humor Effect about Humor?" *Humor* 24 (2011): 22.

51. Carlson, "Impact of Humor on Memory," 22.

52. Peter Derks, John Gardner, and Rohit Agarwal, "Recall of Innocent and Tendentious Humorous Material," *Humor* 11 (1998): 5–19; Avner Ziv, "Teaching and Learning with Humor: Experiment and Replication," *The Journal of Experimental Education* 57 (1988): 5–15. Companies have perceived a similar effect in their analyses of advertising. When used effectively, humor has the ability to increase a consumer's attention, interest, and recall in a particular ad, and humorous advertising has been consistently shown to outperform nonhumorous advertising. On these effects, see Thomas Cline and James Kellaris, "The Influence of Humor Strength and Humor-Message Relatedness on Ad Memorability," *Journal of Advertising* 36 (2007): 56–67; Martin Eisend, "How Humor in Advertising Works: A Meta-Analytic Test of Alternative Models," *Marketing Letters* 22 (2011): 115–32; H. Shanker Krishnan and Dipankar Chakravati, "A Process Analysis of the Effects of Humorous Advertising Executions on Brand Claims Memory," *Journal of Consumer Psychology* 13 (2003): 230–45.

53. Ziv, "Teaching and Learning with Humor," 5–15.

54. Ziv, "Teaching and Learning with Humor," 12–14.

55. Martin, *Psychology of Humor*, 356.

for teachers where students often regard humorous instructors as more affable and engaging. For instance, Melissa Bekelja Wanzer and Ann Bainbridge Frymier conducted an analysis of student attitudes toward professors, asking 314 students enrolled at a midwestern University to fill out a humor-orientation scale for themselves and their professors.[56] They determined that students viewed professors who scored high on the humor-orientation scale more positively, even increasing students' self-perception of learning.[57] Similarly, in a survey of 115 graduate students, Stephen Fortson and William Brown asked respondents to "describe their best and worst instructor in 1 sentence."[58] Upon generating a taxonomy based on various responses, Fortson and Brown determined that, along with course organization, "a sense of humor … [was] perceived as most influencing best choice."[59] In short, the use of humor by instructors, particularly nonaggressive styles, has the potential to increase one's affability and establishes a stronger bond between teacher and student. This effect is particularly salient when considering learning environments.

One of humor's most potent tools in educational settings appears to be its ability to provide a comfortable setting in which to learn, due in part to the decreased distance between educator and student. This phenomenon, which scholars designate "immediacy," refers to the perceived distance between teachers and students and is facilitated by a wide range of behaviors ranging from classroom arrangement and body language to a professor's general demeanor.[60] Increased immediacy on the part of a professor generates a feeling of proximity and comfortability, which in turn has a measurable impact on student learning. In a meta-analytical review of eighty-one studies on immediacy, Paul Witt, Lawrence Wheeless, and Mike Allen concluded that there are statistically significant correlations

---

56. Melissa Bekelja Wanzer and Ann Bainbridge Frymier, "The Relationship between Student Perceptions of Instructor Humor and Students' Reports of Learning," *Communication Education* 48 (1999): 48–62.

57. Bekelja Wanzer and Bainbridge Frymier, "Students' Reports of Learning," 57.

58. Stephen Fortson and William Brown, "Best and Worst University Instructors: The Opinion of Graduate Students," *College Student Journal* 32 (1998): 572–76.

59. Fortson and Brown, "Best and Worst University Instructors," 572.

60. The concept itself is traceable to the work of Albert Mehrabian, who defined it as "the extent to which communication behaviors enhance closeness to and nonverbal interaction with another." Albert Mehrabian, "Some Reference and Measures of Nonverbal Behavior," *Behavior Research Methods and Instrumentation* 1 (1969): 213–17.

between immediacy and student learning.[61] This correlation appears to hold even across cultures.[62] In addition to these features of immediacy, studies have demonstrated a correlation between humor and immediacy. In their survey of 206 students, Joan Gorham and Diane Christophel asked students to track how teachers demonstrated a sense of humor, which they analyzed regarding potential connections to immediacy and learning outcomes.[63] Gorham and Christophel concluded that the use of humorous anecdotes and verbal/nonverbal humor resulted in higher scores from students and "was positively correlated with the frequency of his/her use of other verbal and nonverbal immediacy behaviors."[64] Other researches have reached similar conclusions. For instance, Bekelja Wanzer and Bainbridge Frymier observed that students in their study rated teachers with high humor orientation as more immediate than teachers with low humor orientation.[65] Ultimately, humor helps to enhance teacher immediacy, which, in turn, is "associated with more positive student attitudes toward the class and instructor, greater enjoyment and motivation, and greater perceived learning."[66]

Taken together, these studies demonstrate that humor likely enhances pedagogy and rhetoric. The use of humor by an instructor or speaker enables them to gain and hold an audience's attention, increase the likelihood of remembering content, generate a pleasurable atmosphere for listening and learning, and augment the bond between a speaker and audience. Humor is a powerful rhetorical tool with the

---

61. Paul Witt, Lawrence Wheeless, and Mike Allen, "A Meta-Analytic Review of the Relationship between Teacher and Student Learning," *Communication Monographs* 71 (2004): 184–207.

62. E.g. Scott Johnson and Ann Miller, "A Cross-Cultural Study of Immediacy, Credibility and Learning in the U.S. and Kenya," *Communication Education* 51 (2002): 280–92; Witt, Wheeless, and Allen, "Teacher and Student Learning," 197, support this conclusion: "Although some cultural differences do exist, substantial positive correlations between teacher immediacy and affective and perceived learning were indicated across almost all of the nationalities and cultural groupings that were examined."

63. Joan Gorham and Diane Christophel, "The Relationship of Teachers' Use of Humor in the Classroom to Immediacy and Student Learning," *Communication Education* 39 (1990): 46–62.

64. Gorham and Christophel, "Relationship of Teachers' Use of Humor," 58.

65. Bekelja Wanzer and Bainbridge Frymier, "Relationship between Student Perceptions," 58.

66. Martin, *Psychology of Humor*, 353.

potential to enhance a speaker's standing, an audience's engagement, and the reception of content.

Humor and Society

In addition to its physiological, psychological, and pedagogical value, humor plays a key role in social bonding. In fact, this is often seen as one of humor's most critical functions. While there are many dimensions to humor's social effects, it is helpful to look at four primary uses: group in-bonding, group out-bonding, promotion of social stability, and promotion of social change.[67] Humor plays a powerful role in group dynamics. To begin with, humor is potent as an agent of social bonding. In the context of communication, such bonding occurs by "identifying communicators with their audiences, [and] enhancing speaker credibility."[68] At a broader level of internal cohesion, humor is often efficacious by trading in the common values of a group. That is, humor will jest with those traits that are central to identity and put audiences in a position to emotionally identify with these traits either as an insider or an outsider—either getting a joke or not. Such activity occurs in both positive and negative ways. For instance, humor is often used in workplaces to build corporate identity. In a six week study by Jennifer Terrion and Blake Ashforth, they examined police officers during a professional development course.[69] Terrion and Ashforth observed the use of put-down humor by the officers and concluded that, as the humor shifted from "putdowns of oneself to put-downs of shared identities, external groups, and finally, each other ... [they moved] from a sense of disconnection to one of togetherness, with shared identity and purpose."[70] However, there can be a negative side to such cohesion. Frequently, humorous in-bonding also out-bonds, trading broadly in stereotypes and establishing cohesion at the expense of a one-dimensional Other. This occurs saliently in ethnic humor, where out-groups act as the target of jokes and are constantly depicted as dumb,

---

67. Nilsen, *Humor Scholarship*, 293.

68. John Meyer, "Humor as Double-Edged Sword: Four Functions of Humor in Communication," *Communication Theory* 10 (2000): 318.

69. Jennifer Terrion and Blake Ashforth, "From 'I' to 'We': The Role of Putdown Humor and Identity in the Development of a Temporary Group," *Human Relations* 55 (2002): 55–88.

70. Terrion and Ashforth, "From 'I' to 'We,'" 80.

boorish, dirty, lazy, et cetera. Even when framed in the ambiguous register of humor, social out-bonding along ethnic lines (or other stereotypes) can correlate to more serious discourse, in some cases opening the door to hostility and aggression.[71]

In addition to acting as a bonding agent, many people use humor as a way of policing group identity, values, and boundaries. In this way, humor can be an agent of social stability. It may be used to "embarrass or intimidate groups or individuals … [by using] irony, sarcasm, and satire."[72] Such techniques are especially frequent in teasing. Indeed, teasing is a particularly effective way of maintaining social norms by pointing out in a playful manner behaviors that are otherwise seen as transgressive. In doing so, a person teasing their target is able to correct an undesirable trait or activity without seemingly overly assertive or aggressive.[73] Notably, research has borne this out. In one study concerning the efficacy of irony, it was found that ironic statements were generally perceived to be more humorous and that "irony also seemed to mute the message conveyed by literal language: ironic criticism was perceived as less aggressive and insulting than direct criticism."[74] In sum, humor can play a mediating role in confrontative forms of discourse meant to enforce particular values, singling out groups or individuals in a less direct manner. Finally, humor can also act as a tool for social change by engaging in critique of social norms and values. Humor is particularly suited to subjects attempting to feel out discrete social values and where they might stand relative to such values. Because it trades in ambiguity, humor allows a subject to disguise probative queries on such matters a pathway to retreat to the safety of a different meaning if a given statement is perceived as offensive.[75] This makes humor an indispensable tool for a critic who wishes to establish or criticize a matrix of values. With an established matrix in hand, critics can engage in differen-

---

71. Giselinda Kuipers and Barbara van der Ent, "The Seriousness of Ethnic Jokes: Ethnic Humor and Social Change in the Netherlands, 1995–2012," *Humor* 29 (2016): 605–33.

72. Debra Long and Arthur Graesser, "Wit and Humor in Discourse Processing," *Discourse Processes* 11 (1988): 35–60, 53.

73. Dacher Keltner et. al., "Just Teasing: A Conceptual Analysis and Empirical Review," *Psychological Bulletin* 127 (2001): 229–48. This depends, of course, on the degree of aggression. Persons who are too aggressive in their teasing are often perceived as coercive if they attack a target too much.

74. Martin, *Psychology of Humor*, 120.

75. Martin, *Psychology of Humor*, 118.

tiation, "contrasting themselves with their opponents, their views with an opponents views, their own social group with others, and so on."[76] Indeed, many regard this as one of humor's greatest strengths—its ability to enact social change by means of isolating and humiliating particularly abhorrent practices or values.[77] Or humorists, satirists, and activists may draw a contrast between reality as it is and a humorous reality that could be, such as when Polish peace activists protested the regime of Slobodan Milošević by dressing as elves and carrying out carnivals, even responding to police interdiction with songs and kisses.[78]

While humor has many other social functions, those which I have outlined demonstrate just how potent it can be in society. Because of its proximity to incongruity, mirth, the ludicrous, et cetera, humor is especially adept at fostering and maintaining group boundaries and identities. Yet it is equally adroit when acting as an agent of social protest and change. With a general sketch of the physiological, psychological, educational, and social functions of humor in hand, I turn now to how these categories may apply to the first tier of humor in Mark 4:35–6:6.

Humor Functions in Mark 4:35–6:6

Tier One

The first tier of humor encompasses several script-oppositions bundled together in two major threads: WONDERWORKER/AVERAGE PERSON and PROPER/FOOLISH RESPONSE TO JESUS.[79] These, in turn, occasionally join with one-off script-oppositions and jab lines that further augment incongruity as the narratives develop. These two threads work in complementary fashion, conjointly crafting a portrait of Jesus's identity over against the conceptions characters in the narrative maintain regarding Jesus. All told, humor contributes to the evangelist's narrative and rhetorical strategies,

---

76. Meyer, "Humor as Double-Edged Sword," 321.

77. On the humorous work of John Callahan as a social critique of ableism, see Kara Shultz and Darla Germeroth, "Should We Laugh or Should We Cry? John Callahan's Humor as a Tool to Change Societal Attitudes Toward Disability," *Howard Journal of Communications* 9 (1998): 229–44.

78. Majken Sørensen, "Laughing on the Way to Social Change: Humor and Nonviolent Action Theory," *Peace and Change* 42 (2017): 128–56.

79. For the complete list of script-oppositions extant in tier one, see table 4.6.

raises critical points about Christology and opens up the affective range of the narrative to potentially include mirth and happiness.[80]

The first major thread in Mark 4:35–6:6 engages with the question of Jesus's status as a wonderworker, raising the possibility that he might be an average person. While this may seem strange, as the evangelist so transparently demonstrates Jesus's power and status in the opening chapters of the gospel, I have shown in the analysis so far that Jesus's status in the present miracle catena is more debatable than is sometimes observed. One sees this through particular script-oppositions in each of the major healing stories. In 4:35–41, the evangelist problematizes Jesus's status by stating that he was asleep even as he and the disciples were on the cusp of drowning. While there may be theological layering here (i.e., the sleeping-deity motif), the action is strikingly odd and commensurate with comedic texts that exploited sleep as a comical state. When one reads this passage against contemporary seastorm type-scenes, the contrast grows odder still and may have caused an audience to laugh at the sheer contrast. Yet the moment is fleeting, for immediately Jesus is roused by the disciples and just as quickly dispatches with the storm (4:38).

A similar pattern occurs in 5:1–20. In this case, the man with unclean spirits tests Jesus's abilities. He arguably mocks Jesus through his "worship" (5:6), speaks like an exorcist (5:7), and resists Jesus to the point that Jesus must obtain his name (5:9). This pericope contains the most atypical exorcism in the gospel in that Jesus is not in complete command of the situation. Indeed, he appears more like a typical or struggling exorcist than the Son of God who can command sea and wind. The incongruity rests here, not so much in a person struggling with a powerful demonic force, but rather in *Jesus* struggling with a powerful demonic force. This exceeds the bounds of every other exorcism account and stands as a strikingly odd contrast, strange enough to yield humor for persons in the evangelist's audience. Yet as before, the moment is fleeting, for Jesus ultimately banishes the demonic force and restores the man to health.

A similar pattern emerges in the account of Jairus's daughter, though here too it is more complicated than the first miracle story. The evangelist depicts Jesus as an ordinary or even farcical figure when denoting Jesus's

---

80. Throughout I have drawn upon previous work where I have explored rhetorical, sociological, and theological implications of humor in Mark 4:35–6:6. On these issues see Carman, "Jesus Asleep on the Job?," 99–117; and Carman, "Ancient Quackery," 31–46.

ignorance regarding the woman who touched him (5:30–32). Jesus's actions stand in contradiction to his preternatural knowledge elsewhere and, more obviously, are confusing given that a crowd is pressing upon him (a fact that the disciples emphasize in 5:31). The passage fills out the comical everyman portrait when Jesus declares to a crowd of mourners that the child they are mourning as dead is, in fact, only asleep (5:39). Indeed, Jesus's statement is so oddly incongruous that it elicits derisive laughter from those gathered to mourn (5:40). While the story will go on to vindicate Jesus's statement regarding the girl, with the evangelist folding the script-opposition of DEATH/SLEEP back on itself to generate humor, the incongruity is striking and may have been perceived as humorous from an audience of the gospel, perhaps even unintentionally.

Each of these miracle stories works hand in hand with a complementary thread: PROPER/FOOLISH RESPONSE TO JESUS. In every pericope, Jesus's activities elicit a response from others in the text that is humorously incongruous. In the opening pericope of 4:35–41, the disciples are the first targets of this humor. While scholars often depict them as being overly fearful in the midst of the storm, there is good reason to doubt this interpretation. Instead, the humorous response comes in the form of the disciples' cowardice after the fact. Rather than be grateful that Jesus saved them (4:39), the disciples instead "feared with a great fear." That they should fear the man who secured their safety is incongruous. What precisely did they expect in rousing Jesus in the first place? Ultimately, the disciples are still afraid even though they are now secure. The evangelist targets the disciples, bolstering Jesus's status through juxtaposition with the cowardly men standing beside him in the boat.

The narrative of the man afflicted by demons reads similarly to that of the storm, with the denizens of the area replacing the disciples. As the evangelist describes at the outset of the passage (5:1–5), the man is powerful. He lives in the tombs and cannot be bound even by chains. Miraculously, by the end of his encounter with Jesus, he is calm, clothed, and in possession of his agency (5:15). Yet rather than be joyous at this occurrence, the people who witness this become fearful and ask Jesus to leave the region (5:16–18). As with the disciples before them, the people become the target of the evangelist's humor regarding their ignorance.

This pattern occurs again with the account of Jairus and his daughter. Upon arriving at the scene and declaring that the young girl is sleeping rather than dead, the onlookers laugh at Jesus. Initially, their response to the incongruous statement makes some sense. It is only in light of what

Jesus accomplishes that it turns out to be an improper response. As those before them, the people also misunderstand Jesus and his capacity such that he throws them out and is vindicated when the girl is awakened (5:40–42). Interestingly, the threads of WONDERWORKER/AVERAGE PERSON and PROPER/FOOLISH RESPONSE TO JESUS are upended in the closing pericope.

The scene in 6:1–6 begins in a manner typical of the previous stories. Jesus arrives at his πατρίς and initially his kinfolk welcome him. Upon his teaching in a synagogue, they marvel at his wisdom and works of power (6:3). However, the narrative suddenly shifts, and the audience learns that the initial wonder signals incredulity rather than respect. The people are scandalized (6:3) and Jesus defends himself with a proverb about prophets and hospitality (6:4). After Jesus's repartee, he attempts to do works of power but finds himself unable to do so, with the exception that he can heal only a few (6:5). In response to this outcome, Jesus himself marvels at their unbelief (6:6).

This brief pericope is profound for its presentation of Jesus, especially in light of the previous stories. Within six short verses, the evangelist unravels the intertwined threads of WONDERWORKER/AVERAGE PERSON and PROPER/FOOLISH RESPONSE TO JESUS that have proven elemental thus far. Upon Jesus's failure to heal, it becomes clear that the people's response, while foolish in the larger theological scheme of Mark, is not unfounded. Per their instincts, Jesus is, in fact, just an average person, incapable of the great works and wisdom they have heard rumors about. For his part, the dialectic present in the previous stories ("can he/can't he") is upended. The man asleep in a storm, the typical or struggling exorcist, and the inadvertent healer who showed up late to a miracle—in every case Jesus rescues his reputation. Not so this time, and Jesus himself is shocked at the circumstances. By narrating the story in such a striking manner, the evangelist has flipped both scripts, raising the question: Is this humorous?

To a contemporary reader, the question of whether a gospel writer could make Jesus the target of humor may seem obvious. Presumably, the evangelists set out to craft persuasive portraits of Jesus. This would appear to rule out a priori any notions of the gospel writers making fun of Jesus. Furthermore, even if the Markan evangelist may bend Christology from time to time, surely the evangelist would not go so far as to make Jesus the target of scandalizing incongruity. This would seem like a natural bounding of humor. Yet there are currents in Second Temple Jewish and early Christian literature that are worth noting. In Tobit, Testament of Abraham, and Testament of Job, one finds protagonists who, on the one hand, are laudable figures and, on the other hand, farcical.[81] The authors have no trouble taking pious characters or great individuals from Israelite history and recasting them both as being the target of humor and as conveying significant theological or moral truths. Similarly, it is possible that the depiction of Jesus as a child in the Infancy Gospel of Thomas may have also been construed as humorous, even while making important points about Jesus's development from child to grown man.[82] These examples demonstrate that characters sacred to a community could be cast in a humorous light, even while making important truth claims. Given that such characters could be sources of humor and the evangelist's tendency to make Jesus a target of humor in the previous pericopes, it is possible the evangelist intended this last narrative to be humorous as well.

Taken together, the threads of WONDERWORKER/AVERAGE PERSON and PROPER/FOOLISH RESPONSE TO JESUS generate an engaging series of miracle stories that balance both serious and comical material. These two threads focalize the incongruities present in 4:35–6:6 through the filter of Jesus's identity. Whether the situations are too dire or the people are confused as to how best to respond, the first tier of humor in the miracle cycle is consistently engaging the question raised by the disciples in 4:41: "Who is this, that even the wind and the sea obey him?" The evangelist ends this cycle of powerful stories with a sharply incongruous pericope about Jesus's powerlessness, presenting a Jesus that, if only momentarily, looks very much like an average man, capable of only a handful of remarkable deeds. Naturally, if Jesus's identity is the central point around which humor orbits, it follows that one must consider what role humor plays in the narrative and its rhetorical impact.

---

81. For more on these works see Nancy Klancher, "The Male Soul in Drag: Women-as-Job in the Testament of Job," *JSP* 19 (2010): 225–45; Jared Ludlow, *Abraham Meets Death: Narrative Humor in the Testament of Abraham*, JSPSup 41 (Sheffield Academic, 2022); McCracken, "Narration and Comedy in the Book of Tobit," 401–18; Portier-Young, "Alleviation of Suffering in the Book of Tobit," 35–54. This is to say nothing of the jabs that Greco-Roman writers often take at the gods.

82. On depictions of Jesus's rage and his growth cycle, see Kristi Upson-Saia, "Holy Child or Holy Terror? Understanding Jesus' Anger in the Infancy Gospel of Thomas," *CH* 82 (2013): 1–39; Michael Whitenton, "The Moral Character Development of the Boy Jesus in the Infancy Gospel of Thomas," *JSNT* 38 (2015): 219–40.

Humor, Performance, and Rhetorical Strategy

The presence of humor in the miracle cycle of Mark 4:35–6:6 impacts the performance of the Markan narrative in several critical ways. To begin with, the two threads that weave through these pericopes generate a form of comical drama. The evangelist crafts a pattern of Jesus initially presented as an everyman who is then able to turn and deliver miracles. Rhetorically, such a pattern inserts tension into the stories by subtly or openly raising the question of whether Jesus will, in fact, act as he has in the previous chapters. Remarkably, this pattern appears to be rarely discussed.[83] It is taken for granted that there is no real tension regarding Jesus's standing or capacity to work miracles. Yet such a reading ignores the final scene of 6:1–6 where Jesus struggles with acts of power. By introducing a temporary crisis tinged with comedy, the evangelist generates an expanding and contracting story that is far more engaging than if Jesus were simply capable of doing anything at anytime.

In addition to its dramatic role, the use of humor likely functions as making the present stories more memorable. As noted above, in pedagogical settings, adding humor to one's performance has the potential to increase content recall. By joining particular concepts to humor, one forges a link between content and audience. Yet one critical finding in humor studies is the fact that, for humor to aid memory, it ought to be related to one's topic. Humor that is peripheral to important content can have an adverse effect, as an audience may remember the salient comedy without a connection back to the content. What is striking in 4:35–6:6 is the degree to which the humor consistently revolves around the question of Jesus's identity. To be sure, there are one-liners that may obliquely refer to the topic of identity. Yet on the whole, the surface level humor

---

83. The following scholars do not dwell at length on the issue of Jesus's powerlessness or make no connection to the pattern for which I have argued in the previous miracle episodes. Mary Ann Beavis, *Mark*, Paidea (Baker Academic, 2011), 99–100; Bolt, *Jesus' Defeat of Death*, 91; Boring, *Mark*, 166–67; Broadhead, *Teaching with Authority*, 115; Camery-Hogatt, *Irony in Mark's Gospel*, 140–41; Yabro Collins, *Mark*, 292; Geyer, *Fear, Anomaly, and Uncertainty*, 185–205; Donahue and Harrington, *Mark*, 186–89; Dwyer, *Motif of Wonder*, 120–24; Guelich, *Mark*, 311–13; Macdonald, *Allegiance, Opposition, and Misunderstanding*, 151; van Iersel, *Mark*, 92–93; Marcus, *Mark*, 379–80; Neufeld, *Mockery and Secretism*, 144–54; Stephen Knapp, "He Could Do No Mighty Deed There.... Mark 6:1–6," *Proceedings: Eastern Great Lakes and Midwest Biblical Societies* 12 (1992): 155–66.

of 4:35–6:6 turns on incongruities regarding Jesus's abilities or the incongruous response of people around him. By hitting this theme consistently and comically, the evangelist raises the likelihood that audiences of this gospel would remember the core of these stories. Indeed, it is not difficult to recall the disciples' cowardice, a man possessed by a demonic force using the words of an exorcist, or Jesus fumbling in a crowd to see who touched him and declaring a dead girl asleep. The link between humor, performance, and memory, while having empirical grounding, generally remains beyond considerations of Markan composition and performance.[84] The present analysis indicates that more attention should be given to such concerns. Since it is the case that various scholars have noticed traces of humor in the miracle catena, due consideration must be given to the ways in which this element enhances both the impact of the narrative on the audience through dramatic tension and memory enhancement.

Another factor to consider when analyzing humor in the miracle cycle is the way in which its use facilitates a connection between the author and audience or performer and audience. While Markan scholars have keyed in on the narrative-critical notion of the evaluative point of view of the narrator and traced ways in which the rhetoric of the gospel pushes readers or audiences to accept this as normative for understanding Jesus, by not exploring humor and performance scholars have missed out on a critical way in which the gospel might accomplish this rhetorical task. The education research noted above underscores the ways in which humor builds a link between teachers and students, facilitating immediacy between the two, generating a congenial and affirming atmosphere, and making students more receptive to a teacher's perspective. Such effects are likely at play in gospel performance. By creating comical moments in the gospel, the positive feelings engendered by humor may collapse the distance between author/performer and audience, potentially making them more receptive to the message that the evangelist is putting forward in the text.

Related to increasing the persuasive efficacy of the author/performer is the fact that humor, in its social dimensions, builds in-group/out-group dichotomies in a tangible and visceral way. Studies have demonstrated that being in a group enhances the experience of humor. This enjoyment is

---

84. Iverson, "Incongruity, Humor, and Mark," 2–19 n. 51, notes that humor maintains a variety of functions in gospel presentation including as a memory aid.

often expressed somatically in smiles, laughter, or glancing around to see if others are laughing too. Consequently, there is pressure to be in on a joke, rather than out. Indeed, these lexical designations frequently function as a short-hand for the social reality that to be in on a joke is to be an insider to a group, and vice versa. In the present passage, the evangelist pushes a particular way of thinking about and understanding Jesus's identity, faith, and discipleship (among other themes). In so doing, the narrative directs its audience to be part of the larger group who gets the jokes in the pericopes and who, ultimately, maintains a proper understanding of the issues and values presented therein.

Finally, it is critical to note that humor in the miracle cycle is intentionally targeting a broader range of emotions than scholars generally consider when reading the Gospel of Mark. Indeed, apropos of the Markan Gospel, joy/mirth is not often seen as a primary affective dimension elicited by the narrative.[85] Even robust treatments of emotion in the gospel do not include an emotional state commensurate with humor.[86] Yet as the present study demonstrates, emotional mapping of the Markan text ought to include some elements that correspond to humor as this trait permeates the miracle cycle of 4:35–6:6.

Ultimately, at the level of rhetoric and performance, humor operates in a number of critical ways: (1) humor helps sustain a form of drama in the unfolding question of whether Jesus can or cannot accomplish certain acts of power (i.e., "can he/can't he?"); (2) because it focuses on the topic of Jesus's identity, humor augments the ability of audiences to recall pericopes at a later time; (3) humor acts as a crucial aid in persuasion, inviting the audience to side with the author/performer of the gospel in a visceral manner so that they might be part of those who are in on the jokes of the narrative; (4) humor activates an affective dimension of mirth and joy alongside other emotions such as awe and wonder. In addition to considering the impact of humor on the gospel's rhetoric and performance, there

---

85. Two excellent treatments of emotion in the miracle cycle are found in Bolt, *Jesus' Defeat of Death* and Geyer, *Fear, Anomaly, and Uncertainty*. Both monographs take very seriously the emotional dynamics of Mark's audience and how they would have been impacted by the gospel. I will say more about this below, but it is key to note here that the emotional states they target are those of fear, wonder, or awe. Mirth or happiness do not figure in their accounts.

86. Michael Whitenton, "Feeling the Silence: A Moment-by-Moment Account of Emotions at the End of Mark (16:1–8)," *CBQ* 78 (2016): 272–89.

are two elements that the comic nature of the miracle cycle enhances that bear further discussion: Christology and affect.

Humor and Christology

The present cycle of miracles plays directly into one of the most discussed elements of the Markan Gospel: Christology.[87] Since William Wrede's seminal work advancing his notion of the messianic secret, scholars have wrestled over how to make sense of Markan Christology.[88] One of the issues central to the christological debate concerns how best to balance the elements of power and suffering in the narrative. The gospel is, on the one hand, a story about the powerful Son of God; however, this portrait contrasts with Jesus's suffering, a point Jesus himself returns to poignantly in his passion predictions throughout Mark 8–10.[89] This has led scholars to view the second half of the gospel as qualifying the acts of power in the first half of the gospel. As Susan Henderson observes, there is a "broad consensus of scholarship [that] maintains that only in light of the cross do the disciples (and thus the readers) gain full disclosure of Jesus' identity, which is that of a crucified and raised messiah."[90] It is beyond the present study to weigh in on this aspect of the christological debate. Whatever way one is inclined to construe the manner in which the halves of Mark characterize Jesus, one thing has gone unnoticed—humor in the miracle

---

87. For a helpful survey of christological issues in Mark, see Max Botner, "What Has Mark's Christ to Do with David's Son? A History of Interpretation," *CurBR* 16 (2017): 50–70; Daniel Johannson, "The Identity of Jesus in the Gospel of Mark: Past and Present Proposals," *CurBR* 9 (2010): 364–93; and Andrew Kelley, "Miracles, Jesus, and Identity: A History of Research Regarding Jesus and Miracles with Special Attention to the Gospel of Mark," *CurBR* 13 (2014): 82–106.

88. William Wrede, *The Messianic Secret*, Library of Theological Translations (Clarke, 1971).

89. Bruce Longenecker, "Mark's Gospel for the Second Church in the Late First Century," in *In the Fullness of Time: Essays on Christology, Creation, and Eschatology*, ed. Daniel Gurtner, Grant Macaskill, and Jonathan Pennington (Eerdmans, 2016), 210, highlights this tension well. From the middle of the gospel forward, through Jesus's prophesies about his impending martyrdom and teachings, the presentation of power gets dramatically tempered: "Evidently Jesus' power requires a radical revision of expectations and lifestyle."

90. Susan Henderson, *Christology and Discipleship in the Gospel of Mark*, SNTSMS 135 (Cambridge University Press, 2006), 9.

cycle of 4:35–6:6 raises the possibility that qualifications of Jesus's power are already underway well before the turn to the second half of the gospel.

It is commonplace to locate the turning point of Markan Christology in 8:22–10:52. There are good reasons for this. One finds in this block of material Peter's confession that Jesus is the Christ (8:27–30), characterizing discipleship as a way of suffering (8:34–9:1), the transfiguration of Jesus (9:2–8), and three passion predictions laying out Jesus's dismal fate (8:31–33; 9:30–32; 10:32–34). There is, thus, a marked emphasis on the humiliation and suffering of Jesus in conjunction with revelations about his identity. Yet this tension is already present in the material leading up to this turning point in the gospel. Furthermore, it plays a more significant role than scholars generally suppose.[91] It is not simply the case that there are moments of "humanity in the first portions of the Gospel."[92] Rather, at least in the case of 4:35–6:6, the tension of Jesus's humanity and preternatural power are, in fact, a driving dynamic in the entire miracle cycle. By paying close attention to the comedic incongruities in these stories, the question of "can he/can't he?" becomes a live question, which, in turn, paves the way for the truly stunning events of 6:1–6 where Jesus can only perform a handful of miracles. By unraveling the thread concerning Jesus's identity, the evangelist offers audiences a glimpse into what a powerless Jesus looks like. The narrative adumbrates what Jesus will experience as the dramatic action of the gospel shifts into higher gear and culminates in the tragic death of Jesus who perishes helpless, friendless, and in agony.

Careful attention to the use of humor in 4:35–6:6 thus nuances discussions apropos of tension in Markan Christology. Even before Jesus will qualify his divine sonship in the direction of humiliation and suffering, there are already signs of distress in Jesus's power. Power and powerlessness are bound together in incongruities of this miracle cycle that generate humor as Jesus pulls back from the brink of appearing inert, only for the cycle to become upended in an incongruity focused on Jesus's inability to heal those without faith.

In addition to the tension present in Markan Christology regarding power and suffering, scholars generally have not commented on the

---

91. Scholars that focus on the material here often key in on positive appraisals of Jesus's power rather than the tension generated by extant incongruities. So, for example, Achtemeier, "Origin and Function of the Pre-Marcan Miracle Catenae," 198–220; Broadhead, *Teaching with Authority*, 88–116; Dwyer, *Motif of Wonder*, 92–144.

92. Philip Davies, "Mark's Christological Paradox," *JSNT* 35 (1989): 3–18.

potential comedic elements surrounding questions of Jesus's identity. There is no doubt in Markan scholarship that misunderstanding of Jesus's identity plays a critical role in the narrative. How best to interpret this feature of the narrative remains unresolved. Notably, the presence of humor in the miracle cycle raises an interesting question for this discussion: To what extent might the question of Jesus's identity and misapprehensions concerning his identity be informed by or interpreted in light of comedic texts? For instance, there have been attempts to read scenes of recognition in light of a tragic or Aristotelian framework.[93] What scholars have not considered is to what degree either evangelist or audience might be influenced by comedic texts or stories. As I noted in the previous chapter, misunderstanding is one of the most prevalent tropes in Greco-Roman New Comedy. Indeed, *anagnorsis*, while a common element of tragedies, is equally critical to the action and drama of comedies. Most of the plays in New Comedy generate their humor from fundamental misunderstandings regarding the identity of protagonists, with many culminating in a dramatic, lighthearted reveal and resolution at the end of the play. *Menaechmi* is an excellent example of this with twin brothers getting into increasingly farcical scenarios because of their mistaken identities.

Given that mistaken identity plays such a key role in comedies, when flexing the theme of identity and misunderstanding, Markan texts may be composed or interpreted in light of such comedies. This allows moments of misunderstanding in 4:35–6:6 to be read in a new light. When people around Jesus fail to recognize who is in their midst, not only are these profound moments of irony. Rather, they are very possibly also moments of humor, with the audience being in on the joke time and again, while those who should know better fail to recognize Jesus. Finally, though it is beyond the scope of the present study, it is worth noting that it is possible that the messianic secret, however one might interpret it with respect to the larger narratival scheme, may itself be a consistent source of humor at various points throughout the narrative.[94]

---

93. Adam Wright, "Recognizing Jesus: A Study of Recognition Scenes in the Gospel of Mark," *JGRChJ* 10 (2014): 174–93.

94. Neufeld, *Mockery and Secretism*, 90, offers an intriguing interpretation of the messianic secret and Jesus's characterization throughout the gospel. Rather than viewing secrecy as a well-constructed theological leitmotif, Neufeld raises the possibility that the Evangelist has intentionally created an ambivalent portrait of Jesus.

Humor and Affect

When considering the rhetorical impact of the miracle cycle in 4:35–6:6, scholars generally key in on the emotions of fear or awe. Two authors in particular have offered illuminating readings of the pericopae in light of such emotions: Peter Bolt and Geyer. In their respective monographs, Bolt and Geyer underscore the themes of fear, disease, and death that are present throughout the Markan Gospel and that take startling shape in the present stories. Bolt focuses on the experienced reality of physical and spiritual oppression, paying special attention to healing and exorcism accounts and the ways in which Markan audiences are drawn into these stories.[95]

In particular, Bolt highlights the fear not only of disease, but rather death itself—a fear available to everyone in antiquity. It is precisely in this light that the Gospel of Mark's message becomes so powerful: "Death is no longer the only thing hovering on the horizon of human life.... In the midst of a world crying out in its suffering and mortality, 'Don't you care that we are perishing?', Jesus has defeated death."[96] Geyer offers a similar reading. Operating with the category of the "anomalous frightful," he too focuses on accounts of demonic oppression, disease, and death.[97] Thus, for Geyer, the "Gospel of Mark presents to us material that emphasizes the uncertain, the dreadful, the impure, and the uncanny."[98]

Bolt and Geyer helpfully foreground the broader context in which the miracle stories of 4:35–6:6 would be heard and the potential emotional response that a performer might elicit in rehearsals of the pericopae. Analysis of the Roman socioeconomic context confirms such analyses. As Longenecker notes in his discussion of poverty in ancient Rome, while there was a socioeconomic scale in the Roman Empire that ran the gamut from those below subsistence all the way to imperial elites, most lived in economic uncertainty.[99] Indeed, it is possible that roughly 55 percent of those in the

---

95. Bolt, *Jesus' Defeat of Death*.

96. Bolt, *Jesus' Defeat of Death*, 279.

97. Geyer, *Fear, Anomaly, and Uncertainty*, 38, defines the anomalous frightful as "a strange event that causes fear." Essentially, Geyer probes the worldview of antiquity, paying particular attention to those phenomena that might be considered uncanny within such a *weltanschauung* and the emotions they might elicit.

98. Geyer, *Fear, Anomaly, and Uncertainty*, 271.

99. Bruce Longenecker, "Exposing the Economic Middle: A Revised Economy Scale for the Study of Early Christianity," *JSNT* 31 (2009): 243–78; Longenecker, *Remember the Poor: Paul, Poverty, and the Greco-Roman World* (Eerdmans, 2010),

Roman Empire were either at or below subsistence with an additional 27 percent maintaining stability just above it.[100] Essentially, life in the advanced agrarian economy of Rome, while it brought new wealth to many, was home to endemic strife and poverty: "Economic exploitation was inherent within the structures of Greco-Roman agrarianism, not least with regard to the potential for elite acquisitiveness."[101] What is more, the challenges of life in the empire affected everyone. Though political instability, food shortages, and economic depressions impacted those at subsistence or below the hardest, elites were not immune to such harms. They too were subject to disease, demonic or ghostly afflictions, political intrigue, and martial violence. All told, the Roman Empire was a challenging environment in which to thrive. This raises interesting implications for reading Mark 4:35–6:6.

Bolt and Geyer rightly emphasize the dark character of the narratives in this miracle cycle. Fear of sea-travel, demons, disease, and death were all perennial concerns that would have plagued early Jesus followers. They would have heard stories about such events or experienced maladies themselves, which, in turn, would impact the ways in which they might respond to such narratives. Moreover, a gospel emphasizing Jesus's power over such realities could quite plausibly have inspired hope and awe as many scholars have asserted. It is precisely in this context where humor may have been particularly helpful.

As I noted above, humor has physiological, psychological, and social effects with great potential to act as a bulwark against stressful life events. Researchers have linked humor and laughter to positive health outcomes. Somatically, humor has been linked to positive physiological responses including stress reduction, muscle relaxation, and increased pain tolerance. Psychologically, humor enhances emotional regulation, stress management, and interpersonal relationship management. Socially, humor engenders social bonding and group identity building. These positive aspects of humor offer new ways to consider the reception of the Markan Gospel by its audiences. By balancing stories that confront lived fears of Jesus followers with humor, the evangelist confronts such experiences with a powerful tool. Humor allows one to laugh in the context

---

36–59; Longenecker, "Socio-economic Profiling of the First Urban Christians," in *After the First Urban Christians: The Social Scientific Study of Pauline Christianity Twenty-Five Years Later*, ed. Todd Still and David Horrell (T&T Clark, 2009), 36–59.

100. Longenecker, *Remember the Poor*, 53.
101. Longenecker, *Remember the Poor*, 57.

of nature's unpredictable fury, demonic oppression, sickness, and finally death itself. The very act of reciting these stories not only reinforces the proclamation of Jesus's power, it evokes a somatic response in the form of greater relaxation, increased positive mood and decreased negative mood, and unity with a strong social bond wherein the trials and travails of life are encountered with solidarity. Humor has the potential to blunt the gravity of pain, to put this universal experience at a distance where it can be quantified and diminished through shared mirth. Indeed, performances of this portion of the gospel may themselves be therapeutic acts where the audience can laugh at pain, disease, and death, even if only for a moment. The evangelist underscores these effects through the striking move in the final pericope to depict Jesus as nearly powerless. By refracting the theme of Jesus's powerlessness through a comical lens, the evangelist is able to introduce or engage a troubling affective dynamic for audiences, namely, the problem of suffering on account of conviction. Humor allows this theme to be broached, but to also be kept at arms length. Not only does this prepare an audience for the more difficult passages ahead, it also engages their own affective core to the extent that Jesus's narrative reflects back to them a situation of suffering.

Conclusion

The humor in tier one represents the most obvious or accessible humor in the miracle cycle of 4:35–6:6, focalized through the topic of Jesus's identity and responses to Jesus by narrative actors. The presence of humor in these stories contributes to the narrative and rhetorical strategies of the evangelist, acting as a creator of tension, increasing the likelihood of recall, enhancing the evangelist/performers' standing with audiences, while inviting the audience to be in on the jokes and opening an affective dimension of mirth and joy. Additionally, humor raises new insights into issues of Christology and affect. Regarding the former, the humor of the miracle cycle complicates the question of Jesus's power earlier than scholars often recognize. Concerning the latter, tracking humor brings an entirely new affect of mirth into conversation with readings that highlight fear, awe, and wonder in the text.

Tier Two

The first tier of Markan humor in 4:35–6:6 focuses on Jesus's identity by generating comedic moments from twin threads focused on the topic. The second tier of humor is not as unified in its themes. It is made up of the following script-oppositions: ROMAN IMPERIUM/JESUS'S IMPERIUM, CIVILIZED/BARBARIAN, WORSHIP/OPPOSITION, and DEATH/SLEEP. Of these, the DEATH/SLEEP and CIVILIZED/BARBARIAN script-oppositions qualify as threads while the ROMAN IMPERIUM/JESUS'S IMPERIUM script-oppositions offer humor sustained over a short distance in the text. As noted above, I have placed these script-oppositions into the second tier as they comprise more veiled, abstract, or less *prima facie* humor. Significantly, two of the three primary script-oppositions continue to build on the question of Jesus's identity (ROMAN IMPERIUM/JESUS'S IMPERIUM, DEATH/SLEEP), while one focuses on a different theme altogether (CIVILIZED/BARBARIAN).

Humor and Imperium

The second tier script-opposition of ROMAN IMPERIUM/JESUS'S IMPERIUM is extant in the second miracle story and concerns Jesus's interaction with the man afflicted by a demonic horde. In 5:9, the maleficent force gives its name as "Legion," thereby activating a script of Roman military might and imperium that, while initially powerful, fails to gain control over Jesus. Notably, many scholars have perceived comical elements in the story, while others have commented on the political and satirical nature of the account.[102] Frequently, however, these two trajectories do not meet. Scholars rarely bring out the full impact of humor working in tandem with political critique in the present passage. A notable exception to this is the work of Carter who, in commenting upon the ways the evangelist intentionally cross-genders Roman military might in order to "un-man" it, draws upon comedies to bolster his reading.[103]

As I noted in the previous chapter, there are potentially three jab lines that activate the script-opposition of ROMAN IMPERIUM/JESUS'S IMPERIUM: 5:10, 12, and 13. In each instance, the evangelist breaks down the image of the formerly stalwart force, incapable of being bound. The once mighty Legion is said to beg Jesus for the right to stay in the local-

---

102. On the humorous nature of the passage, see LaMarche, *Evangile de Marc*, 145; Marcus, *Mark*, 350, and Tolbert, *Sowing the Gospel*, 167. On the political/satirical dynamics, see Derrett, "Contributions to the Study of the Gerasene Demoniac," 2–17; Leander, *Discourses of Empire*, 201–19; Adam Winn, *Reading Mark's Christology under Caesar: Jesus the Messiah and Roman Imperial Ideology* (Intervarsity, 2018), 81–85.

103. Carter, "Cross-Gendered Romans," 139–55.

ity and must plead for a porcine host, which they instantly destroy upon their habitation.

The use of humor in the present passage is multifaceted. To begin with, as was the case with humor extant throughout tier one, comedic elements in the present pericope likely augment the story's memorability and overall performance of the text. Additionally, the evangelist has possibly adopted humor in this passage for the express purpose of political protest. While it is an open question whether humor has the ability to act as an effective agent of political change, people have used humor to critique political regimes throughout most of documented history.[104] In this way, humor can function as a tool for physiological and psychological stress reduction. As with the problems listed in tier one, imperial occupation and domination carried its own forms of trauma and pain. For any among Markan audiences who may have been subject to the wrong end of the Roman fasces, portraying Roman imperial power as weak could easily act as a moment of empowerment and reprieve. Even for elites, this might be the case. Not every reification of imperial authority was celebrated even by powerful Roman citizens who were themselves often victims of its capriciousness. Life at the upper echelons of the empire was exceedingly dangerous, with people or their family members often assassinated, compelled to suicide, or imprisoned at the slightest change in the political wind. Indeed, even emperors did not escape imperium's fickle nature, as they were often killed in internal plots or martial exercises. Thus, if there were elites in an audience of Markan performance, it is possible they may have found relief in such a depiction of Roman power.

Finally, the evangelist's injection of humor into the present story also draws upon the social nature of humor. The evangelist contrasts the presence and power of Jesus as a calming, restorative force while simultaneously aligning Roman imperium with the destructive tendencies of

---

104. Majken Sørensen, *Humour in Political Activism: Creative Nonviolent Resistance* (Palgrave Macmillan, 2016), 201–16. Notably, this attitude is observable on the ground in ancient Pompeii. Longenecker, *In Stone and Story*, 139, highlights this tendency in imperial Rome by noting the mocking depiction of Aeneas, his kin, and even Romulus in a Pompeian home: "These two parodies of the famous story of Aeneas exhibit a low-grade form of resistance of the narrative that was supported by huge amounts of pro-Roman money that flowed into Vesuvian towns." For further analysis of anti-imperial humor and the material culture of Pompeii, see Clarke, *Looking at Laughter*, 133–62.

the monstrous demons. The text is not impartial, instead encouraging the audience by the end of the story to laugh and deride one kind of imperium (kingdom of Rome), while applauding a better form of imperium (kingdom of God).[105] The evangelist utilizes humor as a form of social control by pushing those in the audience who catch the subtext of the narrative to side with Jesus's imperium rather than that of Rome. Significantly, this also contributes to a decisive issue in the first tier of humor: Jesus's identity.

Humor and Barbarians

The second major script-opposition the evangelist deploys in the second tier of humor involves the CIVILIZED/BARBARIAN script-opposition and is located in the story of the man afflicted by Legion. The script-opposition potentially plays off of stereotypes regarding foreigners. Beyond this, it is difficult to tell whether the evangelist is trading in generic attitudes towards uncivilized individuals living in the hinterland or seeks to press a JEW/GENTILE distinction to humorous ends. The story never designates individuals in the narrative as gentiles. However, scholars frequently point to the geographic designation on the other side of the Sea of Galilee, the presence of pig-herders, and proximity to the Decapolis as details which could suggest a gentile locale.[106] With this in mind, some have suggested that ethnic tensions potentially lie in the background of the narrative and provide humor along ethnic lines with gentiles acting as the target of humor for their reaction to Jesus.[107] Beyond these observations, little is made regarding the function of humor or its possible recurrence.

With respect to rhetorical impact, the humor here appears to function in a more nuanced way than is generally noticed. Often, scholars note the initial failure of the onlookers in 5:1–20 and say little more about the

---

105. Carter, "Cross-Gendered Romans," 154, makes a similar observation: "This link, of course, is not neutral. Most obviously, it constructs Roman power as demonic.... This fantasy scene cross-genders Rome and its military might, mocked and shamed by male humor that trades in imperial-military, gendered, and sexual innuendo."

106. Several scholars posit a gentile setting for the narrative. So Boring, *Mark*, 149; Yarbro Collins, *Mark*, 267 (though she notes that the "gentileness" of the story should not be overemphasized); Donahue and Harrington, *Gospel of Mark*, 170; Marcus, *Mark*, 341.

107. So Donald Juel, *A Master of Surprise: Mark Interpreted* (Fortress, 1994), 347.

correct response of people at the end of the pericope.[108] Yet the evangelist seems to be making a very intentional point about stages of development regarding the onlookers, possibly doing so in a humorous fashion. The local denizens beyond the sea initially present as ignorant pig herders afraid of the man plagued by demons *after* he has been healed. However, by the end of the story, they marvel at Jesus's work as preached to them by one of their own. In both the subject matter and the rhetorical *telos*, one sees in this transformation a direct invoking of humor's social dimensions. To begin with, the evangelist utilizes a garden-path form of humor. The audience is misdirected initially by the concession of a stereotyped understanding of barbarians only to have this initial heuristic subverted by the jab line at the end of the story wherein the audience realizes that the people are as spiritually capable as the people of Capernaum who witness a similar event (1:21–28). The rhetorical aim is likely didactic, with the evangelist driving the audience to accept the evaluative point of view that it is not only those in the home territory of Jesus who marvel at his work, but also those working in the hinterlands across the Sea of Galilee as well.

It is hard to say for certain whether the script-opposition here is focused on the more abstracted CIVILIZED/BARBARIAN incongruity or a JEW/GENTILE distinction. If the former is at play, then it is possible that the evangelist is challenging the audience to be more open to the abilities of individuals who live beyond typical civilized spaces or who society deems civilized. This could run the gamut from individuals perceived to be for-

---

108. E.g. Beavis, *Mark*, 94, who views this response as an echo of the disciples' cowardice; Donahue and Harrington, *Gospel of Mark*, 167, characterize the people as "suspicious"; Guelich, *Mark*, 284, suggests that, given the final form of the text, the townspeople are upset at their financial loss; Marcus, *Mark*, 346, states that their reaction is "negative, which is unnatural." The fear here is sometimes appraised positively. Yabro Collins, *Mark*, 273, follows Dwyer, *Motif of Wonder*, 113, in viewing this as the proper response to epiphanic experience. Yet this perspective does not take into consideration just how unique such an outcome was in healing stories from antiquity. Werner Kahl, *New Testament Miracle Stories in Their Religious-Historical Setting*, FRLANT 163 (Vandenhoeck & Ruprecht, 1994), 236, in his religious-historical analysis of miracles states that "the motif of the *rejection* of the bearer of numinous powers in the gospels, [is] unique among ancient healing miracle traditions." Marcus, *Mark*, 346, noting Theissen's work makes a similar observation: "This repudiation … is an unusual ending for a miracle story; such stories usually end with acclaim, not rejection. Theissen says that he knows of no analogies outside of the NT, and even within the NT he can only cite distant parallels."

eign to an URBAN/RURAL dichotomy with the city imagined as a civilized space and the country less so. Scholars who emphasize the JEW/GENTILE dichotomy may understand the humor here to play upon in-group/out-group dynamics in a challenge to a certain kind of halakhic perspective of gentiles, pushing the audience to have a more expansive view of the spiritual capacity of gentiles. However, without better information regarding the identity of author/audience, it is challenging to tease out social implications further.

Humor and Sleep

The third major locus of humor in the second tier resides in the story of Jairus's daughter (5:21–43) and builds upon the script-opposition of DEATH/SLEEP found in the latter half of the story (5:35–43). In the midst of this seemingly tragic moment, a potentially humorous script-opposition unfolds in a complicated manner, with humor playing a critical role in narrative movement and a rhetoric of amelioration and persuasion.

As noted in chapter 3, this pericope has already received some attention by scholars regarding potential humor. In particular, both Hatton and Shepherd have found the ambiguity in the pericope to be a possible source of humor.[109] Yet neither Hatton nor Shepherd have addressed the manner in which the ending of the narrative requires a rereading of the account that, while generating humor in the story, also pushes the humor some distance away from the surface of the text.[110] This is due to the fact that the script-opposition involving sleep is dormant in 5:35 and 5:39. The actions in these verses (telling Jairus his daughter is dead; mourning the girl) are perfectly normal in light of the people's limited perspective. However, these are also potentially latent jab lines, for in 5:39 Jesus points out the absurdity of such actions given that the girl is only sleeping—a fact proven by her healing/resurrection in 5:42. Consequently, an interpretation is opened up to the audience that throws new light on earlier activities of the people involved: those in Jairus's house are telling a worried father that his sleeping daughter has passed away, performing funerary rites for her, and even mocking the only person in the story who correctly sees what is going on: Jesus. Such a portrait is potentially comical. Yet such an

---

109. Hatton, "Comic Ambiguity," 91–123; Shepherd, *Markan Sandwich Stories*, 169.

110. Hatton and Shepherd key in on different elements of the narrative without focusing on this particular aspect of the pericope.

interpretation is only activated upon a rereading or reimagining of the earlier details of the story in light of its end. While it is possible that some in a Markan audience might have grasped this and found it humorous, the complex movement of the script-oppositions suggests a more abstract engagement with the narrative. This, in turn, would dilute the comical effect given the presence of such abstraction.

Though the humor is more abstract, it has potential to act in several ways throughout the story. To begin with, humor's social-control element is sharply evident in the passage. Scholars correctly underscore the mention of humor in 5:40 when those in the house "laugh down" (καταγελάω) at Jesus.[111] Yet given the trajectory of the narrative, the evangelist effectively flips the script on those in the story, for it turns out that the girl is not dead after all. Rhetorically, this buttresses the stature of Jesus by making disbelievers the target of humor. What is more, the values of the pericope radiate beyond the narrative and invite those in the audience to agree with the author. For those seeing humor in the narrative, they are invited to affirm a resurrection perspective, rejecting notions of Jesus's incapabilities and affirming the stories of Jesus followers that place Jesus as the powerful hero of their story.

Humor also potentially acts as a crucial affective additive. As noted above, the accounts retold in 4:35–6:6 engage difficult subject matter. In the present portion of the tale concerning the sick girl, the audience comes face to face not only with disease or affliction but death itself. The evangelist and audiences of the Markan Gospel were undoubtedly familiar with the experience of death. Life in the empire could be brutal and challenging, and parents lost children at alarming rates.[112] The evangelist's choice to address this topic with an abstracted touch of ambiguity and humor is significant. For those reflecting at depth on the story, this could allow grief and pain to intersect with an entirely different affective range, namely, hap-

---

111. Halliwell, *Greek Laughter*, 475, views this passage as indicative of early Christianity's suspicion toward laughter.

112. Quintilian offers a poignant account of the loss of his own son: "My younger son, just past his fifth year, went first, and took away one of the two lights of my life. I have no desire to flaunt my troubles or exaggerate the causes of my tears: I only wish there were some way of making them less! But how can I conceal what beauty he showed in his face, what charm in his talk, what flashes of intellect, what solid possession of a calm and even at that age almost unbelievably lofty mind? This was a child who would have deserved love, even if he had been another's" (*Inst.* 6.3.1–8 [Russell]).

piness and mirth. Such a mixture is crucial for keeping pain at a tolerable distance and allowing the audience to engage another truth the evangelist pursues: the hope of resurrection. The present reality of pain and death is softened by a light touch of humor and relativized by the promise of a time and place where death truly is just sleep.

Finally, it is worth noting that the indulgence of humor through the topic of sleep seems to be a recurring Markan trope—a fact not often highlighted.[113] As seen above, the evangelist has likely utilized sleep as a source of humor in the script-opposition ASLEEP/ALERT in Jesus's act of sleeping through a storm (4:38). Significantly, in the poignant narrative of Jesus praying in the garden (14:32–34), the theme of sleep appears once again and in a potentially humorous way. The evangelist seems to play with a script-opposition of SLEEP/WATCHFULNESS, a trope in ancient comedies, when speaking of Jesus and the disciples. In the final hours before his arrest, Jesus implores his closest companions to remain awake with him while he prays (14:32). Yet three times the disciples fall asleep, only to be woken by Jesus, a formulaic interaction that ends with Jesus's exasperated cry: "Are you still sleeping and resting? Enough! The hour has arrived, behold the Son of Man is being delivered into the hands of sinners."[114] The contrast between Jesus's emotional state and the failure of the disciples to remain alert not once, but three times, raises the possibility that the evangelist has deployed a humorous script-opposition regarding sleep here in a manner similar to the pericope of Jairus's daughter. The farcical actions of the disciples may too be blunting the otherwise tragic vector of the gospel story.

Conclusion

Humor in the second tier of 4:35–6:6 trades less directly in farcical moments of humor. In spite of this, script-oppositions continue to labor

---

113. It is a little surprising that this does not come up more often given that both the present pericope and that of Jesus stilling the storm both make direct reference to sleep.

114. The formulaic development of the story may be an intentional way of enhancing both the drama and humor of the narrative. For a similar argument regarding a "3+1" formula in Luke 14:15–24, see Bruce Longenecker, "A Humorous Jesus? Orality, Structure, and Characterisation in Luke 14:15–24, and Beyond," *BibInt* 16 (2008): 179–204.

for the narrative. Through the script-oppositions of ROMAN IMPERIUM/ JESUS'S IMPERIUM and DEATH/SLEEP, the evangelist focuses once more on Jesus's identity by affirming his power over Roman demons and scoffing onlookers. Additionally, the evangelist treats the topic of insiders and outsiders through the lens of CIVILIZED/BARBARIAN, pointedly underscoring that individuals in noncivilized spaces are just as spiritually capable as those society deems civilized. Within these loci, the functions of humor remain multifaceted. One sees its capacity for satire, resistance, in-group/out-group bonding, and salutary effects, even if these remain some distance away from the surface of the text.

Tier Three

The third and final tier of humor is home to the least apparent script-oppositions in 4:35–6:6, primarily because the script-oppositions the evangelist uses remain abstracted far from the surface of the text. It is comprised of one major script-opposition: ROMAN IMPERIUM/JESUS'S IMPERIUM. This humorous locus, though it is distant from obvious farce or incongruity, carries forward questions of Jesus's identity. Ultimately, the script-opposition of imperium is likely a distant echo that may further build up Jesus's identity as an agent of power.

Satire

The incongruity in tier three concerns a possible intertextual link between Jesus and Caesar/Roman imperium in 4:35–41. As discussed in chapter 3, Jesus's command of the sea potentially trades in tropes of imperial figures such as Xerxes and Augustus asserting their dominance over the sea. More pertinently, Aus and Strelan have argued for a direct parallel between Jesus's sea crossing here and that of Julius Caesar in his attempt to cross the Ionian and/or Adriatic (a story narrated by Lucan, Plutarch, Appian, and Cassius Dio).[115] Were this comparison in mind, the story would then read as a satire upon Caesar's imperium, for Jesus accomplishes what he does not: he masters the seas and has a successful crossing. Aus and Strelan are correct that the portrait of the two stands in stark contrast. Whereas Caesar rails against the storms defying fate and the gods, Jesus is roused

---

115. Aus, *Stilling of the Storm*, 56–88; Strelan, "Greater than Caesar," 166–79.

from slumber and calms the raging storm with merely two words (4:39). There is also the tantalizing possibility that this passage stands in juxtaposition to depictions of Venus, a goddess capable of symbolizing Rome. Indeed, a fresco at Pompeii depicts Venus ushering a boat to safety through turbid waters, possibly standing in contrast to Jesus rising from sleep to calm a storm.[116] While the script-opposition of ROMAN IMPERIUM/JESUS'S IMPERIUM is a very real possibility, whether this story would be humorous or not depends on the degree to which the audience would be familiar with the allusion(s). Given the difficulty in determining the evocation of the precise script, it seems possible that the Caesar narrative or stories like it would go unnoticed or perhaps be obtained only through later reflection on the story. Consequently, the humorous nature of the satire may be placed at the outer limits of humor recognition by a Markan audience.

If one grants that the present story does bear some potential for humor, its function would rest primarily in its rhetorical and social dimensions. Rhetorically, this story presents Caesar and, by extension, Roman imperium as a target to be mocked. By deconstructing Caesar and demonstrating Jesus's superiority, Jesus is seen to wield a power far greater than the Roman ruler. Nor is this a neutral attitude. Rather, it is a critical point made by the narrative seeking to persuade or confirm with its audience that Jesus's imperium stands head and shoulders above Caesar's. The evangelist encourages the audience to laugh at or belittle Roman imperium while supporting the assertion that Jesus is more worthy to follow and adore than an impotent emperor shaking his fists and yelling empty threats into the wind.

Rhetorical Effects of Humor: Conclusion

In the present chapter, I have explored the potential moments of humor in Mark 4:35–6:6 and their rhetorical impact on Markan audiences. While at first glance it appears that humor runs rampant through the stories, even to the point of disruption, the presence of overlapping script-oppositions concentrated in single jab lines and the likelihood that there are tiers of humor brings this number down considerably. When combined with humor limiters, variability in performance, and humor competence, obvious moments of potential disruption drop to single digits, as one would

---

116. Longenecker, *In Stone and Story*, 66–67.

expect when encountering a serious text interspersed with humor. Several critical observations arise from noticing humor's presence in the miracle cycle.

To begin with, humor likely generates physiological, psychological, educational, and social effects in the miracle stories that have generally gone unnoticed by scholars. Physiologically and psychologically, humor finds its greatest potential in its ability to generate positive responses in the audience while engaging otherwise difficult topics. By adopting a humorous perspective on topics including demonic affliction, imperial power, disease, and even death, the evangelist potentially elicits positive somatic and psychic responses that may act to minimize these difficult topics, even while offering a word of hope in the scope of broader narrative themes (i.e., divine power, resurrection, communal solidarity, etc.). Furthermore, humor opens up an affective dimension of mirth and joy. Pedagogically, the use of humor has the ability to bolster the persuasiveness of the evangelist by mitigating distance between author/performer and audience, as well as to increase memorability of the stories. Socially, the presence of humor in the miracle stories binds audiences together through shared jokes, encourages audience members to adopt certain social values, and galvanizes communal solidarity behind Jesus over against corrupt leaders (i.e., Rome). Perhaps most significantly, humor plays a direct role in pushing audiences to align with the proper understanding of Jesus's identity as the powerful Son of God, a fact that is lost time and again on characters in the pericopae.

In addition to such functions, tracking the evangelist's use of humor reveals two major threads (PROPER/FOOLISH RESPONSE TO JESUS; WONDERWORKER/AVERAGE PERSON) that function as the primary engines of humor. These threads focalize script-oppositions upon the question of Jesus's identity, creating humorous tension by crafting a cycle of "can he/can't he" when Jesus confronts impossible situations. Strikingly, these threads unravel in the final pericope when Jesus is challenged one final time, only to find himself nearly powerless due to people's lack of belief. By upending the expected cycle of "can he/can't he," the evangelist creates a powerful moment in the narrative raising profound questions about Christology, divine agency and power, the role of the audience as Jesus followers, and the danger of unbelief, among other themes.

Finally, beyond the topic of Jesus's identity, the evangelist uses humor to target particular themes including imperial power, insider/outsider distinctions, and the problem of evil as reified in nature, demons, disease, and death. While treated more obliquely than problems regarding Jesus's identity, the evangelist adopts a humorous outlook with the potential to minimize the pain of powerlessness in the environment of Markan audiences. All told, the evangelist wields humor in a sophisticated manner, weaving humorous materials through stories both as one-off jokes and as long-form comical narratives—all with an eye toward serious *teloi*.

5
Summary

Introduction

In this study, I have taken up the question of whether or not the Gospel of Mark is humorous. More specifically, I have examined the episodes in Mark 4:35–6:6 for their potential humor. I began the study in chapter 1 with a review of gospel scholarship and humor, particularly those few pieces that directly addressed humor in Mark or topics adjacent to humor that signaled its hermeneutical possibility. Based on this review, the possibility and, indeed, the likelihood of some form of humor being present in the text emerged. However, given the relative dearth of studies on Markan humor and humor's supposed subjectivity, I proposed the need for a methodology suited to the task of discovering humor in the text. In chapter 2, I articulated the instrument that I would use in my analysis of the Markan text: a humor methodology interweaving the General Theory of Verbal Humor and ancient humorous comparanda. Utilizing this method, in chapter 3, I mapped the possible script-oppositions in Mark 4:35–6:6. Additionally, I looked for points of contact in humorous comparanda from antiquity. These texts anchored the analysis by providing evidence that ancient authors may have found such script-oppositions humorous. Having teased out these script-oppositions, I set about indexing them in chapter 4. Upon considering potential humor-limiters, I placed each script-opposition in one of three tiers ranking their likelihood of being perceived by an audience as humorous. I then traced the ways in which humor interacted with the text, its themes, and possible impact on interpretations of the text.

Having undertaken such an analysis, I sought to answer the question driving the present study: Is the Gospel of Mark humorous, and can one detect humor through analyzing incongruities in the text?

Based on the work above, I would assert that the answer to this is yes. The intuition of gospel scholars that the Gospel of Mark uses humor in its depiction of Jesus's ministry is well-founded. By tracing incongruities in Mark 4:35–6:6, one sees humor proliferating through these narratives. While the sample size is too limited to speak of an exhaustive definition of Markan humor, there is enough consistency throughout the text to begin to build a humor profile of the Markan evangelist. In what follows, I will comment on what I believe are the first sketches of Markan humor and conclude with a brief discussion of limitations to the present study as well as potential future directions for scholarship.

Markan Humor

Based on the presence of two comedic threads (WONDERWORKER/AVERAGE PERSON; PROPER/FOOLISH RESPONSE TO JESUS) present throughout the entire narrative block, it is likely that the evangelist is capable of, and possibly enjoys, utilizing humor in a sophisticated manner. There is a strong enough pattern of incongruities to suggest that humor is not coincidental to the narrative but vital to its unfolding. This is seen in the fact that the two most obvious threads are present in each pericope, central to plot development, and mutually inform one another.

In the opening miracle (4:35–41), the evangelist initially presents Jesus as sleeping at the most inopportune moment, only for the disciples to wake him in time to deliver everyone on board from certain death. Jesus's actions, rather than sparking admiration, wonder, or clarity about his status as God's beloved child, engenders fear in those closest to him and leaves them more confused than before about his identity. In the second miracle story (5:1–20), Jesus's exorcistic powers appear to be something of an open question as he wrestles with Legion. Ultimately, Jesus proves powerful but, in his success, once more people are initially fearful and send him away rather than thank or admire him. The third miracle story (5:21–43) depicts Jesus as lacking his typical level of prescience and potentially too late to intervene in the death of Jairus's daughter. He is also openly mocked by onlookers when he remarks that the girl is sleeping rather than dead. Their misunderstanding is confirmed when Jesus heals the girl. Most surprisingly, the evangelist upends these threads in 6:1–6. Once more, Jesus encounters misunderstanding as people from his home territory fail to recognize him for the powerful miracle-worker of the previous stories. Yet, their statements turn out to be partially correct, if only temporarily, as he

5. Summary

can only do a handful of powerful deeds—a fact that leaves him marveling at their lack of belief.

The sustained use of humor by the evangelist suggests that the author has some understanding of humor's efficacy. Whether or not the evangelist has explicitly considered the importance of humor for rhetoric, or simply enjoys its use, the evangelist likely has some grasp on humor's ability to enhance a narrative's persuasive force, themes, memorability, and character formation.

The evangelist's tendency to build humor around ambiguity regarding Jesus's abilities is an interesting decision, given the ways in which high-status symbols potentially limit the comedic. But, even here the evangelist handles this delicately. Jesus's status as a wonderworker, troubled as it may be in the stilling of the storm, confronting Legion, healing the woman of faith, and raising Jairus's daughter, only falters in the final episode, with Jesus granted an allowance of some works of power. This deft, comical touch puts the evangelist in a camp similar to humorous Second Temple texts such as Tobit, Testament of Job, and Testament of Abraham, where highly regarded religious figures are at once relatable through their human moments, yet admirable for their character and faithfulness.

Finally, the sustained use of humor suggests that the evangelist may be approaching the topic of Jesus's life and ministry from an intentionally tragicomical perspective. The evangelist deploys humor alongside several serious subjects in the miracle cycle of 4:35–6:6: the destructive power of nature, the terror of demons, the pain of enduring illness and death, and even the near powerlessness of charismatic leaders. By weaving humor into these narratives, the evangelist injects a degree of lighthearted catharsis into otherwise grim topoi.

The topics of humor are significant. One of the most striking conclusions from the present study is that, in the first tier of humor, the Markan evangelist centers humor around the characterization of Jesus, particularly his power and identity. This impacts Markan Christology and current discussions about how best to understand the relationship between Jesus's power and suffering through the gospel. Surfacing the humor extant in 4:35–6:6 reveals that the problematizing of Jesus's powers begin well before the middle of the gospel. What is more, this is anchored in a storytelling pattern of incongruous crisis ("will Jesus succeed or won't he?") that is generally unnoticed by Markan scholarship. The latter point impacts the issue of Jesus's identity and the messianic secret by raising the possibility that mistaken identity is not only a theological consideration but possibly flexed in ways analogous to ancient comedies and novels which treat mistaken identity as a major engine for humor.

The second tier of humor involves a variety of humorous topoi. At this more abstracted level of humor, the evangelist addresses Roman imperium, potentially ethnic difference, and the ambiguity of sleep, among other topics. In offering wry observations on Roman power and cultural superiority, the evangelist joins in well-founded traditions from antiquity. As far back as Aristophanes, one finds these topics to be mainstays of humor and, though its form changes in the imperial era, is still present well into late antiquity. Addressing these issues through humor allows the evangelist to critique attitudes and policies they find deleterious to Jesus followers. The issue of sleep is more complicated. Though sleep is often used in farce, its presence in Mark links to deeper theological concerns around trust and Jesus's possession of power greater than death.

The third tier of humor engages once more in a critique of Roman imperium. However, it does so at a level significantly abstracted from the surface of the text. It is possible that the evangelist is mocking the tradition of Julius Caesar's attempt to cross the sea in Mark 4:35–41. If this is the case, the evangelist is offering not only a satire of Roman power, but a direct comparison between Jesus's abilities and those of Caesar.

The evangelist's use of humor has the potential for significant impact on a Markan audience and the rhetorical aims of the evangelist or a performer of the gospel. Infusing a text with humor gives rise to physical, psychological, social, and pedagogical effects. At the level of somatic impact, humor has the ability to decrease negative physical and mental states while generating or augmenting positive states. By weaving humor into the narrative, recitations and performances of the miracle cycle have the potential to help ease health burdens and increase enjoyment, even if only partially, in early Jesus-follower communities.

Regarding its social impact, the presence of humor in the miracle cycle allows the evangelist and subsequent performers to inculcate and reinforce discrete Jesus-follower values, while subverting other values they do not agree with. Humor acts as a form of indirect communication that facilitates prescriptive values with a softer touch, even while adopting the power of peer-pressure to encourage individuals to be in with the group. The element of group identity, critical as it is to humor's didactic function, also acts as a potent form of solidarity. Humor has the power to bind people within groups, a feature which would have provided a bulwark against the social pressures early Jesus followers faced throughout the empire.

Pedagogically, humor has the potential to aid at several critical junctures in the performance of the text. The use of humor increases the likelihood that audiences will be able to recall these stories later, especially as the two primary threads of humor are related to the overall goals of the narrative to advance important ideas about Jesus's identity. Its presence also reduces the social distance between performers and audiences. This, in turn, lends credibility to the performer as the audience is more likely to trust and respond positively to orators that augment immediacy through humor. These features enhance the rhetorical aims of the evangelist and performers of the gospel who wish to win over audiences and have them adopt a particular perspective regarding Jesus's life and ministry.

Overall, an analysis of humor in Mark 4:35–6:6 reveals an evangelist at home in the world of humor. They deploy humor in sustained, creative, and surprising ways. The evangelist connects humor to a variety of topics, enhancing the potency of the gospel and its performance by unlocking several positive benefits that stem directly from humor.

Limitations and Future Directions

The ground covered in the present study is significant. I have made, to my knowledge, the first monograph-length study of the Markan evangelist's humor and examined its presence and impact in Mark 4:35–6:6. This analysis has opened new lines of inquiry regarding gospel themes, characterization, and rhetorical impact. However, there are limitations to the present study as well.

The first salient limitation concerns sample size. I have foregone an analysis of the entire gospel for the purposes of crafting a method suitable to the task of locating humor in the narrative. The end result is that the present study is a confirmation of humor in 4:35–6:6 and a deposit on future humor studies. If there is a consistent use of humor present in the gospel or a distinctive Markan humor as I have suggested, future studies should bear this out. At first glance, this seems possible as the humor present in the miracle cycle comports with analyses undertaken by Combs, Hatton, and Iverson (see chapter 1) where humor orbits around Jesus's identity or is used to convey important gospel themes such as discipleship and proper understanding of Jesus's character and ministry. All told, the results are promising, but it must be admitted that Markan scholars are only at the beginning stages of unpacking Markan humor.

A second major concern rests in the subjective nature of humor. While humor studies have effectively banished the notion that humor is entirely idiosyncratic and a hopeless enterprise to analyze, it is still the case there is subjectivity in the discipline that scholars must account for. I have attempted to control for this by observing humor-limiters and locating script-oppositions and incongruity in a broader range of texts deemed humorous by dint of *gattung* (i.e., comedies, novels, satire, etc.). Unfortunately, without access to the author or performance and cues accompanying incongruities to help audiences perceive humor, locating humor in script-oppositions will revolve around probability. This need not turn Markan scholars off of the enterprise, as work with historical texts and material culture is often made with similar limitations. But, it is something to always keep at the forefront of one's mind in an attempt to separate a scholar's understanding of humor from that of the text. While such limitations are present, there are exciting implications for Markan studies.

The detection of a carefully crafted, sustained use of humor in Mark engenders new possibilities for the study of the gospel. To begin with, one of the first tasks that scholars should undertake is a study throughout the entirety of the text. Present scholarship has noted the possibility of humor in significant parts of the Markan Gospel (chs. 4–6, 8, 10, 14), but much material remains to be studied. In particular, it would be important to analyze the ways in which the two primary threads detected above play out in other parts of the gospel. That is, in what ways does the evangelist possibly exploit ambiguity around Jesus's identity to humorous effect? And what might the hermeneutical and rhetorical implications be?

Another potential line of inquiry concerns the intersection between potential humor and seemingly odd moments in the Markan narrative. The gospel includes some famously strange turns. I have touched on some of these, but others remain to be explored with respect to the potential for humor. Particularly, the story of the Syro-Phoenician woman, the account of the naked disciple, and even the startling turn at the end of the gospel are all excellent starting points for a humor analysis as there are incongruities floating on the surface of the text. I suspect that the Markan Gospel will be found to be a more lively account than is sometimes recognized and that the evangelist found playful turns in the narrative to be enjoyable and helpful in conveying the story of Jesus to early Jesus followers.

Finally, one of the most important conclusions from the present study concerns the implications for the analysis of Markan performance and its reception by early audiences. Whether analyzing early composition of the gospel, its final form, and/or the interaction between performer, text, and audience, humor is a critical element to keep in mind. Markan scholars should give greater consideration to humor's ability to impact audiences at the somatic, social, and pedagogical levels as this has largely been omitted thus far. It is easy to treat the gospels as liturgical texts with a one-dimensional affect of seriousness or gravity, without paying greater attention to the entertainment value of discrete portions of the gospel. Notably, this can be a mistake for, while the gospels certainly move into the domain of liturgical texts, they are also narratives rooted in the lively exploits of a charismatic wonderworker who appears to have used humor in his own teachings and rhetorical engagements. It is difficult to imagine average people in the Roman Empire not finding mirth in the exploits of Jesus, even if they are hard to gauge from a contemporary position.

One of the ways in which scholars can pursue this is by broadening hermeneutical horizons and engaging with the vast amount of humor literature and material culture in antiquity. Gospel scholars rarely make use of the humor traditions so prevalent in Greece and Rome. To do so is to miss a large part of the cultural zeitgeist that proliferated throughout antiquity. The Greco-Roman world, particularly as one encounters it through its literary traditions, was home to extensive meditations regarding humor's place in society. This is evident in philosophical treatises on humor (e.g., Aristotle), rhetorical expositions on its nature and role in public speech (e.g., Cicero, Quintilian), the use of comedies in early education settings (e.g., translating Plautus and Terence), and even collections of humor found in jokebooks (e.g., *Philogelos*). This was coupled with the presence of humorous media at both elite (e.g., Greek and Roman comedy traditions, satire, novels) and pedestrian levels (e.g., mime). When one regards comedy's breadth, duration, and philosophical reflection in antiquity, it is striking that Markan scholars have not made more use of humorous comparanda. It is my hope that Markan scholars will become acquainted with a new matrix of texts that bear witness to an important aspect of Greco-Roman culture that, while difficult to spot from a contemporary vantage point, was clearly important to inhabitants at every level of the empire.

Bibliography

Abel, Millicent. "Humor, Stress, and Coping Strategies." *Humor* 15 (2008): 365–81.
Achtemeier, Paul. "The Origin and Function of the Pre-Marcan Miracle Catenae." *JBL* 6 (1972): 198–220.
——. "Toward the Isolation of Pre-Markan Miracle Catenae," *JBL* 89 (1970): 265–91.
Anderson, Robert. "'A Man Asleep in a Storm at Sea' as a Biblical Motif." *Proceedings: Eastern Great Lakes and Midwest Biblical Societies* 6 (1986): 32–39.
Anderson, William S. *Barbarian Play: Plautus' Roman Comedy*. University of Toronto Press, 1993.
Apte, Mahadev L. *Humor and Laughter: An Anthropological Approach*. Cornell University Press, 1985.
Apuleius. *Apologia; Florida; De Deo Socratis*. Edited and translated by Christopher P. Jones. LCL. Harvard University Press, 2017.
——. *Books 1–6*. Vol. 1 of *Metamorphoses (The Golden Ass)*. Edited and translated by J. Arthur Hanson. LCL. Harvard University Press, 1996.
Aristophanes. *Acharnians; Knights*. Edited and translated by Jeffrey Henderson. LCL. Harvard University Press, 1998.
——. *Birds; Lysistrata; Women at the Thesmophoria*. Edited and translated by Jeffrey Henderson. LCL. Harvard University Press, 2000.
——. *Clouds. Wasps. Peace*. Edited and translated by Jeffrey Henderson. LCL. Harvard University Press, 1998.
Aristotle. *Art of Rhetoric*. Translated by J. H. Freese. LCL. Harvard University Press, 1926.
Attardo, Salvatore. "The GTVH and Humorous Discourse." Pages 93–105 in *Humorous Discourse*. Edited by Władysław Chłopicki and Dorota Brzozowska. Humor Research 11. de Grutyer, 2017.
——. *Humorous Texts: A Semantic and Pragmatic Analysis*. Humor Research 6. de Gruyter, 2001.

———. *Linguistic Theories of Humor*. Humor Research 1. de Gruyter, 1994.
———. "A Multiple-Level Analysis of Jokes." *Humor* 2 (1989): 417–40.
Attardo, Salvatore, and Victor Raskin. "Script-Theory Revis(it)ed: Joke Similarity and Joke Representational Model." *Humor* 4 (1991): 293–347.
Aus, Roger. *The Stilling of the Storm: Studies in Early Palestinian Judaic Traditions*. International Studies in Formative Judaism and Christianity. Global Publications, 2000.
Banas, John, Norah Dunbar, Dariela Rodriguez, and Shr-Jie Liu. "A Review of Humor in Educational Settings: Four Decades of Research." *Communication Education* 60 (2011): 115–44.
Banting, Blayne Alexander. "Proclaiming the Messiah's Mirth: A Rhetorico-contextual Model for the Interpretation and Proclamation of Humour in Selected Gospel Sayings." DMin thesis. Acadia Divinity College, 1998.
Batto, Bernard. "The Sleeping God: An Ancient Near Eastern Motif of Divine Sovereignty." *Bib* 68 (1987): 153–77.
Baumbach, Lydia. "Quacks Then as Now? An Examination of Medical Practice, Theory, and Superstition in Plautus." *Acta Classica* 26 (1983): 99–104.
Beavis, Mary Ann. *Mark*. Paidea. Baker Academic, 2011.
Beck, Mark. "The Serio-Comic Life of Antony." Pages 137–46 in *A Versatile Gentleman: Consistency in Plutarch's Writing*. Edited by Jan Opsomer, Geert Roskam, and Frances B. Titchener. Plutarchea Hypomnemata. Leuven University Press, 2016.
Bednarz, Terri. *Humor in the Gospels: A Sourcebook for the Study of Humor in the New Testament: 1863-2014*. Lexington, 2015.
———. "Humor-neutics: Analyzing Humor and Humor Functions in the Synoptic Gospels." PhD diss. Texas Christian University, 2009.
———. "Status Disputes and Disparate Dicta: Humor Rhetoric in Luke 16:14–18." *BibInt* 21 (2013): 377–415.
Bekelja Wanzer, Melissa, and Ann Bainbridge Frymier. "The Relationship between Student Perceptions of Instructor Humor and Students' Reports of Learning." *Communication Education* 48 (1999): 48–62.
Bell, Nancy. "Failed Humor." Pages 356–70 in *The Routledge Handbook of Language and Humor*. Edited by Salvatore Attardo. Routledge Handbooks in Linguistics. Routledge, 2017.
Belo, Fernando. *A Materialist Reading of the Gospel of Mark*. Translated by Matthew O'Connell. Orbis, 1981.

Berger, Peter. *Redeeming Laughter: The Comic Dimension of Human Experience*. 2nd ed. de Gruyter, 1997.
Bertrand, D. A. "Le Chevreau d'Anna: La Signification Du l'anecdotique Dans Le Livre de Tobit." *RHPR* 68 (1988): 269–74.
Bilezekian, Gilbert. *The Liberated Gospel: A Comparison of the Gospel of Mark and Greek Tragedy*. Baker Books, 1977.
Bizi, Smadar, Giora Keinan, and Benjamin Beit-Hallahmi. "Humor and Coping with Stress: A Test under Real-Life Conditions." *Personality & Individual Differences* 9 (1988): 951–56.
Blanchard, Alain. *Essai sur la composition des comédies de Ménandre*. Les Belles Lettres, 1983.
Bolt, Peter. *Jesus' Defeat of Death: Persuading Mark's Early Readers*. Cambridge University Press, 2008.
———. "Mark 16:1–8: The Empty Tomb of a Hero?" *TynBul* 47 (1996): 27–37.
Boonstra, Harry. "Satire in Matthew." *Christianity and Literature* 29 (1980): 32–45.
Boring, Eugene. *Mark: A Commentary*. NTL. Westminster John Knox, 2006.
Borthwick, E. Kerr. "Observations on the Opening Scene of Aristophanes' Wasps." *ClQ* 42 (1992): 274–78.
Botner, Max. "What Has Mark's Christ to Do with David's Son? A History of Interpretation." *CurBR* 16 (2017): 50–70.
Bragues, George. "The Market for Philosophers: An Interpretation of Lucian's Satire on Philosophy." *The Independent Review* 9 (2004): 227–51.
Broadhead, Edwin. *Teaching with Authority: Miracles and Christology in the Gospel of Mark*. JSNTSup 74. JSOT Press, 1992.
Buckley, George Wright. *The Wit and Wisdom of Jesus*. West, 1901.
Bultmann, Rudolf. *The History of the Synoptic Tradition*. Translated by John Marsh. Harper & Row, 1963.
Burrow, Andrew. "Bargaining with Jesus: Irony in Mark 5:1–20." *BibInt* 25 (2017): 234–51.
Camery-Hoggatt, Jerry. *Irony in Mark's Gospel: Text and Subtext*. SNTSMS 72. Cambridge University Press, 1992.
Carlson, Keith. "The Impact of Humor on Memory: Is The Humor Effect about Humor?" *Humor* 24 (2011): 21–41.
Carman, Jon. "Ancient Quackery: The Sick Woman and the Cost of Incompetence." Pages 31–46 in *Looking Both Ways: At the Intersection of the*

Academy and the Church; Essays in Honor of Joseph Grana II. Edited by William Curtis Holtzen and J. Blair Wilgus. Claremont, 2021.

———. "Jesus Asleep on the Job? Analyzing an Incongruity in Mark 4:35–41." Pages 99–117 in *Biblical Humor and Performance: Audience Experiences That Make Meaning*. Edited by Peter Perry. Biblical Performance Criticism 20. Cascade, 2023.

Carrell, Amy. "Historical Views of Humor." Pages 303–32 in *The Primer of Humor Research*. Edited by Victor Raskin and Ruch Willibald. Humor Research 8. de Gruyter, 2008.

Carter, Warren. "Cross-Gendered Romans and Mark's Jesus: Legion Enters the Pigs (Mark 5:1–20)." *JBL* 134 (2015): 139–55.

Chapman, Anthony, and Hugh Foot, eds. *Humor and Laughter: Theory, Research, and Applications*. Transaction, 1995.

Choi, Jin Young. "The Misunderstanding of Jesus' Disciples in Mark: An Interpretation from a Community-Centered Perspective." Pages 55–69 in *Mark*. Edited by Nicole Wilkinson Duran, Teresa Okure, and Daniel Patte. Fortress, 2011.

Cicero. *On the Orator: Books 1–2*. Translated by E. W. Sutton and H. Rackham. LCL. Harvard University Press, 1942.

[———.]. *Rhetorica ad Herennium*. Translated by Harry Caplan. LCL. Harvard University Press, 1954.

Clarke, John R. *Looking at Laughter: Humor, Power, and Transgression in Roman Visual Culture, 100 B.C.–A.D. 250*. University of California Press, 2007.

Cline, Thomas, and James Kellaris. "The Influence of Humor Strength and Humor-Message Relatedness on Ad Memorability." *Journal of Advertising* 36 (2007): 55–67.

Coarelli, Filippo. *The Column of Trajan*. Colombo, 2000.

Cohen, Shaye. "Menstruants and the Sacred in Judaism and Christianity." Pages 273–98 in *Women's History and Ancient History*. Edited by Sarah Pomeroy. University of North Carolina Press, 1991.

Colston, Herbert. "Irony and Sarcasm." Pages 234–49 in *The Routledge Handbook of Language and Humor*. Edited by Salvatore Attardo. Routledge Handbooks in Linguistics. Routledge, 2017.

Combs, Jason Robert. "A Ghost on the Water? Understanding an Absurdity in Mark 6:49–50." *JBL* 127 (2008): 345–58.

Coon, Raymond. *The Foreigner in Hellenistic Comedy*. PhD diss, The University of Chicago, 1920.

Cooper, Lane. *An Aristotelian Theory of Comedy: With an Adaptation of the Poetics and a Translation of "Tractatus Coislinianus."* Harcourt, 1922.

Cormier, Henri. *Le Humour de Jésus.* Editiones Paulines, 1974.

Cotter, Wendy. "Cosmology and the Jesus Miracles." Pages 118–31 in *Whose Historical Jesus.* Edited by William Arnal and Michel Desjardins. Studies in Christianity and Judaism 7. Wilfrid Laurier University Press, 1997.

Cowan, Robert. "Lucan's Thunder-Box: Scatology, Epic, and Satire in Suetonius' 'Vita Lucani.'" *HSCP* 106 (2011): 301–13.

Crossan, John Dominic. *Raid on the Articulate: Comic Eschatology in Jesus and Borges.* Harper & Row, 1976.

Culpepper, R. Alan. "Humor and Wit: The New Testament." *ABD* 3:333.

D'Angelo, Mary. "Power, Knowledge and the Bodies of Women in Mark 5:21-43." Pages 81–106 in *The Woman with the Blood Flow (Mark 5:23–34).* Edited by Barbara Baert. Art and Religion 2. Peeters, 2014.

Davies, Philip. "Mark's Christological Paradox." *JSNT* 35 (1989): 3–18.

De Saint Denis, Eugene. "Le Sourire de Virgile." *Latomus* 23 (1964): 446–63.

Diebart, Richard. *Mark.* Interpretation Bible Studies. Geneva, 1999.

Deppe, Dean. *The Theological Intentions of Mark's Literary Devices: Markan Intercalations, Frames, Allusionary Repetitions, Narrative Surprises, and Three Types of Mirroring.* Wipf & Stock, 2015.

Derks, Peter, John Gardner, and Rohit Agarwal. "Recall of Innocent and Tendentious Humorous Material." *Humor* 11 (1998): 5–19.

Derrett, J. D. "Contributions to the Study of the Gerasene Demoniac." *JSNT* 3 (1979): 2–17.

———. "Mark's Technique: The Hemorrhaging Woman and Jairus' Daughter." *Bib* 63 (1982): 474–505.

———. "Spirit-Possession and the Gerasene Demoniac." *Man* 14 (1979): 286–93.

Dinkler, Michal Beth. "Suffering, Misunderstanding, and Suffering Misunderstanding: The Markan Misunderstanding Motif as a Form of Jesus' Suffering." *JSNT* 38 (2016): 316–38.

Donahue, John R., and Daniel J. Harrington. *The Gospel of Mark.* SP 2. Liturgical, 2005.

Dorey, T. A. "Aristophanes and Cleon." *Greece & Rome* 3 (1956): 132–39.

Dossey, Leslie. "Watchful Greeks and Lazy Romans: Disciplining Sleep in Late Antiquity." *JECS* 21 (2013): 209–39.

Duckworth, George. *The Nature of Roman Comedy: A Study in Popular Entertainment.* Princeton University Press, 1952.

Dunbar, R. I. M., Rebecca Baron, Anna Frangou, Eiluned Pearce, Edwin van Leeuwen, Julie Stow, Giselle Partidge, Ian Macdonald, Vincent Barra, and Mark van Vugt. "Social Laughter Is Correlated with an Elevated Pain Threshold." *Proceedings: Biological Sciences* 279 (2012): 1161–67.

Dwyer, Timothy. *The Motif of Wonder in the Gospel of Mark.* JSNTSup 128. Sheffield Academic, 1996.

Eckman, George P. *The Literary Primacy of the Bible.* The Mendenhall Lectures, second series. Methodist Book Concern, 1915.

Edwards, James. "Markan Sandwiches: The Significance of Interpolations in Markan Narratives." *NovT* 31 (1989): 193–216.

Eisend, Martin. "How Humor in Advertising Works: A Meta-Analytic Test of Alternative Models." *Marketing Letters* 22 (2011): 115–32.

Emanuel, Sarah. "On the Eighth Day, God Laughed: 'Jewing' Humour and Self-Deprecation in *Crazy Ex-Girlfriend* and the Gospel of Mark." *Journal of Modern Jewish Studies* 19 (2020): 29–50.

Ermida, Isabel. *The Language of Comic Narratives: Humor Construction in Short Stories.* Humor Research 9. De Gruyter, 2008.

Evrard, Franck. *L'Humor.* Hachette, 1996.

Feder, Lillian. *Madness in Literature.* Princeton University Press, 1990.

Figueroa-Dorrego, Jorge, and Cristina Larkin-Galiñanes, ed. *A Source Book of Literary and Philosophical Writings about Humour and Laughter: The Seventy-Five Essential Texts from Antiquity to Modern Times.* Edwin Mellen, 2009.

Fontaine, Michael. "Between Two Paradigms." Pages 516–35 in *The Oxford Handbook of Greek and Roman Comedy.* Edited by Michael Fontaine and Adele C. Scafuro. Oxford University Press, 2014.

———. *Funny Words in Plautine Comedy.* Oxford University Press, 2010.

Forehand, Walter E. *Terence.* Twayne's World Authors Series 745. Twayne, 1985.

Fortson, Stephen, and William Brown. "Best and Worst University Instructors: The Opinion of Graduate Students." *College Student Journal* 32 (1998): 572–76.

Fowler, Robert. "Irony and the Messianic Secret in the Gospel of Mark." *Proceedings: Eastern Great Lakes and Midwest Biblical Societies* 1 (1981): 26–36.

France, R. T. *The Gospel of Mark: A Commentary on The Greek Text*. NIGTC. Eerdmans, 2002.
Furly, William. *Menander: Perikeiromene or The Shorn Head*. Bulletin of the Institute of Classical Studies Supplement 127. Institute of Classical Studies, 2015.
Gamel, Brian. "Salvation in a Sentence: Mark 15:39 as Markan Soteriology." *JTI* 6 (2012): 65–78.
Gelardini, Gabriella. *Christus Militans: Studien Zur Politisch-Militärischen Semantik Im Markusevangelium Vor Dem Hintergrund Des Ersten Jüdisch-Römischen Krieges*. NovTSup 165. Brill, 2016.
Gervais, Matthew, and David Wilson. "The Evolution and Functions of Laughter and Humor: A Synthetic Approach." *The Quarterly Review of Biology* 80 (2005): 395–430.
Geyer, Douglas W. *Fear, Anomaly, and Uncertainty in the Gospel of Mark*. Scarecrow Press, 2002.
Given, John. "When Gods Don't Appear: Divine Absence and Human Agency in Aristophanes." *CW* 102 (2009): 107–27.
Goldberg, Sander M. "The Dramatic Balance of Terence's *Andria*." Pages 216–23 in *Oxford Readings in Menander, Plautus, and Terence*. Edited by Erich Segal. Oxford University Press, 2001.
———. *Understanding Terence*. Princeton University Press, 1986.
Gorham, Joan, and Diane Christophel. "The Relationship of Teachers' Use of Humor in the Classroom to Immediacy and Student Learning." *Communication Education* 39 (1990): 46–62.
Grassi, Joseph. *God Makes Me Laugh: A New Approach to Luke*. Wipf & Stock, 1986.
Guelich, Robert A. *Mark 1–8:26*. WBC 34A. Word Books, 1989.
Guidi, Annarita. "Humor Universals." Pages 17–33 in *The Routledge Handbook of Language and Humor*. Edited by Salvatore Attardo. Routledge Handbooks in Linguistics. Routledge, 2017.
Gundry, Robert. *Mark: A Commentary on His Apology for the Cross*. Eerdmans, 1993.
Haber, Susan. "A Woman's Touch: Feminist Encounters with the Hemorrhaging Woman in Mark 5:24–34." *JSNT* 26 (2003): 171–92.
Halliwell, Stephen. *Greek Laughter: A Study of Cultural Psychology from Homer to Early Christianity*. Cambridge University Press, 2008.
Hatton, Stephen. "Comic Ambiguity in the Markan Healing Intercalation (Mark 5:21–43)." *Neot* 49 (2015): 91–123.

———. "The Gospel of Mark as Comedy." *Downside Review* 120 (2002): 33–56.

———. "Mark's Naked Disciple: The Semiotics and Comedy of Following." *Neot* 35 (2001): 35–48.

Henderson, Jeffrey. *The Maculate Muse: Obscene Language in Attic Comedy*. Yale University Press, 1975.

Henderson, Susan. *Christology and Discipleship in the Gospel of Mark*. SNTSMS 135. Cambridge University Press, 2006.

Hendrickx, Herman. *The Miracles Stories*. Studies in the Synoptic Gospels. Chapman, 1987.

Henze, Matthias. *The Madness of King Nebuchadnezzar: The Ancient Near Eastern Origins and Early History of Interpretation of Daniel 4*. JSJSup 61. Brill, 1999.

Herodotus. *The Persian Wars*. Translated by A. D. Godley. LCL117. Harvard University Press, 1920.

Hesiod. *Theogony; Works and Days; Testimonia*. Edited and translated by Glenn W. Most. LCL. Harvard University Press, 2007.

Horsley, Richard. *Hearing the Whole Story: The Politics of Plot in Mark's Gospel*. Westminster John Knox, 2001.

Hull, Robert. *Hellenistic Magic and the Synoptic Tradition*. SBT 28. SCM, 1964.

Hyde, Thomas Alexander. "Christ as Orator." *The North American Review* 156 (1893): 750–53.

———. *Christ the Orator, or Never Man Spake Like This Man*. Arena, 1893.

Iersel, Bas van. *Mark: A Reader-Response Commentary*. Translated by W. H. Bisscheroux. JSNTSup 164. Sheffield Academic, 1998.

Iverson, Kelly. "Incongruity, Humor, and Mark: Performance and the Use of Laughter in the Second Gospel." *NTS* 59 (2013): 2–19.

———. "Jews, Gentiles, and the Kingdom of God: The Parable of the Wicked Tenants in Narrative Perspective (Mark 12:1–12)." *BibInt* 20 (2012): 305–35.

Janko, Richard. *Aristotle on Comedy: Towards a Reconstruction of Poetics*. Vol. 2. University of California Press, 1984.

Johansson, Daniel. "The Identity of Jesus in the Gospel of Mark: Past and Present Proposals." *CurBR* 9 (2010): 364–93.

Johnson, Scott, and Ann Miller. "A Cross-Cultural Study of Immediacy, Credibility and Learning in the U.S. and Kenya." *Communication Education* 51 (2002): 280–92.

Josephus. *Books 78*. Vol. 3 of Jewish *Antiquities*. Translated by Ralph Marcus. LCL. Harvard University Press, 1934.
Juel, Donald. *An Introduction to New Testament Literature*. Abingdon, 1978.
———. *A Master of Surprise: Mark Interpreted*. Fortress, 1994.
Kahl, Werner. *New Testament Miracle Stories in Their Religious-Historical Setting*. FRLANT 163. Vandenhoeck & Ruprecht, 1994.
Kelley, Andrew. "Miracles, Jesus, and Identity: A History of Research Regarding Jesus and Miracles with Special Attention to the Gospel of Mark." *CurBR* 13 (2014): 82–106.
Keltner, Dacher, Lisa Capps, Ann Kring, Randall Young, and Erin Heerey. "Just Teasing: A Conceptual Analysis and Empirical Review." *Psychological Bulletin* 127 (2001): 229–48.
Kennedy, George. *Progymnasmata: Greek Textbooks of Prose Composition and Rhetoric*. WGRW 10. Society of Biblical Literature, 2003.
Kiffiak, Jordash. *Responses in the Miracle Stories of the Gospels: Between Artistry and Inherited Tradition*. WUNT 2/429. Mohr Siebeck, 2017.
Kinukawa, Hisako. *Women and Jesus in Mark: A Japanese Feminist Perspective*. The Bible and Liberation. Orbis, 1994.
Klancher, Nancy. "The Male Soul in Drag: Women-as-Job in the Testament of Job." *JSP* 19 (2010): 225–45.
Kilinksi, Karl, II. "Boeotian Trick Vases." *AJA* 85 (1986): 153–58.
Knapp, Sheppard "Traces of Humor in the Sayings of Jesus." *The Biblical World* 29 (1907): 201–7.
Knapp, Stephen. "He Could Do No Mighty Deed There ... Mark 6:1-6." *Proceedings: Eastern Great Lakes and Midwest Biblical Societies* 12 (1992): 155–66.
Konstan, David. *Greek Comedy and Ideology*. Oxford University Press, 1995.
Krishnan, H. Shanker, and Dipankar Chakravarti. "A Process Analysis of the Effects of Humorous Advertising Executions on Brand Claims Memory." *Journal of Consumer Psychology* 13 (2003): 230–45.
Kuipers, Giselinde, and Barbara van der Ent. "The Seriousness of Ethnic Jokes: Ethnic Humor and Social Change in the Netherlands, 1995–2012." *Humor* 29 (2016): 605–33.
Kynes, Will. "Beat Your Parodies into Swords, and Your Parodied Books into Spears: A New Paradigm for Parody in the Hebrew Bible." *BibInt* 19 (2011): 276–310.
LaMarche, Paul. *Evangile de Marc*. EBib 33. Gabalda, 1966.

Lane, William. *The Gospel according to Mark*. NICNT. Eerdmans, 1974.

Lang, Candace. *Irony/Humor: Critical Paradigms*. The Johns Hopkins University Press, 1988.

Larkin-Galiñanes, Cristina. "An Overview of Humor Theory." Pages 4–13 in *The Routledge Handbook of Language and Humor*. Edited by Salvatore Attardo. Routledge, 2017.

Leander, Hans. *Discourses of Empire: The Gospel of Mark from a Postcolonial Perspective*. SemeiaSt 71. Society of Biblical Literature, 2013.

Lindheim, Sarah. "Hercules Cross-Dressed; Hercules Undressed: Unmasking the Construction of the Propertian *Amator* in Elegy 4.9." *American Journal of Philology* 119 (1998): 43–66.

Lloyd, Robert. "Humor in the 'Aeneid.'" *CJ* 72 (1977): 250–77.

Long, Debra, and Arthur Graesser. "Wit and Humor in Discourse Processing." *Discourse Processes* 11 (1988): 35–60.

Long, Timothy. *Barbarians in Greek Comedy*. Southern Illinois University Press, 1986.

Longenecker, Bruce. "Exposing the Economic Middle: A Revised Economy Scale for the Study of Early Christianity." *JSNT* 31 (2009): 243–78.

———. "A Humorous Jesus? Orality, Structure, and Characteristics in Luke 14:15–24, and Beyond." *BibInt* 16 (2008): 179–204.

———. *In Stone and Story: Early Christianity in the Roman World*. Baker Academic, 2020.

———. "Mark's Gospel for the Second Church of the Late First Century." Pages 197–214 in *In the Fullness of Time: Essays on Christology, Creation, and Eschatology*. Edited by Daniel Gurtner, Grant Macaskill, and Jonathan Pennington. Eerdmans, 2016.

———. *Remember the Poor: Paul, Poverty, and the Greco-Roman World*. Eerdmans, 2010.

———. "Socio-economic Profiling of the First Urban Christians." Pages 36–59 in *After the First Urban Christians: The Social Scientific Study of Pauline Christianity Twenty-Five Years Later*. Edited by Todd Still and Todd Horrell. T&T Clark, 2009.

Lucan. *The Civil War (Pharsalia)*. Translated by J. D. Duff. LCL. Harvard University Press, 1928.

———. *The Dead Come to Life or The Fisherman; The Double Indictment or Trials by Jury; On Sacrifices; The Ignorant Book Collector; The Dream or Lucian's Career; The Parasite; The Lover of Lies; The Judgement of the Goddesses; On Salaried Posts in Great Houses*. Translated by A. M. Harmon. LCL. Harvard University Press, 1921.

Ludlow, Jared. *Abraham Meets Death: Narrative Humor in the Testament of Abraham*. JSPSup 41. Sheffield Academic, 2002.

———. "Are Weeping and Falling Down Funny? Exaggeration in Ancient Novelistic Texts." Pages 165–77 in *Reading and Teaching Ancient Fiction: Jewish, Christian, and Greco-Roman Narratives*. Edited by Sara Johnson, Christine Shea, and Rubén Dupertuis. WRGWSup 11. Atlanta: SBL Press, 2018.

Ludwig, Paul. "The Portrait of the Artist in Politics: Justice and Self-Interest in Aristophanes' Acharnians." *The American Political Science Review* 101 (2007): 479–92.

Luke, Trevor. "Ideology and Humor in Suetonius' 'Life of Vespasian' 8." *CW* 103 (2010): 511–27.

Macdonald, Dennis. *The Gospels and Homer: Imitations of Greek Epic in Mark and Luke-Acts*. The New Testament and Greek Literature 1. Rowman & Littlefield, 2015.

Macdonald, Deven. *Allegiance, Opposition, and Misunderstanding: A Narrative Critical Approach to Mark's Christology*. Pickwick, 2018.

Marcus, Joel. *Mark 1–8*. AB 27. Doubleday, 1999.

Martial. *Books 1–5*. Vol. 1 of *Epigrams*. Edited and translated by Walter C. A. Ker. LCL. Harvard University Press, 1919.

Martin, Rod. *The Psychology of Humor: An Integrative Approach*. Elsevier, 2007.

Martineau, William. "A Model of the Social Functions of Humor." Pages 101–25 in *The Psychology of Humor: Theoretical Perspectives and Empirical Issues*. Edited by Jeffrey Goldstein and Paul McGhee. Academic Press, 1972.

Mather, Judson. "The Comic Art of The Book of Jonah." *Soundings* 65 (1982): 280–91.

McCracken, David. "Narration and Comedy in the Book of Tobit." *JBL* 114 (1995): 401–18.

Mehrabian, Albert. "Some Referents and Measures of Nonverbal Behavior." *Behavioral Research Methods and Instrumentation* 1 (1969): 213–17.

Melo, Wolfgang David Cirilo de. "Plautus' Dramatic Predecessors and Contemporaries in Rome." Pages 447–61 in *The Oxford Handbook of Greek and Roman Comedy*. Edited by Michael Fontaine and Adele C. Scafuro. Oxford University Press, 2014.

Meltzer, Gary. "The Role of Comic Perspectives in Shaping Homer's Tragic Vision." *CW* 83 (1990): 265–80.

Menander. *Heros; Theophoroumene; Karchedonios; Kitharistes; Kolax; Koneiazomenai; Leukadia; Misoumenos; Perikeiromene; Perinthia.* Edited and translated by W. G. Arnott. LCL. Harvard University Press, 1997.

Meyer, John. "Humor as Double-Edged Sword: Four Functions of Humor in Communication." *Communication Theory* 10 (2000): 310–31.

Myers, Ched. *Binding the Strong Man: A Political Reading of Mark's Gospel.* Orbis, 1988.

Miles, John A. "Laughing at the Bible: Jonah as Parody." *JQR* 65 (1975): 168–81.

Miller, Geoffrey. "An Intercalation Revisited: Christology, Discipleship, and Dramatic Irony in Mark 6:6b–30." *JSNT* 35 (2012): 176–95.

Miniconi, P. "La Joie Dans l' Eneide." *Latomus* 21 (1962): 563–71.

Monro, D. H. *Argument of Laughter.* Melbourne University Press, 1951.

Montiglio, Silvia. *The Spell of Hypnos: Sleep and Sleeplessness in Ancient Greek Literature.* Tauris, 2016.

Morreall, John. "Sarcasm, Irony, Wordplay, and Humor in the Hebrew Bible: A Response to Hershey Friedman." *Humor* 13 (2001): 293–301.

———. *Taking Laughter Seriously.* State University of New York, 1987.

Myers, Ched. *Binding the Strong Man: A Political Reading of Mark's Gospel.* Orbis, 1988.

Myers, Doris. "Irony and Humor in the Gospel of John." *Occasional Papers in Translation and Text Linguistics* 2 (1988): 1–13.

Neufeld, Dietmar. *Mockery and Secretism in the Social World of Mark's Gospel.* LNTS 503. Bloomsbury, 2014.

Nilsen, Don. *Humor Scholarship: A Research Bibliography.* Bibliographies and Indexes in Popular Culture. Greenwood, 1993.

Nissin, Laura. "Sleeping Culture in Roman Literary Sources." *Arctos* 49 (2015): 95–133.

Noble, Joseph Veach. "Some Trick Greek Vases." *Proceedings of the Philosophical Society* 112 (1968): 371–78.

Norwood, Gilbert. *Plautus and Terence.* Cooper Square, 1963.

Ogden, Daniel. "The Apprentice's Sorcerer: Pancrates and His Powers in Context (Lucian, Philopseudes 33–36)." *Acta Classica* 47 (2004): 101–26.

———. "The Love of Wisdom and the Love of Lies: The Philosophers and Philosophical Voices of Lucian's Philopseudes." Pages 177–203 in *Philosophical Presences in the Ancient Novel.* Edited by J. R. Morgan and Meriel Jones. Ancient Narrative Supplementum 10. Barkhuis, 2007.

Ovid. *Tristia; Ex Ponto.* Translated by A. L. Wheeler. Revised by G. P. Goold. LCL. Harvard University Press, 1924.

Padel, Ruth. *Whom Gods Destroy: Elements of Greek and Tragic Madness.* Princeton University Press, 1995.

Palmer, Earl. *The Humor of Jesus: Sources of Laughter in the Bible.* Regent College Publishing, 1987.

Palmer, Humphrey. "Just Married, Cannot Come." *NovT* 18 (1976): 241-57.

Paterson, William Romaine. "The Irony of Jesus." *The Monist* 9 (1899): 345-58.

Perera, S., E. Sabin, P. Nelson, and D. Lowe. "Increases in Salivary Lysozyme and IgA Concentrations and Secretory Rates Independent of Salivary Flow Rates Following Viewing of Humorous Videotape." *International Journal of Behavioral Medicine* 5 (1998): 118-28.

Perks, Lisa Glebatis. "The Ancient Roots of Humor Theory." *Humor* 25 (2012): 119-32.

Petronius; Seneca. *Satyricon; Apocolocyntosis.* Translated by Michael Heseltine and W. H. D. Rouse. Revised by E. H. Warmington. LCL. Harvard University Press, 1913.

Philostratus. *Life of Apollonius of Tyana, Books 1-4.* Vol. 1 of *Apollonius of Tyana.* Edited and translated by Christopher P. Jones. LCL. Harvard University Press, 2005.

Phipps, William. *The Wisdom and Wit of Rabbi Jesus.* Westminster John Knox, 1993.

Plato. *Books 7-12.* Vol. 2 of *Laws.* Translated by R. G. Bury. LCL. Harvard University Press, 1926.

———. *Euthyphro; Apology; Crito; Phaedo.* Edited and translated by Christopher Emlyn-Jones and William Preddy. LCL. Harvard University Press, 2017.

Plautus. *Amphitryon; The Comedy of Asses; The Pot of Gold; The Two Bacchises; The Captives.* Edited and translated by Wolfgang de Melo. LCL. Harvard University Press, 2011.

———. *Casina; The Casket Comedy; Curculio; Epidicus; The Two Menaechmuses.* Edited and translated by Wolfgang de Melo. LCL. Harvard University Press, 2011.

Plebe, Armando. *La teoria del comico da Aristotele a Plutarco.* Giappichelli, 1952.

Pliny. *Books 28-32.* Vol. 8 of *Natural History.* Translated by W. H. S. Jones. LCL. Harvard University Press, 1963.

Plutarch. *Agesilaus and Pompey. Pelopidas and Marcellus.* Vol. 5 of *Lives.* Translated by Bernadotte Perrin. LCL. Harvard University Press, 1917.

Portier-Young, Anathea. "Alleviation of Suffering in the Book of Tobit: Comedy, Community, and Happy Endings." *CBQ* 63 (2001): 35–54.

Price, Lucian, ed. *Dialogues with Alfred North Whitehead.* Little, Brown, 1954.

Provine, Robert. *Laughter: A Scientific Investigation.* Penguin, 2000.

Puhlick-Doris, Patricia. "The Humor Styles Questionnaire: Investigating the Role of Humor in Psychological Well-Being." University of Western Ontario, 2004.

Quintilian. *Books 6–8.* Vol. 3 of *The Orator's Education.* Edited and translated by Harold Edgeworth Butler. LCL. Harvard University Press, 1921.

———. *Books 9–10.* Vol. 4 of *The Orator's Education.* Edited and translated by Donald A. Russell. LCL. Harvard University Press, 2002.

Răchită, Constantin. "Why Does Jonah Snore in the LXX Translation (Jonah 1:5-6)? From the Theological Sobriety of the Patristic Exegesis to the Facetiousness of a Hellenizing Translation." *Vulgata in Dialogue* 1 (2017): 71–82.

Raskin, Viktor. *Semantic Mechanisms of Humor.* Synthese Language Library 24. Reidel, 1985.

Robinson, Timothy. "In the Court of Time: The Reckoning of a Monster in the 'Apocolocyntosis' of Seneca." *Arethusa* 38 (2005): 223–57.

Robson, James. *Humour, Obscenity, and Aristophanes.* Narr Verlag, 2006.

Roeckelein, Jon. *The Psychology of Humor: A Reference Guide and Annotated Bibliography.* Greenwood, 2002.

Rosen, Ralph. *Old Comedy and the Iambographic Tradition.* American Classical Studies 19. Scholars Press, 1988.

Ruch, Willibald. "State and Trait Cheerfulness and the Introduction of Exhilaration: A FACS Study." *European Psychologist* 2 (1997): 328–41.

Rusten, Jeffrey. ed., *The Birth of Comedy: Texts, Documents, and Art from Athenian Comic Competitions, 486-280.* Translated by Jeffrey Henderson et. al. The Johns Hopkins University Press, 2011.

———. "In Search of the Essence of Old Comedy: From Aristotle's Poetics to Zieliński, Cornford, and Beyond." Pages 33-49 in *The Oxford Handbook of Greek and Roman Comedy.* Edited by Michael Fontaine and Adele C. Scafuro. Oxford University Press, 2014.

Salzmann, Andrew. "'Do You Not Still Understand?' Mark 8:21 and the Mission to the Gentiles." *BTB* 39 (2009): 129–34.

Schenke, Ludger. *Die Wundererzählungen des Markusevangeliums*. Katholisches Bibelwerk, 1974.
Segal, Erich. *Roman Laughter: The Comedy of Plautus*. 2nd ed. Oxford University Press, 1987.
Seidensticker, Ernd. *Palintonos Harmonia: Studien zu komischen Elementen in der grieschen Tragödie*. Hypomnemata 72. Vandenhoeck & Ruprecht, 1982.
Sharrock, Alison. *Reading Roman Comedy: Poetics and Playfulness*. Cambridge University Press, 2009.
———. "Roman Comedy." Pages 309–12 in *The Edinburgh Companion to Ancient Greece and Rome*. Edited by Edward Bispham, Thomas Harrison, and Brian Sparkes. Edinburgh University Press, 2010.
Shelly, Cameron. "Plato on the Psychology of Humor." *Humor* 16 (2003): 351–67.
Shepherd, Tom. *Markan Sandwich Stories: Narration, Definition, and Function*. Andrews University Seminary Doctoral Dissertation Series 18. Andrews University Press, 1993.
———. "The Narrative Function of Markan Intercalation." *NTS* 41 (1995): 522–40.
Shultz, Kara, and Darla Germeroth. "Should We Laugh or Should We Cry? John Callahan's Humor as a Tool to Change Societal Attitudes Toward Disability." *Howard Journal of Communications* 9 (1998): 229–44.
Shutter, Marion. "The Element of Humor in the Bible." *BQR* 7 (1885): 443–53.
Slater, Niall W. *Plautus in Performance: The Theatre of the Mind*. Princeton University Press, 1985.
Sliter, Michael, Aron Kale, and Zhen Yuan. "Is Humor the Best Medicine? The Buffering Effect of Coping Humor on Traumatic Stressors in Firefighters." *Journal of Organizational Behavior* 35 (2014): 257–72.
Sørensen, Majken. *Humour in Political Activism: Creative Nonviolent Resistance*. Palgrave Macmillan, 2016.
———. "Laughing on the Way to Social Change: Humor and Nonviolent Action Theory." *Peace and Change* 42 (2017): 128–56.
Snijder, G. A. S. "Eine zaubervase im Allard Pierson Museum zu Amsterdam." *Mnemosyne* 5 (1997): 40–52.
Spaeth, John. "Martial Looks at His World." *CJ* 24 (1929): 361–73.
Stacy, Robert. "Fear in the Gospel of Mark." PhD diss., The Southern Baptist Theological Seminary, 1979.

Stone, Arthur, John Neale, Donald Cox, Anthony Napoli, Heiddis Valdimarsdottir, and Eileen Kennedy-Moore. "Daily Events Are Associated with a Secretory Immune Response to an Oral Antigen in Men." *Healthy Psychology* 13 (1994): 440–46.

Strawn, Brent A. "On Vomiting: Leviticus, Jonah, Ea(a)Rth." *CBQ* 74 (2012): 445–64.

Strelan, Mark. "A Greater than Caesar: Storm Stories in Lucan and Mark." *ZNW* 91 (2000): 166–79.

Szabo, Attila. "The Acute Effects of Humor and Exercise on Mood and Anxiety." *Journal of Leisure Research* 25 (2003): 152–62.

Taylor, Vincent. *The Gospel according to St. Mark*. 2nd ed. Macmillan, 1966.

Terence. *The Woman of Andros; The Self-Tormentor; The Eunuch*. Edited and translated by John Barsby. LCL. Harvard University Press, 2001.

Terrion, Jennifer, and Blake Ashforth. "From 'I' to 'We': The Role of Putdown Humor and Identity in the Development of a Temporary Group." *Human Relations* 55 (2002): 55–88.

Theophrastus, Herodas, and Sophron. *Characters; Herodas: Mimes; Sophron and Other Mime Fragments*. Edited and translated by Jeffrey Rusten and I. C. Cunningham. LCL. Harvard University Press, 2003.

Thimmes, Pamela. "The Biblical Sea-Storm Type-Scene: A Proposal." *Proceedings: Eastern Great Lakes and Midwest Biblical Societies* 10 (1990): 107–22.

———. *Studies in the Biblical Sea-Storm Type-Scene: Convention and Invention*. Mellen Research University Press, 1992.

Thompson, Mary. *The Role of Disbelief in Mark: A New Approach to the Second Gospel*. Paulist, 1989.

Thumiger, Chiara. "Ancient Greek and Roman Traditions." Pages 42–61 in *The Routledge History of Madness and Mental Health*. Edited by Greg Eghigian. Routledge Histories. Routledge, 2017.

Tolbert, Mary Ann. *Sowing the Gospel: Mark's World in Literary Perspective*. Fortress, 1989.

Trueblood, Elton. *The Humor of Christ*. Harper & Row, 1964.

Tsakona, Villy. "Genres of Humor." Pages 489–503 in *The Routledge Handbook of Language and Humor*. Edited by Salvatore Attardo. Routledge, 2017.

Upson-Saia, Kristi. "Holy Child or Holy Terror? Understanding Jesus' Anger in the Infancy Gospel of Thomas." *CH* 82 (2013): 1–39.

Vartejanu-Joubert, Madalina. "Representations of Madmen and Madness in Jewish Sources from the Pre-exilic to the Roman-Byzantine Period."

Pages 19–41 in *The Routledge History of Madness and Mental Health*. Edited by Greg Eghigian. The Routledge Histories. Routledge, 2017.

Velleius Paterculus. *Compendium of Roman History; Res Gestae Divi Augusti*. Translated by Frederick W. Shipley. LCL. Harvard University Press, 1924.

Via, Dan. *Kerygma and Comedy in the New Testament: A Structuralist Approach to Hermeneutic*. Fortress, 1975.

Vickers, Michael. "Another Dirty Trick Vase." *AJA* 84 (1980): 183–84.

———. "A Dirty Trick Vase." *AJA* 79 (1975): 282

Waetjen, Hermen. *A Reordering of Power: A Sociopolitical Reading of Mark's Gospel*. Fortress, 1989.

Wakshlag, Jacob J., Kenneth D. Day, and Dolf Zillman. "Selective Exposure to Educational Television Programs as a Function of Differently Paced Humorous Inserts." *Journal of Educational Psychology* 73 (1981): 27–32.

Walsh, Robyn Faith. *The Origins of Early Christian Literature: Contextualizing the New Testament within Greco-Roman Culture*. Cambridge University Press, 2021.

Wefald, Eric. "The Separate Gentile Mission in Mark: A Narrative Explanation of Markan Geography, the Two Feeding Accounts and Exorcisms." *JSNT* 60 (1995): 3–26.

Whitenton, Michael. "Feeling the Silence: A Moment-by-Moment Account of Emotions at the End of Mark (16:1–8)." *CBQ* 78 (2016): 272–89.

———. *Hearing Kyriotic Sonship: A Cognitive and Rhetorical Approach to the Characterization of Mark's Jesus*. BibInt148. Brill, 2017.

———. "The Moral Character Development of the Boy Jesus in the Infancy Gospel of Thomas." *JSNT* 38 (2015): 219–40.

Whitlark, Jason, and Jon Carman. "Hearing Humor in the Invective against Esau: A Performance-Critical Analysis of Hebrews 12:16." Pages 164–90 in *Biblical Humor and Performance: Audience Experiences That Make Meaning*. Edited by Peter Perry. Biblical Performance Criticism 20. Cascade, 2023.

———. "Humor in Hebrews: Rhetoric of the *Ridiculus* in the Example of Esau." Pages 246–66 in *Practicing Intertextuality: Ancient Jewish and Greco-Roman Exegetical Techniques in the New Testament*. Edited by Max J. Lee and B. J. Oropeza. Cascade, 2021.

Wijewardena, Nilupama, Charmine Ej Härtel, and Ramanie Samaratunge. "Using Humor and Boosting Emotions: An Affect-Based Study of

Managerial Humor, Employees' Emotions and Psychological Capital." *Human Relations* 70 (2017): 1316–41.

Wild, Barbara, Rodden Frank, Wolfgang Grodd, and Willibald Ruch. "Neural Correlates of Laughter and Humor." *Brain* 126 (2003): 2121–38.

Willi, Andres. *The Languages of Aristophanes: Aspects of Linguistic Variation in Classical Attic Greek*. Oxford University Press, 2003.

Winn, Adam. *Reading Mark's Christology Under Caesar: Jesus the Messiah and Roman Imperial Ideology*. Intervarsity, 2018.

Witt, Paul, Lawrence Wheeless, and Mike Allen. "A Meta-Analytical Review of the Relationship between Teacher and Student Learning." *Communication Monographs* 71 (2004): 184–207.

Wood, Ralph. *The Comedy of Redemption: Christian Faith and Comic Vision in Four American Novelists*. Notre Dame University Press, 1988.

Worthington, Ian. "Aristophanes' Knights and the Abortive Peace Proposals of 425 B.C." *L'Antiquité Classique* 56 (1987): 56–67.

Wrede, William. *The Messianic Secret*. Library of Theological Translations. Clarke, 1971.

Wright, Adam. "Recognizing Jesus: A Study of Recognition Scenes in the Gospel of Mark." *JGRChJ* 10 (2014): 174–93.

Yarbro Collins, Adela. *Mark: A Commentary*. Fortress, 2008.

Young, Philip. "Fighting in the Shade: What the Ancient Greeks Knew About Humor." *Soundings* 74 (1991): 289–307.

Zagagi, Netta. *The Comedy of Menander: Convention, Variation and Originality*. Indiana University Press, 1995.

Zimmerman, Bernhard. "Aristophanes." Pages 132–59 in *The Oxford Handbook of Greek and Roman Comedy*. Edited by Michael Fontaine and Adele C. Scafuro. Oxford University Press, 2014.

Ziv, Avner. "Teaching and Learning with Humor: Experiment and Replication." *The Journal of Experimental Education* 57 (1988): 5–15.

Zumbrunnen, John. "Elite Domination and the Clever Citizen: Aristophanes' 'Archarnians' and 'Knights.'" *Political Theory* 32 (2004): 656–77.

———. "Fantasy, Irony, and Economic Justice in Aristophanes' Assemblywomen and Wealth." *The American Political Science Review* 100 (2006): 319–33.

Zuver, Dudley. *Salvation by Laughter*. Harper & Row, 1933.

Ancient Sources Index

Hebrew Bible/Old Testament

Joshua
  22:24 — 94

Judges
  11:12 — 94

2 Samuel
  16:10 — 94

Job
  27:20 — 70
  34:25 — 70
  34:30 — 70

Psalms
  7:7 — 74
  35:23 — 74
  43:24–27 — 74
  59:5–6 — 74
  77:65–66 — 74
  91:5 — 70
  107 — 68
  107:23 — 68
  107:23–28 — 78
  107:25–29 — 68

Proverbs
  23:34 — 72–73

Isaiah
  34:14 — 70

Daniel
  4:33 — 90

Jonah
  1:5 — 74
  1:5–6 — 63

Deuterocanonical Books

Tobit
  3:8 — 83
  6:15 — 83
  6:18 — 83
  8:3 — 83

Ancient Jewish Writers

Josephus, *Antiquitates judaicae*
  8.2.5 — 92

New Testament

Matthew
  12:38–42 — 72
  13:58 — 121

Mark
  1:1 — 79, 119
  1:7 — 88
  1:10 — 79
  1:12 — 88
  1:21–28 — 98, 119, 163
  1:23 — 90
  1:23–28 — 90
  1:24 — 91

Mark (continued)

Reference	Pages
1:25	90
1:26	90, 95
1:27	98, 119
2:6–7	110
2:8	111
3:5	112
3:11	91, 95
3:14	99
3:27	88
4:1–34	20
4:27	71
4:35–6:6	4, 20, 23, 58, 59–60, 79, 99, 115, 120–21, 123–29, 131, 133–34, 146–47, 150–53, 155–59, 165–68, 171–73, 175
4:33–34	79
4:35–6:56	18
4:35–41	20, 60, 67, 69, 73, 75–78, 98, 124, 147–48, 167, 172, 174
4:37	70
4:38	67, 71, 124–27, 147, 166
4:39	67, 75–76, 124–25, 127, 148, 168
4:40	77
4:41	59, 67, 76, 78–79, 124–27, 150
5:1–5	89–90, 107, 148
5:1–20	6, 16–17, 20, 79, 98, 124, 128, 160, 172
5:2	89
5:3	89
5:3–4	89
5:3–5	88, 97
5:5	89
5:5–13	128
5:6	89, 91, 124, 126–27, 147
5:6–13	89, 91, 125,
5:7	7, 89, 92, 124–27, 147
5:8	89, 94, 124–27
5:9	95, 147, 160
5:10	89, 95, 124–25, 127, 160
5:11	89, 95–96
5:12	96, 124–25, 127, 160
5:13	89, 91, 95–96, 124–27, 160
5:13–17	99
5:14	97, 98
5:14–15	98
5:14–17	89, 97
5:15	98, 148
5:16	97
5:16–18	148
5:17	89, 97–98, 124–27
5:18	89, 99
5:18–20	89, 99
5:19	99
5:20	99, 121, 125, 127
5:21–23	108
5:21–24	108
5:21–43	7, 10, 20, 99, 107–9, 124, 128, 164, 172
5:23	108
5:24	111
5:24–34	109
5:25	109
5:25–26	107, 109
5:25–34	108
5:26	7, 108, 110, 124, 128
5:28	110
5:30	7, 108, 110–11, 124–27
5:30–32	109, 148
5:31	108, 111, 124–27, 148
5:32	108, 112, 124–27
5:34	112
5:35	20, 112, 114, 124–27, 164
5:35–42	128
5:35–43	108, 112, 164
5:38	112, 114, 124–27
5:39	71, 108, 112, 114, 124–27, 148, 164
5:39–40	7
5:40	20, 108, 114, 124–27, 148, 165
5:40–42	112, 149
5:41–42	20
5:42	108, 114, 125, 127, 164
6:1–2	118
6:1–6	20, 67–68, 115, 118–19, 124, 151, 155, 172
6:3	118–19, 124–27, 149
6:4	120, 149
6:5	120–21, 124, 126–27, 149

6:5–6	120	Luke	
6:6	59, 121, 124–27, 149	4:16–30	121
6:6–13	20	8:22–25	71
6:14–29	20	11:29–32	72
6:30	20	14:15–24	3, 166
6:45–52	70, 77–78		
6:48–50	77	Acts	
6:49	77	19:11–20	90, 92
6:50	70	19:13	92
6:51–52	77		
6:59–50	11	Hebrews	
7:1–23	119	12:16	134
7:24–30	90, 120		
7:29	90	Rabbinic Works	
7:31–37	120		
8:1–10	120	b. Pesahim	
8:11–13	120	112b	96
8:14–21	13, 120		
8:17	112	Greco-Roman Literature	
8:21	120		
8:22–26	94	Apthonius, *Progymnasmata*	
8:22–10:52	155	34R	44–45
8:27–30	155		
8:31–33	155	Apuleius, *Florida*	
8:34–9:1	155	19	105–6
9:2–8	155		
9:14–29	90–91	Apuleius, *Metamorphoses*	
9:25	90	1.6	107
9:30–32	155		
10:32–34	155	Aristophanes, *Equites*	
12:1–12	120	115–117	61
13:35–37	71	820–826	84
13:36	71		
14:32	166	Aristophanes, *Lysistrata*	
14:32–34	166	521–528	84–85
14:37	71	538	84–85
14:37–38	71		
14:37–41	71	Aristophanes, *Nubes*	
14:38	71	1–10	62
14:40–41	71	5–11	61
14:51–52	9	95–96	35
15:19	91	145	35
15:39	120	165	35
16:1–8	153	193–195	103
		225–230	103

Aristophanes, *Nubes* (continued)

231–234	103
347–355	103
695	63
701–705	63
710–715	63
731	63

Aristophanes, *Ranae*

479–493	66
720	87

Aristophanes, *Vespae*

1–9	62

Aristotle, *De anima*

429a7	72

Aristotle, *Poetica*

1449a	28

Aristotle, *Rhetorica*

3.1412b	40

Cicero, *De oratore*

2.62.254	31
2.63.255	31
2.70.254	31

Galen, *De symptomatum causis*

1.8	72

Herodotus, *Historiae*

7.34	75
7.35	75

Hesiod, *Opera et dies*

687–693	69

Hesiod, *Theogonia*

211–214	70

Homer, *Illias*

2.211–70	57

Homer, *Odyssea*

10.1–69	73
13.73–90	73

Lucan, *Pharsalia*

5.577–586	64
5.654–571	64
5.671–575	64

Lucian, *Philopseudes*

16	82
29	104
30	104
31	104
32	105

Martial, *Epigrammata*

1.47	101
8.74	101
9.96	101

Menander, *Perikeiromene*

172–174	39
172–177	86
175–177	39
467–550	38
484–475	38
505–507	39
513–525	86–87
526–531	38
708–827	38

Nicolaus, *Progymasmata*

63	93
63–67	93

Ovid, *Tristia*

19–36	69

Papyri Graecae Magicae

4.3045	92

Philostratus, *Vita Apollonii*

4.45	106

Ancient Sources Index

Plautus, *Bacchides*
50–507   41–42

Plautus, *Menaechmi*
367–380   116
394–401   117
819   42
820–1000   101
831–833   81
841–845   81
847–848   42
854–860   81
860–861   42
860–870   42
870–877   81
885–900   101
910–913   101
923–934   102
950–955   102

Plato, *Apologia*
18d   29
19bc   103
19c   29

Plato, *Leges*
2.669e   29

Plato, *Respublica*
452b   29

Plato, *Timaeus*
71e4–6   72

Pliny the Elder, *Naturalis historia*
29.1–21   100
29.11   100
29.7   100
29.21   101

Plutarch, *Marcellus*
20.5–6   80

Psuedo-Hermogenes, *Progymnasmata*
20–22   93

Quintilian, *Institutio oratoria*
6.2.3   32
6.3.1–8   165
6.3.22   32
6.3.24   32
6.3.84   32
6.3.50   32
9.2.30–31   93

Res gestae divi Augusti
1.3   75
1.4   75
1.25   75

Rhetorica Ad Herrenium
4.52.65   93

Seneca, *Apocolocyntosis*
10   85

Suetonius, Vespasianus
8.3   57

Terence, *Andria*
315–317   45
338   45
748–758   46
996–973   117–18

Theon, *Progymasmata*
115   93
115–118   93
116   93

Theophrastus, *Characteres*
25   65–66

Virgil, *Aeneid*
5.143–5.148   57

Modern Authors Index

Abel, Millicent	138	Borthwick, E. Kerr	62
Achtemeier, Paul	59, 155, 179	Botner, Max	154
Agarwal, Rohit	141	Bragues, George	104
Allen, Mike	143	Broadhead, Edwin	77, 111, 151
Anderson, Robert	72–73, 179	Buckley, George Wright	3
Anderson, William	42, 179	Bultmann, Rudolf	6, 94
Apte, Mahadev	27, 179	Burrow, Andrew	17, 92
Ashforth, Blake	144	Camery-Hogatt, Jerry	17, 114, 151
Attardo, Salvatore	12–13, 17–18, 25–26, 30, 51, 53–56, 96, 124–25, 129–32, 179	Capps, Lisa	145
		Carlson, Keith	140–41
		Carman, Jon	61, 67, 99, 103, 134, 147
Aus, Roger	65, 72, 75, 167, 180	Carrell, Amy	26, 27
Bainbridge, Frymier Ann	142–43, 180	Carter, Warren	16, 95, 160, 162
Banas, John	140, 180	Chakravarti, Dipankar	141
Baron, Rebecca	136	Chapman, Anthony	28
Brown, William	142	Christophel, Diane	143
Barra, Vincent	136	Choi, Jin Young	18
Batto, Bernard	74, 180	Clarke, John R.	48, 161
Baumbach, Lydia	102, 180	Cline, Thomas	141
Beavis, Mary Ann	151, 163, 180	Coarelli, Filippo	48
Beck, Mark	58, 180	Cohen, Shaye	109
Beit-Hallahmi, Benjamin	138, 181	Colston, Herbert	17
Bednarz, Terri	2–5, 180	Combs, Jason Robert	8, 11–13, 70, 175
Bekelja Wanzer, Melissa	142–43, 180	Coon, Raymond	87
Bell, Nancy	130, 180	Cooper, Lane	30–31
Belo, Fernando	18, 180	Cormier, Henri	3
Berger, Peter	28, 181	Cotter, Wendy	76
Bertrand, D.A.	83, 181	Cowan, Robert	57–58
Bizi, Smadar,	138, 181	Cox, Donald	136
Bilezekian, Gilbert	17, 181	Crossan, John Dominic	3, 5
Blanchard, Alain	37, 181	Culpepper, Alan	6–7, 107
Bolt, Peter	69, 76, 151, 153, 157, 158	D'Angelo, Mary	109
Boonstra, Harry	3	Davis, Philip	155
Boring, Eugene	88–89, 92, 94, 97, 98, 111, 114, 151, 162	Day, Kenneth	140
		De Saint Denis, Eugene	57

Modern Authors Index

Deibert, Richard 88
Deppe, Dean 109
Derks, Peter 141
Derrett, John Duncan 16, 95, 109, 160
Dinkler, Michal Beth 18
Donahue, John 70, 92, 94, 98, 111, 114, 120, 151, 162–63
Dorey, Thomas Alan 84
Dossey, Leslie 72
Dwyer, Timothy 79, 151, 155, 163
Duckworth, George 41, 44
Dunbar, Norah 140, 180
Dunbar, R. I. M. 136
Eckman, George 5
Edwards, James 109
Eisend, Martin 141
Ej Härtel, Charmine 137
Emanuel, Sarah 8, 14–15
Ermida, Isabel 17–18, 132
Evrard, Franck 18
Figueroa-Dorrego, Jorge 50–51
Fontaine, Michael 40–41
Forehand, Walter 43
Fortson, Stephen 142
Fowler, Robert 17
Foot, Hugh 28
France, R. T. 94
Frank, Rodden 135
Frangou, Anna 136
Furly, William 37
Gamel, Brian 120
Gardner, John 141
Germeroth, Darla 146
Gelardini, Gabriella 75
Gervais, Matthew 135
Geyer, Douglas 18–19, 69–70, 78, 151, 153, 157–58
Given, John 35
Goldberg, Sander M 44–45
Gorham, Joan 143
Graesser, Arthur 145
Grassi, Joseph 3
Grodd, Wolfgang 135
Guelich, Robert 70, 111, 114, 151, 163
Guidi, Annarita 130

Gundry, Robert 92, 97
Haber, Susan 109
Halliwell, Stephen 1, 28, 34, 113, 165
Harrington, Daniel 70, 92, 94, 98, 111, 114, 120, 151, 162–63
Hatton, Stephen 8–11, 20, 107, 111, 113–14, 164, 175
Heerey, Erin 145
Henderson, Jeffrey 34–35
Henderson, Susan 154
Hendrickx, Herman 75
Henze, Matthias 90
Horsley, Richard 95
Hull, Robert 94
Hyde, Thomas Alexander 5
van Iersel, Bas 94, 96, 151
Iverson, Kelly 1, 8, 13–15, 120, 152, 113–14, 152, 175
Janko, Richard 30–31
Johansson, Daniel 154
Juel, Donald 17, 97, 162
Kahl, Werner 163
Kale, Aron 138
Keinan Giora 138, 181
Kellaris, James 141
Kelley, Andrew 154
Keltner, Dacher 145
Kennedy, George 93
Kennedy-Moore, Eileen 136
Kiffiak, Jordash 79
Kinukawa, Hisako 109
Klancher, Nancy 150
Kilinksi, Karl, II 49
Knapp, Sheppard 3
Knapp, Stephen 151
Konstan, David 34
Kring, Ann 145
Krishnan, H. Shanker 141
Kuipers, Giselinde 141
Kynes, Will 63
LaMarche, Paul 67, 88, 160
Lane, William 88, 94, 111, 114, 120
Lang, Candace 18
Larkin-Galiñanes, Cristina 50–51
Leander, Hans 16, 95, 160

Leeuwen, Edwin van	136	Palmer, Earl	3
Lindheim, Sarah	48	Palmer, Humphrey	3
Lillian, Feder	90	Partridge Giselle	136
Liu, Shr-Jie	140, 180	Paterson, William Romaine	3
Lloyd, Robert	57	Pearce, Eiluned	136
Long, Debra	145	Perera, S.	136
Long, Timothy	87	Perks, Lisa Glebatis	29, 31–32
Longenecker, Bruce	3, 76, 154, 157–58, 161, 166, 168	Phipps, William	3
		Plebe, Armando	30
Lowe, D.	136	Portier-Young, Anathea	83
Ludlow, Jared	91, 150	Price, Lucian	1
Ludwig, Paul	83	Provine, Robert	135, 139
Luke, Trevor	57–58	Puhlick-Doris, Patricia	139
Macdonald, Dennis	73	Răchită, Constantin	63
Macdonald, Deven	19, 151	Raskin, Viktor	13, 26, 51–54, 56
Macdonald, Ian	136	Robinson, Timothy	85
Marcus, Joel	6–7, 74, 88, 92, 94, 97–98, 100, 111–12, 114, 120, 151, 160, 162	Robson, James	34
		Rodriguez, Dariela	140, 180
Martin, Rod	137–39, 143, 145	Roeckelein, Jon	138
Martineau, William	26–27	Rosen, Ralph	35
Mather, Judson	63	Ruch, Willibald	135, 137
McCracken, David	83, 150	Rusten, Jeffrey	33–34
Mehrabian, Albert	142	Sabin, E.	136
Melo, Wolfgang David Cirilo de	40	Salzmann, Andrew	120
Meltzer, Gary	57	Samaratunge, Ramanie	137
Meyer, John 144	146	Schenke, Ludger	70
Miles, John A.	63	Segal, Erich	40–41, 43, 45
Miller, Geoffrey	17	Seidensticker, Ernd	57
Miniconi, P.	57	Sharrock, Alison	41, 116–17
Monro, D. H	27	Shelly, Cameron	29
Montiglio, Silvia	61	Shepherd, Tom	6–7, 107, 109, 111, 113, 164
Morreall, John	1, 30, 51		
Miller, Ann	143	Shultz, Kara	146
Myers, Ched	16, 95	Shutter, Marion	5
Myers, Doris	3	Slater, Niall W.	41
Napoli, Anthony	136	Sliter, Michael	138
Neale, John	136	Sørensen, Majken	146, 161
Nelson, P.	136	Snijder, G. A. S	49
Neufeld, Dietmar	112, 151, 156	Spaeth, John	101
Nilsen, Don	134, 144	Stacy, Robert	79
Nissin, Laura	72	Stone, Arthur	136
Noble, Joseph Veach	49	Stow, Julie	136
Norwood, Gilbert	44	Strawn, Brent A.	63
Ogden, Daniel	104	Strelan, Mark	75, 167
Padel, Ruth	90	Szabo, Attila	137

Taylor, Vincent	88
Terrion, Jennifer	144
Thimmes, Pamela	73–74
Thompson, Mary	19
Thumiger, Chiara	90
Tolbert, Mary Ann	6–7, 88, 99, 160
Trueblood, Elton	3, 5
Tsakona, Villy	129
Upson-Saia, Kristi	150
Valdimarsdottir, Heiddis	136
Vartejanu-Joubert, Madalina	90
Via, Dan	8–9, 11
Vickers, Michael	49
van Vugt, Mark	136
Waetjen, Hermen	16
Wakshlag, Jacob	140
Walsh, Robyn Faith	22
Wefald, Eric	120
Wheeles, Lawrence	142–43
Whitenton, Michael	74, 150, 153
Whitlark, Jason	134
Wilson, David	135
Wijewardena, Nilupama	137
Wild, Barbara	135
Willi, Andres	35
Winn, Adam	160
Witt, Paul	142–43
Wood, Ralph	1
Worthington, Ian	83–84
Wrede, William	154
Wright, Adam	156
Yarbro Collins, Adela	68, 75, 98, 101, 105, 111, 114, 121, 151, 162–63
Young, Philip	49
Young, Randall	145
Yuan, Zhen	138
Zagagi, Netta	38–39
Zillman, Dolf	140
Zimmerman, Bernhard	33
Ziv, Avner	141
Zumbrunnen, John	83
Zuver, Dudley	5